The Plays, Screenplays and Films of David Mamet

STEVEN PRICE

Consultant editor: Nicolas Tredell

palgrave
macmillan

First published 2008 by
PALGRAVE MACMILLAN
Houndmills, Basingstoke, Hampshire RG21 6XS and
175 Fifth Avenue, New York, N.Y. 10010
Companies and representatives throughout the world

PALGRAVE MACMILLAN is the global academic imprint of the Palgrave Macmillan division of St. Martin's Press, LLC and of Palgrave Macmillan Ltd. Macmillan® is a registered trademark in the United States, United Kingdom and other countries. Palgrave is a registered trademark in the European Union and other countries.

ISBN-13: 978–0–230–55534–1   hardback
ISBN-10: 0–230–55534–9   hardback
ISBN-13: 978–0–230–55535–8   paperback
ISBN-10: 0–230–55535–7   paperback

This book is printed on paper suitable for recycling and made from fully managed and sustained forest sources. Logging, pulping and manufacturing processes are expected to conform to the environmental regulations of the country of origin.

A catalogue record for this book is available from the British Library.

A catalog record for this book is available from the Library of Congress.

10   9   8   7   6   5   4   3   2   1
17   16   15   14   13   12   11   10   09   08

Printed and bound in China

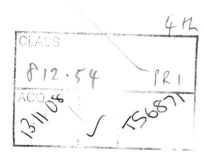

Contents

Introduction

David Mamet (born 1947) is a unique figure in American culture. Arguably the finest living American playwright, whose distinctively profane dialogue is so widely recognised that the term 'Mametspeak' has entered common usage, he is also by general consent the only major American dramatist to have achieved significant success as a Hollywood screenwriter. In addition, he has directed, to date, nine feature films, and in so doing has developed an equally unmistakable cinematic style.

Scope and structure of this guide

This is a study of the critical material published on Mamet's plays, screenplays and films. His many essays and innumerable interviews are beyond its scope, although I have sometimes drawn on them in discussing other works. The first four volumes of essays, which contain the most frequently cited pieces, are collected in *A Whore's Profession* (1994), while Leslie Kane's essential *David Mamet in Conversation* (2001) is a wisely chosen and skilfully edited anthology of 26 interviews and profiles conducted between 1976 and 1999. Brilliant insights abound, but like Orson Welles (1915–85), or Bob Dylan (born 1941) in the mid-1960s, Mamet often appears to treat the interview as an art form, and not all critics have treated his public comments with enough caution; he is sufficiently changeable, humorous, irascible, ironic and contradictory that one can quote selectively to produce almost any Mamet one likes. This should be kept in mind, particularly when reading the many essays that attribute misogynistic attitudes not only to the characters, but also to the author himself.

Biographical studies are also excluded. The most significant to date is John Lahr's article 'Fortress Mamet' (1997), although Ira Nadel's book-length biography, which is sure to become the standard work, was published as this book went to press. I have confined myself to studies published in English, and in keeping with the series brief have given lesser attention to scholarship focused on the plays in performance. Newspaper articles and reviews have been omitted unless these have materially affected subsequent criticism or are otherwise genuinely substantial. A vast number of theatre reviews to 2001 are surveyed in David and Janice Sauer's *David Mamet: A Research and Production Sourcebook* (2003), a remarkably comprehensive annotated bibliography that also includes judicious and pithy single-paragraph responses to the scholar-ship on the plays (though not the films). Several important studies have appeared in more than one form, usually as both a journal article and a book chapter; unless the differences are crucial I have silently pre-ferred one version to the other. For reasons of space I have passed over many survey articles, as well as other material that now appears dated or otherwise unremarkable.

Some book-length studies receive less emphasis than might be expected. Anne Dean's *David Mamet: Language as Dramatic Action* (1990) and Gay Brewer's *David Mamet and Film: Illusion/Disillusion in a Wounded Land* (1993) give an exceptionally detailed close reading of five selected plays and the first three films, respectively. Dean's book in particular is undoubtedly influential, but each presents a difficulty for the present study in being exceptionally hard to summarise, since they tend not to offer arguments as such but instead to describe how each passage of the play or film achieves its particular effects. Moreover, they are untheo-rised and take a very benign view of Mamet, often with the result that a cutting edge is missing; they rarely consider why the same work can mean very different things to different audiences, or indeed whether the text possesses the internal self-contradictions that from some theoretical perspectives are almost mandatory.

For almost directly the opposite reasons, I have also mentioned only briefly Ilkka Joki's (in many ways splendid) *Mamet, Bakhtin, and the Dra-matic* (1993). Half of this book, derived from a doctoral dissertation, is devoted to the work of Mikhail Bakhtin (1895–1975), whose theories of 'dialogism' notoriously and rather inexplicably fail to address theatre; the remaining hundred or so pages use a range of Mamet's works in an attempt to redress this. Joki very valuably details the intermingling of high and low ('demotic') speech in Mamet's work, but much of the emphasis is narrowly sociological, focused for example on the 'super-addressee', such as the regulatory mechanisms of television and radio that dictate what can and cannot be uttered. In general Mamet is used to illuminate Bakhtin, rather than the other way round, while the restricted theoretical focus, and the severely limited distribution, mean that Joki's work has only a very specific kind of usefulness, and has not significantly influenced subsequent criticism.

Each chapter of the present book focuses on a work or works, organ-ised approximately chronologically in order of first performance of a play or release of a film. The chronology of the critical reception, of course, does not simply shadow the development of Mamet's career; the appearance of *House of Games* and *Speed-the-Plow* in the late 1980s, for example, prompted much revision of previously accepted views con-cerning the plays of the 1970s. Therefore, a brief chronological survey of the major developments in criticism now follows.

A short history of Mamet criticism

The serious study of Mamet's work arguably began on 5 July 1976. On that day he was the subject of not one but two prominent profiles, for *The New York Times* and the *Village Voice*, which for the first time brought him significant recognition outside his home city of Chicago.[1] They reveal the 28-year-old playwright as an exceptionally articulate commentator on his own work and on contemporary American culture. Significantly, in light of what was to follow, both Mamet and the feature writers perceive him to be acutely influenced by feminism, and consider that the plays offer a critique of present-day masculinity. This remained the prevalent view until the mid-1980s.

Several articles in the following years contributed to the assumption that his dialogue was realistic – 'people *really speak* as Mamet's characters do'[2] – although this was usually qualified by the recognition that there was 'something beyond realism', 'a desperate energy behind [the] apparent incoherences, a passion for speaking that is so intense as to become authentically lyrical'.[3] At this time, it was also commonplace to note the episodic rather than plot-based construction, the apparently sociopolitical critique of American capitalism, the subliminal hints of a need for moral responsibility and ethical engagement, and the remarkable range of the work. Indeed, in the 1970s Mamet was so prolific – in one two-and-a-half-year stretch no fewer than nine different plays of vastly differing kinds were produced in New York – that it could hamper serious discussion. The trickle of articles that began to appear in scholarly journals in the late 1970s, and the chapters on Mamet that would soon be contributed as a matter of course to essay collections appraising the contemporary American theatrical scene, often had to take the form of a career survey rather than a critical analysis, even when the playwright was barely out of his twenties.

Mamet's profile increased markedly and inexorably in the 1980s. As the decade began he was writing screenplays for successful Hollywood movies with big-name stars and directors, such as *The Postman Always Rings Twice* (Bob Rafelson, 1981), *The Verdict* (Sidney Lumet, 1982), and later *The Untouchables* (Brian De Palma, 1986). He won the Pulitzer Prize in 1984 for *Glengarry Glen Ross*, the epoch-defining play about corrupt real estate salesmen first performed in London the previous year. The first book-length studies were published, helping to establish his position in the increasingly contested 'canon' of writers whose work was considered obligatory on respectable university curricula; and in 1988 *Speed-the-Plow*, his stage satire about Hollywood, featured Madonna (born 1958) in a production that allowed critics to excoriate her performance while praising the play and elevating its writer to celebrity status.

The first and still one of the best books about Mamet was written by C. W. E. [Christopher] Bigsby, who was then (and arguably still is) the most important and influential living academic commentator on American theatre. Between 1982 and 1985 he published his monumental *Critical Introduction to Twentieth-Century American Drama*, the final volume of which contains a substantial chapter on Mamet; his short monograph *David Mamet*, also published in 1985, presents effectively the same material and arguments in expanded form. Bigsby sees Mamet as an essentially absurdist dramatist, concerned with the economic and spiritual decline of an America in which the characters' inability to act is governed by a metaphysical and ontological crisis of self. Any belief that social change can be actively sought, any urge towards redemption, is erroneous, ironic or sentimental; the characters' obsessive storytelling is a demand for illusion, for a shape to be imposed on lives governed by the evasion of human relationships and the fearful if unstated apprehension of death. At best, the choice is between enabling fictions and those that suffocate, and between the kind of action that involves risk and responsibility, and that which is mere performance and artifice. Bigsby has returned to Mamet's work several times since, in a substantial chapter in his *Modern American Drama, 1945–1990* (1992), later revised to take the story up to the year 2000, and in editing and contributing to *The Cambridge Companion to David Mamet* (2004). He remains a persuasive critic, though one would hardly guess from his account that Mamet could reasonably be described as 'American drama's most brilliant comic writer'.[4]

Dennis Carroll's *David Mamet*, published in 1987, offers a contradictory view in almost every way. Carroll treats positively the movements towards communion that Bigsby regards ironically, not least because, where Bigsby considers the characters to be trapped in a kind of static absurdist image, Carroll seeks to identify a dynamic at work both between characters and in the organisation and placement of scenes. Carroll accordingly gives narrative structure a much higher status, especially concerning the paradigm of departure, initiation and return that Mamet perhaps draws from Joseph Campbell (1904–87), and which provides an underlying, structural myth of progression, transformation and redemption; as the title of Mamet's 1988 film puts it, *Things Change*.

This phase of criticism draws to a close with the aforementioned books by Anne Dean and Gay Brewer. Much of the material published before 1993 is now dated, partly of course because Mamet has continued to write prolifically, but also because later, more explicitly theoretically minded critics have at least implicitly challenged the (usually unstated) critical assumptions of their predecessors. More significantly, earlier commentators could not have perceived fully the ideological fissures that were beginning to open up in American culture, of which Mamet's work would soon come to be regarded as emblematic. In particular, with *Oleanna* (1992), in which a female student accuses a male professor of rape, Mamet almost seemed to be goading his detractors, setting himself up as a lightning-rod for issues that encapsulated the 'culture wars' that remain as starkly apparent today as they did then. A work that provoked fights in the audience, written by a man who was now arguably America's most important living playwright, that attracted opprobrium and support in not-quite-equal measures, and landed like a Molotov cocktail on a complex of contemporary American tensions over 'political correctness', sexual harassment, and the Clarence Thomas–Anita Hill hearings some six months previously, generated a paperstorm of debate.

In retrospect the prominent position of *Oleanna* in popular perceptions of Mamet is unfortunate, as it draws attention from major work of the 1990s that showed him continuing to branch out in all directions. Moreover, the ideological arguments that continue to rage around it obscure, to some extent, the widespread feeling that it is not representative of his best work. An influential early review by Elaine Showalter helped to kick-start the controversy surrounding its ideological implications, but less frequently noted is her argument that the play 'gives Mamet little scope for his usual gifts', since the institutional setting precludes much of the humour and 'the staccato, aphasic obscenity which [elsewhere] gives his dialogue its driving rhythms'; in *Oleanna*, this 'fall[s] flat because these characters do not speak the same language; they simply declaim to each other'.[5]

One healthier consequence of *Oleanna* was that it brought into stark focus the ideological tensions of the earlier plays that had previously remained relatively obscure. For example, the treatment of masculinity in such all-male plays as *American Buffalo* and *Glengarry Glen Ross* had been discussed in detail in a surprisingly small number of essays published between 1986 and 1991 by Guido Almansi, Hersh Zeifman and David Radavich; this topic was now unavoidable, and would soon be the subject of a rigorous analysis by Robert Vorlicky in *Act Like a Man* (1995). These writers largely concur with a long-established view that Mamet exposes the myths of masculinity, but this position was coming under pressure from the much more hostile vantage point of feminist theory. Such criticism had commenced in the wake of *Speed-the-Plow* and his first film as writer-director, *House of Games* (1987), in each of which a female character becomes the problematic victim of a male plot against her. This apparently confirmed a suspicion that many had long entertained: the men-only settings of Mamet's best-known plays were in fact a more or less direct expression of the writer's own misogynistic tendencies, and the ubiquitous confidence games were part of a masculine discourse directed against women. Carla J. McDonough and others noted that, with the publication of his essay collections *Writing in Restaurants* (1986) and, in particular, *Some Freaks* (1989), Mamet was voicing quite insistently a defence of such all-male worlds in language which – so the argument goes – shadows the misogynistic discourse of the plays, suggesting a certain complicity with, even celebration of, their macho environments.

Some Freaks signalled the public emergence of another side to the writer that has become increasingly prominent. A brilliant but little-known short play, *The Disappearance of the Jews*, had been performed in 1983, but it was in some of the essays in *Some Freaks* that Mamet first expounded a growing interest in his identity as a Jew, which forms the thematic backbone of his third film, *Homicide*, in 1991. Toby Silverman Zinman and Christopher Hudgins both argued in essays published in 1992 that the dialogue of the plays was influenced by Jewish rhythms and inflections; Hudgins was especially perspicacious in recognising that 'Mamet [was] moving towards a more overtly religious vision', one that resembles, to Hudgins's mind, that of the Jewish theologian Martin Buber (1878–1965).[6] This is the territory that Leslie Kane explores in exhaustive detail in her monumental *Weasels and Wisemen: Ethics and Ethnicity in the Work of David Mamet* (1999), which is in many ways a major advance upon earlier studies. Kane argues for a specifically Jewish inflection at every level of syntax, structure, theme and moral vision, even in those works without any overtly Jewish context at all, such as *Oleanna*. Although many of her arguments are open to dispute, they are much stronger if considered as revelations of what Mamet's work looks like when viewed through the lens of Jewish teachings on education that are undoubtedly attuned to much of his own thinking; and the notes are an education in themselves.

Meanwhile, Kane had been editing a series of essay collections that together represent the most sustained ongoing critical commentary on the writer, including an entire book devoted to *Glengarry Glen Ross*. These studies were complemented throughout the 1990s by the growing number of articles in scholarly journals that dissected all aspects of his work. A disproportionate number of these focused on *Oleanna*, but most of the earlier plays were revisited productively, and there was much interest also in the seemingly autobiographical plays *The Cryptogram* (1994) and *The Old Neighborhood* (1997), while film experts devoted much attention to *House of Games* and specialists in Jewish American studies produced several substantial analyses of *Homicide*.

Crucially, however, few critics have been comfortable in considering the films alongside the plays; with some notable exceptions, Mamet scholars coming from theatre backgrounds have proved ill-equipped in the analysis of cinema, with the frequent result that many such studies focus inappropriately on theme without giving due attention to the peculiar qualities of the 'Mamet movie'. A significant exception is Bruce Barton's *Imagination in Transition: Mamet's Move to Film* (2005), which remarkably is only the second book (after Brewer's) to consider the films in depth, and only the second monograph (after Kane's) to have appeared since 1993. For all of these reasons it is most welcome, although it considers in detail only the handful of plays and films that Barton thinks best illustrate the transition that is his subject. Unfortunately, its greatest strength is also one of its greatest weaknesses. 'I am not here to smother you in theory', insists Teach in *American Buffalo*;[7] but Barton is, and the often lucid insights are swamped by relentless theoretical overkill. It is also typical of the most recent Mamet criticism in paying little if any attention to the problematic works that have appeared since the highly accessible film *State and Main* (2000). To the extent that these have had any effect it has been in compelling the recognition that his dialogue, and much else, is profoundly and increasingly stylised, while pushing critics towards the ongoing reappraisal of earlier work, as if in nervous anticipation of what this extraordinary and unpredictable writer might do next.

CHAPTER ONE

Early Plays: *Lakeboat* (1970), *The Duck Variations* (1972), *Sexual Perversity in Chicago* (1974)

David Mamet has always been a prolific writer; he was also a precocious one. Between 1965 and 1969 he was a student at Goddard College in Vermont, spending his junior year of 1968–69 studying acting under the tutelage of Sanford Meisner (1905–97) at the Neighborhood Playhouse in New York. Goddard staged the first production of a Mamet play, a satirical revue called *Camel*, written by the 20-year-old undergraduate in 1968 to fulfil the requirements of his senior thesis. After taking up a post the following year to teach drama at Marlboro College, also in Vermont, Mamet wrote another play, *Lakeboat* (1970), for his students to perform. He returned to Goddard in 1971 as artist in residence, and formed the St. Nicholas Theater Company with students William H. Macy (born 1950) and Steven Schachter, staging the first productions of *The Duck Variations* and *Reunion*; the St. Nicholas would continue to perform Mamet's work after he returned to Chicago in 1972.

Lakeboat

Although most surveys of Mamet's work begin with *Lakeboat*, criticism of this play usually refers to the revised version produced by the Milwaukee Repertory Theater in 1979 and published by Grove Press in 1981.[1] The revision added little that was strictly new; instead it was condensed and restructured to produce a play of 28 scenes, set aboard a merchant marine ship travelling from port to port in the Great Lakes of North America. The two thin storylines anticipate much of Mamet's later work. The first concerns the rapport that develops between Joe, the middle-aged loser who has spent more than 20 years on the boats, and Dale, the young student of English literature who is working to earn money during his summer vacation. It is an example of the teacher–pupil relationship common in Mamet's work, and Carla J. McDonough argues that here it is bound up with the transmission of masculine values.[2] As she points out, Joe's mentorship of Dale is relatively successful, because Joe has a more rounded and sophisticated understanding of manhood than is found among his fellow workers. For this very reason, however, *Lakeboat*, like *Sexual Perversity in Chicago*, does not elsewhere display the ideal masculine community about which Mamet has written in essays, but that seems to be a chimera in the world of the plays.

The second storyline concerns Guiliani, the missing cook whose absence provokes many lurid fantasies but who appears merely to have overslept. As Bigsby notes, the cook's disappearance allows the sailors to invoke a talent for the mock-heroic, self-delusional storytelling that Mamet would soon develop more fully in *Sexual Perversity in Chicago*, but he also observes that the sailors' tales occasionally touch on an apparently real desperation – there are references to divorce and other personal tragedies, and even suggestions that Joe is contemplating suicide. All these qualities provide the perfect starting-point for Bigsby's influential construction of an absurdist Mamet. The work of Samuel Beckett (1906–89) is recalled, perhaps, in the repeated and circular voyage that gives a kind of aimless structure to the sailors' existence, while there is enough in the play for Bigsby to maintain his parallel argument that Mamet is also a kind of social critic. Indeed, for Bigsby, these two strands are largely inseparable: Mamet addresses alienation, discontinuity, fragmentation and loss as both social fact and 'absurdist image'.[3]

Although Carroll at least implicitly acknowledges much of this, his account is in many ways diametrically opposed.[4] He notes that in production the single set of the whole boat means that apparently discontinuous scenes in fact flow readily into one another, so that in this sense the fragmentation is illusory. Moreover, Carroll thinks the lakeshoremen accept and are relatively content with a working life that many of them regard as easy, in which competition is ritualised rather than threatening, and which affords them regular outlets for the drinking and extramarital sex that are their principal preoccupations. Most significantly, Carroll regards this as one of Mamet's plays about 'learning'. Dale's temporary position on board ship gives him the status of both outsider and catalyst, and although Fred is unable fully to let go of his self-defensive illusions, Joe finally lets the mask drop, letting Dale see into his vulnerability. In this sense the play has a certain narrative as well as thematic progression; more importantly, Dale has prompted a positive change for the better in the older man while he himself has undergone a significant rite of passage.

Michael Hinden casts Dale as a 'liminal' (threshold or marginal) figure who brings about change in the other men but remains unchanged himself. Hinden also introduces a useful distinction between 'community as an idealized nexus of human relationships', and the merely 'physical setting' that includes the political, legal and social organisation of a particular society.[5] The former is of greater interest to Mamet: for example, the story about the cook becomes a kind of communal effort, modified in each retelling so that it becomes a collectively produced myth. Hinden notes that the 1983 version published by Samuel French includes an additional scene in which Stan briefly discusses Robin Hood, a myth that introduces the idea of rebellion against the exploitative rich. The sailors never develop this insight, however, and instead channel their energies into an anger directed against the very few people below them in social status: impoverished women.

In retrospect, the most significant moment in *Lakeboat* occurs when Stan refers to such women as 'soft things with a hole in the middle',[6] words that a remarkable number of critics have used to frame their general arguments about Mamet. Guido Almansi returns almost obsessively to the line in what is less a critical analysis than a thought-piece that celebrates the playwright as 'a virtuoso of invective'. While noting that there is something celebratory and even poetic about Mamet's use of such language, he observes that at the same time as the character says the line, 'someone somewhere thinks that it is a rather eccentric definition of women'.[7] This seemingly obvious point about irony would sometimes get lost in the invective later directed against the playwright from critics such as Jeanne-Andrée Nelson, who used the same line as an epigraph to her essay, almost as if to imply that it represented the actual views of the playwright himself.[8] Other, more sympathetic critics have consequently found it necessary to confront the line head-on to explain why 'David Mamet had been on a collision course with feminist criticism since 1970'.[9] Almansi's piece provides a worthwhile corrective to the many early critics who either damn Mamet for the language or assume that he is a moralist who expects his audiences automatically to take a dim view of its obscenity; instead, he is a 'poet of swearwords, artist of invectives, and virtuoso of obscene expressions'.[10] Nevertheless, although Almansi is surely right to insist that those who value Mamet's work must at some level cherish this kind of language, his tone is ill-judged, as when he states that such speech is often directed against women 'or that more forward, buxom, and aggressive woman, America, who has bestowed upon them a dream, the Great American Dream, only to prove a prick-teaser'.[11]

Although in some respects rudimentary, *Lakeboat*, at once a bleak dramatisation of masculine self-exclusion from the company of women, a celebration of the linguistic resources of all-male dialogue, and a jeremiad for the working man, is a calling card for the plays, and the criticism, that would follow.

The Duck Variations

The Duck Variations is a sequence of 14 short dialogues in which two old men, Emil and George, sit on a park bench, passing the time by watching the birds and drawing sometimes unintentionally comic connections to the human condition. A familiar verdict is encapsulated in the words of Henry I. Schvey, who suggests that it 'betrays all too obviously the influence of [Harold] Pinter [born 1930] and Beckett in its static plotlessness, and attempts to fill the time with meaningless banter'.[12] More subtle readings detect a certain philosophy of language in that banter. In an early interview, Mamet made the oft-quoted remark that 'the language we use, its rhythm, actually determines the way we behave, more than the other way around'.[13] In one of the most impressive early analyses of Mamet's work, Robert Storey suggests that '*The Duck Variations* dramatizes the comic aspiration of attitudes from the melting-pot of speech', as the men regurgitate phrases and attitudes derived from newspapers, popular culture, half-remembered biblical allusions and the storehouse of everyday sentiment; in their comic attempts to forge meaningful argument from such sources 'the balance of power between the characters shift[s] with their shifts in verbal perspective'.[14]

Bigsby's is much the most eloquent and discriminating reading along these lines. He observes that the setting resembles *Zoo Story* (1959) by Edward Albee (born 1928), while the comically ironic contrast between the banality of the men's observations and the inflated register in which they espouse them recalls Pinter. A more central influence, in Bigsby's eyes, is Beckett, to whom he routinely compares the American writer, nowhere more consistently than in his analysis of this play. The men have a fear of mortality which they cannot bring themselves to discuss; whenever the conversation about the ducks brings them too close to this fear they change the subject, which, however, perpetually re-emerges in their cogitations on the ducks' lives. Like the characters of *Lakeboat*, George and Emil incessantly tell stories, but here too they fall victim to a paradox: narrative gives a shape and meaning to lives that might otherwise appear to be empty, and indeed ending, but 'all true stories if continued far enough end in death', a remark Bigsby borrows from Ernest Hemingway (1898–1961).[15] It's either habit or the grave, and their attempts to find something better – the survival of the species, for example, or the consolations of storytelling – are mere evasions. This is a world in which community is meaningless, in which personal mortality is the trump card, and in which the environment (a recurrent concern of the play, in the startling images of dying birds and ducks addicted to nicotine) is a personal context but not a site for sustained engagement with anything outside the self.

Not everyone sees *The Duck Variations* in these terms. Carroll notes that Mamet is here developing his approach to dialogue as music, an analogy present in both the title and the stage directions, and detects a greater degree of social realism or verisimilitude in the play, placing greater emphasis on the environmental references and carefully distinguishing between the two characters. George is more authoritative, the major storyteller, and a man prone to lose himself in generalisations; Emil is more logical, though this is counteracted by sentimentality and fear, so that in different ways the characters are equally liable to take refuge in platitudes. Carroll also sees the relationship in less static terms; notably, tension between the pair erupts in scene 11 in Emil's short-lived challenge to George's authority, while the play moves towards a climax of sorts in the penultimate variation, where both characters are finally willing to confront and accept images of death. In contrast to Bigsby, then, Carroll sees this as a 'positive' play, with the relationship between George and Emil unfolding 'in a dynamic bond of friendship',[16] well brought out in William Herman's observation that the pair show 'immensely moving courtesy toward each other', finishing one another's sentences so that each 'act[s] as a kind of amen chorus' for the other.[17]

Although Carroll's detailed dissection of this relationship provides a valuable alternative to Bigsby's absurdism, less convincing is his placement of *The Duck Variations* in a 'group' of plays about 'learning'; as he concedes, there is little here of the mentor–protégé relationship. Both Bigsby and Carroll treat with a certain solemnity a play that is marked throughout by a comic sensibility that is obvious on the page and on the stage, yet rarely receives its due in critical discussion. For this reason, Philip C. Kolin's analysis of the play as a parody of a Socratic dialogue seems, in this respect, closer to the mark.[18] Kolin sees the resemblance both formally, in the dialogic structure of a dialectic or a question-and-answer debate, and in the construction of a dominant metaphor via which George and Emil consider the typically Socratic topics of history, procreation, evil, friendship, government, transience, death and fate. It is a parody, however, because instead of tending towards knowledge the dialogues repeatedly and comically undercut the philosophical pretensions of the characters, whose debating style depends on spurious analogies, unverifiable sources, and an ultimate determination not to connect the mortality of the ancient Greeks to their own situation. Pascale Hubert-Liebler identifies a similarly 'Socratic' method in the 'interactive' mode of teaching in many of Mamet's mentor-and-pupil relationships, such as that between Don and Bobby in *American Buffalo*.[19] Also valuable to an understanding of the play's form is Deborah R. Geis's observation that while George and Emil resemble the choric figures in a Greek drama, the play has no protagonist, producing 'a void or absence' that generates a 'comic desperation' in the dialogue.[20]

Sexual Perversity in Chicago

In the most substantial of these early plays, Mamet for the first time creates female characters in an uproariously comic if finally dark and alienating dissection of the relentlessly predatory environment of the 1970s singles bar. It begins with Bernie expounding a bizarre sexual fantasy in what the audience soon realises is his destructive role as self-appointed sexual mentor to his friend Dan; this relationship is paralleled by that between two women, Joan and Deb. Dan and Deb begin a sexual affair which collapses, partly, it seems, due to the machinations of the older figures; the play ends with Bernie and Dan on the beach, ogling women from whom they are now more completely alienated than ever.

Although most critics regard the fragmented form of the play as a direct comment on the contemporary urban environment, two essays find in *Sexual Perversity* not so much a modern form as a variation on some very old ones. David Skeele compares it to the medieval homiletic tragedy, which presented alongside the redeemed Everyman figure of the morality play tradition a second, unrepentant sinner who is finally damned. *Sexual Perversity* enacts this split: the opening scene shows Danny to be a blank, 'bear[ing]' an uncanny resemblance to the Humanum Genus figure', and 'completely subordinate' to Bernie, the Vice, who is amusing but, through his attempted corruption of Danny, increasingly dark and sinister.[21] The strains in Skeele's approach become apparent as he hunts for a role for Deb – she is both a virtuous figure and a second Everyman alongside Danny – and he does not even mention Joan.

Douglas Bruster suggests a more plausible comparison, to the city comedies of Ben Jonson (1572–1637). Where Skeele considers Danny in particular 'almost a universalised type ... endowed ... with a curious facelessness',[22] Bruster sees Mamet's characters in general as 'incomplete' and empty.[23] He is on stronger ground than Skeele in connecting Mamet 'with the long tradition of western drama satirizing urban venality',[24] a tradition that arguably also informs *Edmond*, and that Bruster both illuminates and obscures by concentrating almost exclusively on the connections and divergences between Mamet's Chicago and Ben Jonson's depiction of Jacobean London. Bernie resembles the charlatan of Jonsonian comedy, just as the 'entirely credulous' Dan is the gull,[25] although Geis convincingly counters that their dialogues have the quality of ritual exchanges.[26] Bruster also sees linguistic connections in the 'nonsense' the characters often speak: the colloquial, repetitive, fragmented idiolects of their apparently realistic although actually stylised – even 'surrealistic' – language.[27] More revealing, however, are the contrasts. The carnivalesque narrative of Jonsonian comedy brings about the expulsion of the wrongdoer and the restoration of communal order, aided by the purgation of the 'humours' through the exercise of free will. This is unavailable to Mamet's characters, who aim less for achievement than sheer survival in a closed and institutionalised capitalist system, causing Bruster in the end to perceive a 'conscious didacticism' in Mamet's work.[28]

This proposed didacticism is extremely problematic. At around the same time as Bruster's article, David Savran published in 1991 an essay in which he placed Mamet within contemporary 'new realist' theatre, which Savran regards as more confrontational and questioning than either the experimental theatre of the 1960s or the 'theatre of good intentions' in which moral values and decisions are clear-cut. New realism fractures the relations of cause and effect that produce the rationalist ideology of conventional realism (or naturalism). This is further undermined by a critical view of language itself, since the characters are shaped by a received language rather than masters of it, and therefore are sufficiently lacking in self-knowledge that their environment seems permanently confusing or suspect.[29] All of this describes very well the world of Mamet's early plays, except that in his case it is hard to know precisely what is being questioned or confronted. Bigsby starkly asserts that in *Sexual Perversity* Mamet offers a 'virtually Marxist analysis ... of capitalism in a state of decline',[30] although the symptoms of a profound social malaise lie obscurely in the isolation and alienation of characters who discuss sex with modish aggression while avoiding intimacy. Savran similarly remarks on the play's 'almost cubistic illumination of the multifaceted nature, the "perversity" of erotic relationships in a fragmented and compartmentalised society'.[31] As Mamet's career progresses it becomes still harder to detect precisely the object of the satire, or where the implied author's sympathies lie, which helps to account for the radically divided and divisive responses to such works as *Speed-the-Plow*, *Homicide* and *Oleanna*.

As usual with the early plays, Carroll's analysis is thorough and illuminating.[32] In what is almost a scene-by-scene dissection he shows how the scenes break down into groups, pairings and contrasts, their arrangement contributing to the sense that the 'protégés' are being subtly undermined by the insecurities of the 'mentors'. He demonstrates the dynamism of the construction, both within individual scenes – when Bernie encounters Joan in the singles bar he begins by wanting sex and ends by rejecting it, while Joan's trajectory is the reverse – and in the sequence of scenes between Dan and Deb that show why their relationship falls apart. The rapid juxtapositions and minimalist settings also mean that the audience never settles into a secure recognition of place, while the repeated device of having a character deliver a speech to unseen others gives the impression of a teeming urban environment, yet makes the characters appear utterly isolated. The same ambiguity causes Geis to observe the possibility that these unseen audiences may not be present at all; in any case, throughout the play the characters 'talk to themselves and talk at rather than with each other'.[33] Similarly, for Savran the 'poetry' of the play is 'based not on eloquence but on the disjunction between language and desire, on the failure of speech to articulate need' – in Bernie's rant against the women on the beach, for example.[34]

Varun Begley develops the recognition that spatial disorientation is crucial to the effect of the play in his comparison of *Sexual Perversity* to its adaptation for film, *About Last Night...* (Edward Zwick, 1986). Doubtless this first Hollywood appropriation of a Mamet play came about in part because of its apparently cinematic qualities, as well as its title and potentially racy subject matter. Most critics have perceived the film as a travesty on account of the rewrites that transformed Mamet's script into a feel-good romantic comedy, but Begley sees a more fundamental transformation in the treatment of space. Where the play 'uses metonymic shorthand – a few barstools, a desk, and a bed – to denote the range of public and private space', thereby contributing to the effects of fragmentation and alienation, the film 'lingers lovingly on the urban landscape', and in so doing transforms what in the theatre is an exploration of a sexual and social urban 'pathology' into an comforting environment of 'benevolent opportunity'.[35]

In an important analysis that questions the comparison to cinema while taking issue with previous readings of the relationship between Bernie and Dan, Bruce Barton insists upon 'the particularly *theatrical* nature of the *performance* of personality' (Barton's emphasis).[36] Like Ditsky and Geis, Barton sees Danny as an audience for Bernie, whose speeches therefore do not indicate solipsism or describe a state of affairs, but are performative utterances in which veracity is not important. Instead, the two characters tacitly agree to participate in the creation of a speech event, although in the end they become so consumed by this that the 'macro speech act' becomes self-deceiving. On the other hand, while the performative conditions of speech acts can allow the speaker to indulge in this kind of gleeful irresponsibility, speech also *acts*: it creates effects and has consequences in the world.

Barton here latches onto a crucial problem in Mamet's work. Storey encapsulates a whole tradition of Mamet criticism in stating that 'Bernie cannot really be described as a "character"' because he is 'a mélange of received verbal gestures'.[37] Figures such as Bernie, however, often desire independence and autonomy, so their apparent refuge in language masks frustration and the ever-present danger of physical violence. In Barton's view, the speakers in later plays become less and less protected from the effects of language and the presence of the listener or audience, but in *Sexual Perversity* the characters ultimately deny the efficacy of language and retreat into delusion. In the final scene at the beach Danny's aggressive interventions, abandoning his responsibilities as both performer and listener, are as discomfiting for Bernie as the previous silences, and Bernie's struggle to recover his former authority is revealed when, in a rare moment of self-consciousness also highlighted by Savran, he suddenly lets his mask slip and exclaims, 'What the fuck am I talking about?' Barton argues that such moments of self-revelation become more frequent and significant as Mamet's career progresses. The final lines show the extent of the two men's alienation: there are women on the beach, but they are not an audience, and the men display 'a *willed* ignorance generated by fear' of intimacy [Barton's emphasis]. This accounts for the peculiar effect of the play in the theatre: the riotous comedy of the dialogue provokes laughter, but the dynamic of the performance moves the characters into 'a safety zone of alienation'[38] and removal from the dangerous presence of an audience.

In these three short plays of the early 1970s, the failure of the characters to establish significant relationships, along with the experiments in fragmented forms, implied a critique of contemporary masculinity that most of Mamet's first critics took for granted. Yet he was soon championing in interviews a more conventional, linear dramatic structure seemingly at odds with his own practice. In retrospect, it is clear that with *Sexual Perversity* Mamet's apprenticeship, if that is what it can be called, was already at an end, and within a year he would have completed a work that most critics have subsequently accepted as a masterpiece, if not one of the greatest American plays of the twentieth century.

CHAPTER TWO

American Buffalo (1975)

American Buffalo is now generally acknowledged as Mamet's first dramatic masterpiece. Formally, it broke new ground for him in being a relatively lengthy, two-act play, and with only three cast members it implied a more complex, and perhaps a more realistic, notion of 'character' than its predecessors. Like *Lakeboat*, however, whatever plot it has seems to vanish like the mist: Teach and Don, two underclass hoodlums preparing to rob a coin collector who has purchased an apparently valuable nickel from Don's resale store, eventually call off the job on discovering that the third character, Bob, has lied about their proposed victim's whereabouts. Although several reviewers seemed to feel almost cheated by this turn of events, the play was the first to bring Mamet's name to national attention when it transferred to New York in 1977.

Stage history and early critical reception

In his seminal study *Broadway Theatre* (1994), Andrew Harris, a stage director as well as an academic, chose *American Buffalo* as one of just six plays through which to study Broadway theatre in general, and the processes by which a play finds its way to the stage. His chapter begins by sketching the theatrical culture of Chicago in Mamet's early years, and outlines the effect of Sanford Meisner's teaching on the budding playwright. Meisner had been a member of the Group Theatre in the 1930s, but eschewed the close analysis and 'emotional memory' of the 'method' of his colleague Lee Strasberg (1901–82). Meisner concentrated instead on 'action-based objective exercises' that complemented the improvisational work the young Mamet saw at Chicago's Second City.[1] Harris lucidly explains the effect of these influences on *American Buffalo*: instead of the lyrical or political reflections so common in the classical American play, Mamet's characters, focused on the immediate present and their future objective, make almost no references to the past or to a world beyond their immediate concerns. Mamet has consistently stated that Donny is the protagonist, but this was not clear to audiences even of the Chicago production, because as Harris explains, any recognition and reversal that Donny undergoes is passive, the result of receiving the telephone call from Ruthie about Fletcher. Audiences considered Teach the major character, and his role became still more dominant when the play was rewritten under the aegis of Ulu Grosbard (born 1929), director of the New York production in 1977, to the point that 'Teach completely took over the play'. Although *American Buffalo* was still not a realistic work, 'there was a feeling that a Broadway production demanded more consistent characterization. This meant eliminating ambiguities and anchoring every significant detail of the action in psychological motivation'.[2] Harris gives a short but detailed account of the textual changes, and this, along with the identification of how Meisner's teaching translated into Mamet's playwriting practice, and the account of the performances of Robert Duvall (born 1930) and, in a later Broadway revival, Al Pacino (born 1940) as Teach, make this an excellent starting-point for serious study of Mamet's first major play.

Not that all the New York critics were impressed: Harris lists the positive and negative reviewers, the latter being in a comfortable majority. It is important to be aware of the terms in which some of the most influential columnists rejected Mamet's work, since they contributed to a widespread perception of the playwright that helped to set the context for much of the subsequent academic criticism of the play. Their charges – that nothing happens, that the work lacks a moral framework, and that the incessant profanity was pointlessly shocking – would characterise popular opposition to Mamet's work for years to come.

Capitalism and ethics

At first, favourable critical responses predictably took the path of defending the play's artistic quality and thematic and moral seriousness. Most did so by underlining the implied critique of American capitalism. Jack V. Barbera attempts to counter the objections of reviewers by establishing *American Buffalo* as 'a play of intellectual content'.[3] He defends the language, noting that Teach's verbal annihilation of Ruthie is conducted 'in a rain of hammering trochees' (units of sound in which a stressed syllable is followed by an unstressed syllable), while suggesting that the elliptical nature of much of the dialogue is essentially urban realism.[4] Barbera anticipates many later critics both in suggesting that the 'content' of the play is to be found not in theme but in relationships, and in developing Mamet's frequent references in interview to the American economist Thorstein Veblen (1857–1929), from whom 'Mamet got the idea of an identical ethical perversity existing at both ends of the urban economic spectrum', with Mamet's underclass characters resenting a higher class that has appropriated notions of American democracy for its own ends.[5] June Schlueter and Elizabeth Forsyth observe that notions of business have infected all the relationships in the play.[6]

The most substantial and best study along these lines remains C. W. E. Bigsby's discussion in *David Mamet*, which presents the play as 'an assault on the American business ethic and an assertion of the collapse of morale and morality in America'.[7] Like Barbera, Bigsby connects the 'predatory' world of the play to Veblen, and in the course of an expert analysis of how the language of public service, business, and crime become interchangeable, argues that because *American Buffalo* emerged in the wake of Watergate and the end of the Vietnam war, 'Teach's parody of American revolutionary principles . . . is not quite the caricature it may appear'.[8] Rules of behaviour become at best a matter of negotiation and at worst wholly arbitrary – an insight that will inform both *Glengarry Glen Ross* and much subsequent criticism of both plays. *American Buffalo* also prompts perhaps the most vividly written chapter in Bigsby's book, with some wonderfully illuminating phrases: the moments when a character resorts to '[t]he language of classical liberalism', in a world in which such values have largely disappeared, 'are like the occasional intact buildings in a deserted city'.[9]

Money

Much of the best writing on *American Buffalo* has focused on how perceptions of money trouble Teach and Don, who are concerned about the language of 'facts'. This phenomenon is pointed out in Thomas L. King's essay of 1991, which may be read in one way as a helpful condensation of and advance on Anne Dean's contemporaneous book-length study. Like Dean, King is primarily concerned to break down the distinction between 'talk' and 'action', in his case in a more theorised way via Aristotle (384–322 BC), the structuralism that developed from the work of Ferdinand de Saussure (1857–1913), and the neopragmatist philosophy of Richard Rorty (1931–2007). In essence, his argument is simple: much of the drama revolves around Teach's demand for words to correspond to facts, to a verifiable external reality, as opposed to Don's pragmatic adherence to what King sees as a Rorty-like belief that 'truth is what it is better for us to believe'.[10] Within this framework King discusses such episodes as the conversation about the purely hypothetical safe that is almost willed into existence, the many negotiations concerning the value of the buffalo nickel, and the ending: in a fine insight, King notes that it is the final collapse of Teach's belief in 'facts' which causes him to state that '[t]here is nothing out there'.

Johan Callens, William Little and Jon Dietrick have all built on these foundations. Callens connects the slipperiness of linguistic value in the play to the shift towards a postmodern, context-bound notion of economic value. He develops a 'rapprochement' between *American Buffalo* and the eighteenth-century economist Adam Smith (1723–90), which at first seems a curious conjunction; but Callens uses Smith heuristically, to bring out with splendid clarity the long-recognised dramatic interplay of 'business' and 'friendship' in *American Buffalo*. These, he notes, are closely analogous to Smith's 'self-interest' and 'sympathy', categories that also appear at first to be distinct, yet which have a similarly 'precarious relationship': Smith's arguments concerning economic self-interest are inextricable from those that connect it to a socialising economic co-operation.[11] Unlike the other characters, Teach 'is exclusively driven by self-interest', and his habit of extrapolating from this to supposedly altruistic generalities, as when he states that he hit Bobby 'for the good of all', constitutes 'a parody of Smith's deriving communality from the serving of self-interest'.[12] Teach is a kind of entrepreneur, opposed to the division of labour in corporate business, and is paradoxically fond of the police because he sees them in Smith's terms, as protectors of private property. In short, Teach 'acts egotistically yet passes it off as selflessness'.[13]

The radically changed emphasis since Smith's time from production to consumption helps to account for the unstable notions of value in *American Buffalo*, evidenced particularly in the shifting value accorded the buffalo nickel, although Callens also agrees with King that what is really exchanged are 'human motives and desires'. *American Buffalo* therefore presents a parody, 'a shameless travesty of Smith's "natural" market' in which thieves set up a wholly artificial (and yet, in Teach's rhetoric, natural and 'free') market of supply and demand in scarce commodities by stealing the very goods they provide.[14] The role of the audience and the relationship of Donny and Bobby allows Callens rather optimistically to oppose Teach's manipulative 'instrumental reason' to the ideas of the 'public sphere' and 'communicative reason' advanced by Jürgen Habermas (born 1929), although Callens qualifies this by noting the corrosive effects of power in Mamet's world.[15]

Although William Little's brilliant analysis does not cite Callens's article, it takes many of the implications even further. Like Callens, Little notes the circularity of the trade in commodities and money, pointing out that this happens by definition because Don trades in second-hand goods. Little connects this to the characters' anxieties about contemporary free-market capitalism: unsettled by its inherent instability, ceaseless and rapid change, and tendency to generate crises, they wish to withdraw goods from circulation. Other kinds of circulation similarly worry them: the movements of other characters across stage space and other geographical areas, and (in the notoriously scatological language) movements associated with bodily functions. This makes the play a good subject for the abjection theory, concerned with boundaries and the division between inside and outside, that discreetly underpins Little's analysis. The characters long for 'figures that are *backed* by an authoritative standard of significance or value', but it is characteristic of Mamet's work in general to imply that if one assumes such backing exists behind 'a material sign – a word, a story, a piece of money, a piece of junk . . . one is bound to be conned'.[16]

Like Linda Dorff in her essay on *Glengarry Glen Ross* (see Chapter Seven), Little distinguishes idealistic 'real money' (or 'classical' money, in Don's term) that has intrinsic value, from 'representative money' that is merely a promise of value, and contaminated by figuration. Worried by the latter, Don runs through various possible ways of assessing the worth of the buffalo nickel – its cultural importance as an artefact, its physical condition, the value of the silver – and perhaps hopes that taking it out of circulation by stealing and sitting on it will put a stop to its unstable signification. Instead it would become, in an analogy repeated many times in the play, like 'unrelieved, unvoided shit', 'transcendent' and 'not affected and made ambiguous by figures' of whatever kind. Therefore, the characters '*want* to be full of shit because to be full of shit is to back out of the world', and the failure of the heist can be seen as an unconscious wish-fulfilment that illustrates these anxieties: 'they want the same old shit', because if the plot is put in motion it cannot be taken back, and yet the characters are always trying to take things back, as in Teach's constant self-contradictions.[17] There is a death instinct at work here, but when they give up on the heist to take Bobby to the hospital, they finally enter the figural world of circulation from which the shop has offered a fantasy of escape.

In another outstanding recent essay that must have gone to press before Little's article was published, Jon Dietrick advances many related arguments, while carefully distinguishing between Don and Teach and drawing together lines of reasoning concerning naturalism, talk and action that have long surrounded the play. Rather like Little and Dorff, Dietrick establishes the distinction between the paper money (Little's 'representative' money) that circulates in an economy based on signification, and the 'natural' money of a precious metal itself, which can only function in a barter economy. When Don refers to valuable coins as '[f]reak oddities of nature', he is therefore invoking a desire for the end of money. Dietrick draws on King's essay in showing that Don fears talk because he knows it can create a state of affairs rather than simply refer to it, while Teach insists that facts are transparent and exist independently of language; talk can therefore be manipulated to control Don, particularly where his relationships with Fletcher and Bobby are concerned. Noting that the proposed robbery makes little economic sense and that Don's motive – revenge – is personal, Dietrick argues that this is one more example of Don's desire to be free of a money economy, as is the nickel, which as a collector's item is no longer 'representative' money but a commodity, and one whose precise dollar value he is conspicuously unwilling to discuss. Teach's desire for a laissez-faire economy, meanwhile, is threatened by the personal, especially by the bond between Don and Bobby. Dietrick concludes that there is an 'anxiety over money at the heart of the logic of naturalism', whereby it 'must either be *only* paper and nothing else, or else it must somehow magically become the thing that it purports to represent'; this 'excludes the possibility of a paper money that signifies an agreed-upon value'. Dietrick suggests that a similar contradictory logic underlies Mamet's views on acting, the written text and business itself, so that *American Buffalo* ultimately becomes a condemnation of neither 'the money economy [nor] the language economy ... both [are] problematic but necessary systems of signification'.[18]

Masculinity and gender

In bringing out the complex and multiple metaphors that surround money in this play, both Callens and Little offer crucial qualifications to the widely accepted but simplistic view that 'rape and prostitution, primarily of men by men, becomes the central metaphor for American capitalism in Mamet's later plays'.[19] Nonetheless, the frequency with which Mamet constructs all-male worlds is striking, and became the subject of many analyses in the 1990s. Carla J. McDonough contends that Donny tries to establish his masculinity and preserve his position at the top of the hierarchy by choosing, in Bobby, a feminised character for a protégé; Teach exploits Don's anxiety about this status throughout the play. Although one might offer a more sympathetic reading, McDonough is surely right that 'fear of emasculation' motivates much of the action, and that this is intimately connected to the 'fear of the feminine' manifested in each character's view of Grace and Ruthie. Most obviously, Teach hates them because they threaten his own status, but more illuminating is the recognition that perceptions of the women are inextricably bound up with the characters' views of another absent figure, Fletcher. Don thinks of Ruthie as a friend but less admirable than Fletcher, his 'ultimate representative of masculine power and knowhow',[20] who ironically will fall victim to a mugging, while in accusing Fletcher of cheating at cards Teach implicitly pairs him with Ruthie.

Hersh Zeifman details the moral inversions, interchangeable insults, repetitions and contradictions of Teach's language, but denies that *American Buffalo* and *Glengarry Glen Ross* invite us to share the homophobia and misogyny of the characters. Instead, Zeifman suggests that if Mamet is to be accused of misogyny it can only be in the sense that the women who never appear on the stage but are frequently mentioned implicitly possess superior, yet stereotypically feminine, values. Their absence suggests to Zeifman that the relentlessly masculine world of the play is 'literally ruthless and graceless [Zeifman's emphasis]'.[21] Those who believe that the ending reveals the presence and persistence of charity and compassion (in Ruthie's telephone call to ask after Bobby, and in Don and Bobby's final reconciliation) challenge the import of this superb witticism.

Robert Vorlicky, for example, contends that such a movement towards intimacy is remarkable, indeed almost prohibited, in male-cast dramas. Vorlicky draws an important distinction between *American Buffalo* and *Glengarry*: in the later play the characters restrict themselves to social talk, but in *American Buffalo* this mingles with a more personal discourse, producing what Vorlicky terms 'sociopersonal talk',[22] as for example in the opening exchanges between Don and Bobby, and in the combination of notions of business and friendship in the play in general. Don, for example, segues effortlessly from an assertive mode in discussing business to compassionate concern for Bobby's welfare, and Vorlicky argues that the play is replete with this kind of dialogue because *American Buffalo* is a kind of family drama, albeit a family apparently composed entirely of single, heterosexual men. He carefully distinguishes the play's seven 'dyads' (two-handed dialogues) from its five 'triads' (three-handed conversations), and notes that Don participates in all twelve, as Teach and Bobby compete for his attention. In trying to detach Don from both Bobby and Fletcher, Teach pays lip service to Don's feelings of loyalty and personal concern for Bobby, while framing the job in a social context that would exclude the youngster; conversely, he implies that Fletcher's alleged dishonesty makes him a dangerous associate while he, Teach, is both friend and business partner to Don. Bobby is the only one who knows the heist must fail, and therefore replaces the buffalo nickel 'to save Don from his worst side: revenge'.[23] Teach's assault on Bobby, with whom he has more or less ceased communication, is characteristic of American all-male plays, and he trashes the shop because he has now been exposed, and so destroys the things he cannot have.

Language, dialogue and performance

The assumption of many early reviewers that the language of *American Buffalo* was little more than condensed, mundane realism is no longer tenable. Jeanette R. Malkin's positioning of the characters in relation to their capitalist environment recalls Bigsby's analysis, but she sees the language in unconvincingly monologic terms: 'Mamet's characters are soldered into their language ... and no alternate speech idiom or option is offered' to a language that is 'almost unintelligible', '[o]verburdened by incoherence', and contributes materially to a moral debasement in which 'human contact or compassion' is an 'impossibility'.[24] Consequently much of the aggression results from an inability to 'read' another character's meaning.

By contrast, Christopher C. Hudgins's substantial essay on Mamet's humour highlights the array of linguistic resources exploited by the characters. Contrary to the familiar arguments for a Beckettian absurdism or an anti-capitalist realism in the play, Hudgins proposes that it possesses a 'spirit of ironic celebration, even defiant celebration', not only in a more ambivalent treatment of business than many have been willing to concede, but also in the ethical dimension expressed in Don's essentially loving, paternalistic feelings for Bob.[25] The emotional reunion of this pair suggests the formal structure of comedy, but Hudgins is more interested in the dialogue, and he identifies an impressively broad range of sources and effects of the humour, including the innumerable verbal mistakes, elisions, profanities, self-contradictions and tall stories. For example, Teach's habitual malapropisms generate comic double meanings by unintentionally revealing his true feelings, while also perhaps causing the audience to make the mistake of assuming their superiority to him. Similarly, Hudgins cites a number of authorities in arguing that swearing is associated with the lower classes (the middle classes prefer blasphemy) and wrong-foots an audience that may begin by feeling uncomfortable with the threat of such language but, perhaps, ends by applauding its vivacity.

The range of different linguistic approaches that have been applied to the play is testament to this vitality. Stanton B. Garner's brief analysis considers deixis: the methods by which a speaker establishes his or her relation to the immediate context in which the utterance is made. The most obvious examples include the use of personal pronouns, and Garner contends that modern drama often exhibits a 'theatricalized deixis' that undercuts the presumption of realism. To illustrate this point he cites Teach's account of the poker game with Grace and Ruthie. Teach uses the first person pronoun 'I' repeatedly in a very short passage, and although he occasionally widens the circle to include Don, the only other character on the stage at this moment, nevertheless '[w]hat Teach displays so forcefully is true, to varying extents, for all of Mamet's characters: they tend to talk *at* each other'.[26] Yet, as many other critics also observe in different contexts, this is quite the opposite of a confessional mode: instead characters present themselves as performers, much as Teach does in Garner's example, where he is principally a storyteller. Similarly, Deborah R. Geis notes that most of the 'homiletic' speeches belong to Teach, the irony of whose nickname escapes no critic. She borrows the term from Shakespearean criticism to argue that Teach's soliloquies purport to offer a kind of rhetorical and philosophical, rather than personal and introspective, comment on life in general. When Teach delivers his deathless analysis of free enterprise, for example, the audience perceives the gap between his restricted knowledge of the world and his confident assertions about it, in lines that suggest that he also believes his response to the world to be that of 'a deeply moral human being'.[27]

This emphasis on performance helps to explain why it is invariably Teach who strikes audiences as the central character. Bruce Barton neatly summarises Mamet's view of character as 'an acquired behaviour motivated by isolated desire': the characters, particularly in the early plays, try to avoid interactive engagement with a spectator.[28] These defensive strategies are incompatible with spontaneous live perform- ance, accounting for much of the tension in the theatre. For example, when Teach feels threatened by Don's responses he improvises, and 'the momentum of personal turmoil [is] desperately disguised as com- mon sense'.[29] His impassioned language, the sign of a rage at source, is a performance, and always has the effect of deferring the action he insists he wants. Accordingly, Barton pinpoints the moment of reversal as occurring when Teach shifts from performance to action in assault- ing Bob, apparently because of an intuitive grasp that Bob's story is bogus, which brings about a succession of closing events marked by action and understanding rather than inconsequential storytelling and evasion. This approach allows Barton to establish a crucial difference from a play to which *American Buffalo* is compared with distracting regu- larity: *Waiting for Godot* (1953 in French, 1955 in English). Beckett's characters unfailingly, and paradoxically, make sense of their seemingly meaningless world, whereas Mamet's try unsuccessfully to manufacture a kind of rationality from the shards of a culture they barely understand. However, because the characters lack self-awareness, this attempt can only be tentative.

Toby Silverman Zinman argues for a specifically Jewish rhythm and cadence to Mamet's dialogue. In a telling example, she notes that Don's line 'You don't have *friends* in this life' can be read interrogatively, meaning 'something like, "if you don't have *friends* in this life, life is intolerable"', a reading that arguably makes more sense than the nihilis- tic world-view that otherwise emerges.[30] Leslie Kane makes a similarly convincing case for seeing the syntax, at least, as inescapably marked by Yiddish inflections, and her provocative claim that Teach is 'one of Mamet's great Jewish characterizations' is well supported. As ever, some of Kane's suggestions are quite brilliant, if not necessarily persuasive; for example, she interprets the surreal moment when Teach makes him- self a paper hat as a reference to medieval anti-Semitic propaganda, in which Jews were sometimes represented 'clothed in the abhorrent *pileum cornutum*, a three-cornered horned hat'.[31]

Alain Piette has recently argued that there is far more action in the play than is generally conceded: offstage happenings are often violent, those onstage frequently a good deal more so. Meanwhile, arithmetic alone suggests that the putative collection of coins is probably not worth very much, and what happens onstage is a good deal more exciting than the failure of the heist that upset many of the play's earliest reviewers. Piette concludes with a few largely speculative suggestions that Bobby may be smarter than he looks, and may indeed have been double-crossing Teach and Don.[32]

The Broadway staging of *American Buffalo* immediately established Mamet's reputation as a master of urban profanity, but reviewers quickly began to recognise an extraordinary range to his work that belied the superficial realism. The most significant additional plays to be staged in that same landmark year of 1977 were both marked by a metadramatic quality, but otherwise were as radically different from one another as each is to *American Buffalo*.

CHAPTER THREE

A Life in the Theatre (1977),
The Water Engine (1977),
Mr. Happiness (1977)

A Life in the Theatre

First performed in 1977, and revived many times thereafter, this has been one of Mamet's most durable plays. One obvious reason is that it is highly theatrical, with the relationship between a younger and an older actor being explored, in part, via a series of pastiches and parodies of familiar genres. Crucial to the effect of the play, in the first production at least, is that during these 'onstage' scenes the characters are positioned upstage with their backs turned towards the audience, which witnesses them from behind as they perform to a second, imaginary audience in an imaginary theatre, while during the 'backstage' scenes they are positioned conventionally downstage, facing us.

Anne Dean discusses *A Life in the Theatre* as a kind of character study in which Robert 'struggles to find meaning in banality because to admit the frailty of his position as a third-rate actor struggling to make a living on the very fringe of the profession would be to invite terror and despair'.[1] Most critics perceive a similarly tragic element to the backstage story (William Herman's claim that this is 'one of Mamet's most optimistic works'[2] is hard to fathom), and its ironic treatment of the hoary question of the relationship between acting and life has been discussed many times. C. W. E. Bigsby, for example, suggests it invites speculation about the ways in which lives outside the theatre can seem to follow a scripted pattern spoken in language not of our own making, while noting that here the fusion of theatrical and external worlds is not absolute. This would suggest that it is not quite a postmodernist play in the manner of Samuel Beckett or Tom Stoppard (born 1937), although Bigsby frequently invokes these playwrights, and he perhaps is the target of an uncharacteristically petulant remark by Carroll, who has a tendency to see John and particularly Robert as rounded, realistic characters, and dismisses the idea of 'zipping [the play] up in a Beckett–Stoppard bag'.[3]

The bag has looked sturdy enough to most critics, and indeed Deborah R. Geis uses a post-structuralist terminology that takes the argument beyond Bigsby's humanist emphases. Her most important insight here concerns the nature of John's soliloquies. Soliloquies often indicate introspection, and therefore, perhaps, the kind of psychological characterisation to which Mamet is averse on principle. However, Geis notes that Robert's soliloquies indicate the inability of the actor to turn off the performance, as well as his loneliness. In the final scene, John eavesdrops on Robert addressing a deserted theatre in the presence of a non-existent imaginary audience (and yet in the presence of those watching Mamet's play), a paradoxical moment that captures the essential quality of the soliloquy: 'the presence of the audience is both ignored in the intimacy of the moment and acknowledged in the vocalization of the speaker's thoughts'.[4] Geis's insight concerning Teach's homiletic soliloquies in *American Buffalo* is therefore equally applicable to *A Life in the Theatre*: Robert's speeches tend to generate a dramatic irony whereby the audience is alerted not to his perceptiveness but to his inadequacies.

Geis argues that instead of being a mentor, Robert is instead 'in the process of becoming a cipher, a character, an empty sign that has a floating referent',[5] and suggests that while another playwright might have made Robert a tragic hero, Mamet's treatment of him is bound up with the 'metadramatic' quality of the play; he can offer John no real insight into 'life'. This provides an important gloss on Pascale Hubert-Liebler's analysis of the teacher–pupil relationship via the study of power and knowledge provided by the French philosopher Michel Foucault (1926–84). As Hubert-Liebler sees it, most of Mamet's characters are losers without access to power, and channel their frustrated desire for authority either through storytelling or by adopting the role of teacher or mentor to another, usually younger, character; yet in Mamet's world there are no fixed or uncorrupted values, and therefore little worthwhile knowledge or experience to be transmitted. Robert, for example, is a ham actor who knows little of life beyond the theatre, and is jealous of John both socially and professionally. The teacher, as Hubert-Liebler puts it in distinctly Foucauldian vein, 'exercises the prerogatives of questioning, testing, and punishing, while the student has to submit to his probing and accept his decisions'.[6] This 'professorial discourse' may be conducted in either the 'autonomous' (monologic) mode, as in Robert's disquisitions on the subject of acting in *A Life in the Theatre*, or the 'interactive' (question-and-answer) mode, as in the opening exchanges between Don and Bob in *American Buffalo*, where the teacher may be assessing the pupil while attempting to stimulate him towards self-learning. The relationship may provide a surrogate father–son relationship or, in *The Shawl* and *A Life in the Theatre* in particular, a potential or actual realisation of the sexual dynamic between the older and younger man that Hubert-Liebler compares to the merging of pedagogy and pederasty in ancient Greece. This is very clear in scene 8, which contains numerous double entendres as John assists Robert in fixing the broken zipper on his trousers.

The power relationship, however, is inherently unstable, and in Mamet's plays is already compromised through the teacher's inarticulacy or incompetence. The older character fears age and decline, for which some statistical evidence is usually offered (Robert's bad reviews, for instance, or Levene's position on the sales chart in *Glengarry Glen Ross*), and he therefore needs the student as a mirror that will reflect back to him a more potent self-image. This, however, transfers power to the student, who already threatens to rival or even eclipse the teacher if the mentorship is successful, as is all too apparent in Robert's anxious peevishness concerning John's performances and reviews. The last chance for the teacher is to belittle the student or even resort to verbal or physical violence, actions which all entail the likelihood that the relationship will be ended altogether by the student who, as Hubert-Liebler astutely observes, usually has relatively little incentive for entering into or preserving the relationship since he merely 'consents to it rather than actively seeks it'.[7] The younger man is generally less interested in following an apprenticeship than in getting quick results.

Hubert-Liebler offers discriminating ways of investigating what was already a well-worn topic in Mamet criticism, and must be credited as one of the first critics to introduce a rigorous theoretical method to the study of the plays. The only real weakness lies, oddly enough, in the approach via Foucault's essay 'The Subject and Power' (1982), which is specifically concerned with how such relationships function within scholastic institutions. Mamet has remarked that his plays unfold in a 'closed moral universe',[8] but their physical settings are a good deal more porous, and therefore less amenable to the methods of Foucauldian surveillance, than is often conceded. In *A Life in the Theatre*, for example, much of the tension derives from the fact that John apparently conducts a full and rounded social life, with the ready ironies of the play deriving from the fact that it is only Robert who spends his life almost exclusively, it would seem, *in the theatre*.

To the extent that Robert is a teacher, his particular field of knowledge is the stage, and much of the comedy comes from the combination of pomposity and banality in his observations on the subject. As Jerry Dickey observes, Mamet's views on acting, published at book length in *True and False* (1998), have remained remarkably consistent, although most agree that his objections to acting schools are more appropriately directed at the American Method than at the ideas of Konstantin

Stanislavsky (1863–1938).[9] Dickey takes a left-field approach by looking at six excerpts from *A Life in the Theatre* to illustrate Mamet's ideas in *True and False*, concluding that while the play suggests a certain admiration for Robert's capacity to endure, he is nevertheless emblematic of 'all that Mamet feels is wrong with American acting'.[10]

The Water Engine

The metadramatic quality of *A Life in the Theatre* connects it to the contemporaneous and far more complex *The Water Engine*, which Mamet originally wrote as a short story, before reconceiving it for National Public Radio's *Earplay* in 1977, a successful stage play in the same year, and even an original screenplay completed in 1978. In a final incarnation, it was produced for American television in 1992, in a version directed by Steven Schachter, who had also directed the 1978 stage premiere. This complicated history is in part to be explained by the remarkably intricate set of media interactions at work in what is, in essence, a simple story – 'an American fable', as the subtitle has it – set during the Century of Progress Exhibition in Chicago in 1933. Its protagonist is Charles Lang, an inventor who creates the eponymous contraption but who is threatened, kidnapped and finally murdered by the industrial concerns whose power is challenged by the existence of a machine that can use water as fuel. Throughout the play a Chainletter, which functions as a kind of oblique narratorial commentary on the action, has insisted that all people are connected, and before his demise Lang mails the plans for his invention to the technologically minded boy, Bernie, who works in the local store.

Most accounts of the play engage with Schachter's production, of which Dennis Carroll gives a particularly detailed account. In this landmark presentation the stage was set up as a radio station in 1934, in which actors were sometimes reading from a script and at other times acting out their parts, while the theatre audience was prompted to respond on cue, as if they were really at the studio. The action was prefaced by the monologue of an onstage announcer and a set of 1930s songs performed by Annie Hat, neither of which is included in the published script; instead, in some productions *Mr. Happiness* (below) has functioned as a curtain-raiser. In Carroll's opinion this apparently complicated staging, the juxtapositions of different places and time-frames that can look jumbled on the page, worked so fluidly and fluently in the theatre that even the Chainletter was 'organically integrated'. The use of the radio effects allowed the story to appear variously credible or ironic, and spectators became progressively more involved in the action and less diverted by the medium, although Carroll still argues that the play prompts a 'historification' in the manner of Bertolt Brecht (1898–1956), whereby the audience reflects critically on both the distinctions between its own time and the 1930s, and the construction of contemporary and equally misleading fables.[11]

Bigsby notes that in some respects *The Water Engine* offers a parody of 1930s protest theatre, with the apparent critique of American capitalism counterpointed by a mode of staging that suggests that while 'America' may be an ideological myth, audiences have a need for explanatory fictions that create a national consensus about history and identity; as Bigsby puts it, in this play Mamet is 'having his social and philosophic cake and eating it, too'. This produces an arresting argument about the choric role of the many minor characters, as when a knife grinder passes Lang just as he is about to be betrayed, or when the elevator attendant announces 'we're going down' just after the lawyer has described his vision of a capitalist nirvana. Such moments are not simply ironic; they are 'an assertion of interconnection, of equivalence between public and private experience and between different fictional worlds'.[12] The difficulty lies in how to decide between these worlds, since in Geis's words, the 'multiple voices...offer us different "layers" of fiction, and Mamet plays with our (in)ability to determine which, if any, can be considered reliable or authoritative'.[13] In this way the play asks us to act as jurors in assessing what are also different kinds of address, from the declamatory mode of the soapbox speakers to the general circulation of gossip. No 'truth' can be determined, and instead the play celebrates the act of communication and the various media of transmission.

Such considerations lead Bigsby to suggest that the play 'is perhaps best read as a gesture of complicity', since of course Mamet himself is contributing to the circulation of fictions and part of the play's appeal lies in the 'comic-book narrative'[14] and the urge to acquire something for nothing that Mamet elsewhere sees behind an American ideology ostensibly founded on hard work and equal opportunity. This is as true of the relatively sympathetic characters as of the overbearing representatives of big business: Lang, after all, has stolen equipment from his employers to make a machine powered by fuel that drops from the sky, while at the end of the play Bernie discovers that the plans for this miraculous invention have almost literally fallen into his lap. In this sense the consumers of such narratives are also, perhaps, complicit in the perpetuation of the rags-to-riches myth derived from the novels for boys of Horatio Alger (1832–99) – a myth to which Bigsby appositely compares Mamet's fable.

This approach has recently been theorised and taken further in Johan Callens's superb analysis, which builds on two earlier essays by Steven Price and develops a highly sophisticated reading via Jay David Bolter and Richard Grusin's *Remediation: Understanding New Media* (1999). Writing in 1995, Price had argued that a recurrent but then rarely noted aspect of Mamet's work was the frequency with which different media interact on Mamet's stage, and suggested that 'Mamet's figures of authority retain their power by using media as a semi-permeable membrane: information flows only one way'.[15] Callens briefly notes in Mamet's work the intertextual references to other authors, the multiple registers in the dialogue, and Mamet's transformation of his own plays or other works into film scripts, before considering *The Water Engine*. He traces the history of the work's various incarnations and argues that each incorporates 'remediation', in the specific sense that 'the earlier medium', and not just the plot and characters, 'is represented in the remedial process'.[16] Each new transformation modifies the use of the media within it (including telephones, transportation and the mail service, as well as radio, theatre and film), since these may contribute to the actual narration of the story as well as being represented within the story itself. The remediation in *The Water Engine* comments ironically on the naively simple urban legend of a thwarted environmental utopia, much as Callens sees the work of Bolter and Grusin superseding the utopian vision of connectedness in the media-enabled 'global village' offered by Marshall McLuhan (1911–80). All these media in *The Water Engine* are in the service of capital and commercial interests, leading Callens to dispute the many reviews that saw the play as basking in a kind of nostalgia for the lost innocence of radio.

Equally important is Callens's rethinking of the 'frame' and 'inset' stories. The Chainletter appears to function as part of the 'frame' story, casting an ironic perspective on the 'inset' of the story about Charles Lang; yet the situation is more complicated, because at times the Chainletter also appears within the inset, producing a tension between them that highlights 'Bolter & Grusin's double logic of remediation'.[17] According to this 'double logic', the invisibility and apparent transparency of radio can, on the one hand, give it great immediacy, notably when the Chainletter intervenes on several occasions as if to transmit authorial intention; on the other hand, there may be a failure to 'repress the mediation', resulting in the medium becoming very visible and opaque, as when the Chainletter appears within the story (especially in the stage version) as a material text, rather than as a simple voiceover. Via extensive discussion of Schachter's stage and television productions in particular, and of Mamet's essay 'Encased by Technology' (in *Some Freaks*), Callens suggests that Mamet belongs to a 'metatheatrical tradition',[18] yet retains a 'lingering nostalgia for a non-existing, total transparency'.[19] This is a crucial conclusion, because its emphases are repeated in Jon Dietrick's analysis of money in *American Buffalo* (discussed in Chapter Two), and indeed in many discussions of Mamet's approach to Judaism.

Mr. Happiness

Some productions of *The Water Engine* were prefaced by this short but brilliant companion piece, a one-man performance in which a radio agony aunt reads from the letters he has received and offers his advice; the intertextual reference appears to be to the short novel *Miss Lonelyhearts* (1933) by Nathanael West (1903–40). Steven H. Gale considers that *Mr. Happiness* is 'nothing very deep or inspiring – merely an entertainment',[20] but this is plainly too simple; as Bigsby observes, although on the face of it there is something reassuring about Mr Happiness's 'mixture of pieties, popular philosophy and cant mixed in with common sense', one cannot ignore 'the orchestrated cries of suffering, the sense of incompletion, loss, and pain, the desperation that lies behind the letters'.[21] Moreover, Mr Happiness himself is a potentially disturbing figure, since he exerts complete control over the programme and, by implication, its audience, to the extent that John Ditsky considers him a 'chillingly disembodied speaking voice, one which holds power over its listeners because they, like good fascisti, have eagerly handed it over'.[22] As with *The Water Engine*, then, sophisticated approaches to *Mr. Happiness* are alert to Mamet's fascination with the workings of power, an ever-present aspect of his dialogue but here embedded in the technological media of communication and deception.

In retrospect, *The Water Engine* has appeared significant in portending the extraordinary range of experimentation in a vast range of genres and media that continues to characterise Mamet's work. As we shall see in the next chapter, however, even in the 1970s he was extending his range beyond the realism of *American Buffalo* and the metadrama of *A Life in the Theatre* or *The Water Engine* to include children's theatre, family dramas, historical plays, and even a mythic romance in quasi-musical form.

CHAPTER FOUR

Other 1970s Plays: *The Woods* (1977), *Reunion* (1976), *Dark Pony* (1977), Children's Plays, *Squirrels* (1974), *Marranos* (1975), *Lone Canoe* (1979)

M amet's early reputation as a realist was largely based on a certain reading of *Sexual Perversity in Chicago* and *American Buffalo*, but he was equally renowned as a remarkably prolific writer in a varied range of styles. Although his 1970s output is best represented by the plays considered in the first three chapters of this Guide, many others remain of interest, although none has achieved comparable critical recognition.

The Woods (1977)

This two-hander about a young couple attempting to develop their relationship on a trip to the woods has struck some commentators as a major work. John Russell Taylor briefly discusses *The Woods* and *American Buffalo*, alongside some of the work of Sam Shepard (born 1943), to illustrate the commonplace argument that, in place of the classical myths that animated William Shakespeare (1564–1616) and other dramatists of early modern Europe, contemporary American writers are drawn to discover mythic resonance through the woods and the West.[1] Nevertheless, he suggests that the university-educated Mamet must have been drawing on classical Greek myths of Orestes and Oedipus in *The Woods*. Although there is something in his suggestion that Nick and Ruth use mythic storytelling to people their world with heroes, he does not establish this by exploring the play in any detail, so it appears disproportionately light in view of the burden Taylor expects it to carry.

This imbalance between implicit intention and perceived achievement, between what some reviewers saw as a profoundly archetypal presentation of human relationships and what others considered sentimental or banal, helps to explain more generally why Dennis Carroll was not wholly wide of the mark in suggesting, in his 1987 study of the writer, that *The Woods* was 'Mamet's most controversial play' to date. A second source of controversy was that the play attempts, or appears to attempt, a more fully realised depiction of a male–female relationship than is found in *Sexual Perversity in Chicago*; yet it could be and was seen by many critics, in Carroll's summation of a familiar response, 'as a deeply misogynist play masquerading as a feminist one'.[2] Like Dan and Deb in *Sexual Perversity*, Nick and Ruth are very young, and often appear to be younger still. This creates a potential difficulty, because the play concerns their attempts to overcome their fears about sex and commitment, and since they lack maturity and linguistic resources there can be a discrepancy between the language and the apparent import of the action. In this respect, Deborah R. Geis's passing comment is illuminating. Placing *The Woods* alongside several other plays of the 1970s, Geis rightly observes that Mamet eschews the psychological soliloquy and substitutes storytelling, so that any suggestion of the character's inner life tends to be emerge, if at all, through dialogue with other characters.[3]

Bigsby finds much to admire in *The Woods*, but recognises that what is apparently a movement towards 'a moment of grace' as the play closes is instead 'a declaration of faith'.[4] More successful, for Bigsby, are the ways in which Mamet brings out the emotional pressures lying under the surface of dialogue which on the face of it is, in turn, portentous, banal and repetitive. He compares this to two of Hemingway's short stories, 'Hills Like White Elephants' (1927), in which it becomes evident that the relationship between a man and a woman is undergoing a crisis and the woman is about to have an abortion, even though none of this is stated as such; and 'Big, Two-Hearted River' (1924), in which a character seeks to contain the emotional turmoil that threatens to engulf him through a fastidious attention to the details of language and action. In later years it would become routine to compare Mamet to Hemingway, for all the wrong reasons (masculinity, men in the woods, etc.); here Bigsby provides much more impressive grounds for the connection.

And yet, as with *The Duck Variations*, his reading seems to rest heavily on certain prior assumptions about the nature of drama itself. He notes that endings are constructed by the writer, but this is obviously true of all plays (as opposed to performance art), so mentioning it adds nothing; and although he recognises that at times the stories carry a measure of threat, this line is soon dropped, so that by the end of his discussion he is arguing that Ruth and Nick escape from the pressures of sexuality by means of 'pure fiction'.[5] Carroll notes that storytelling can also be used as a form of aggression or genuine revelation, and *The Woods* provides him with a convincing case in point. In the first scene, Ruth's story of the babes in the wood is framed by the story of her grandmother, married to a man whose sexual potency is an implicit challenge and threat to Nick. He responds with the story of his father's wartime companion who went insane and killed himself after visiting the house to which Nick has just brought Ruth. Ruth adjusts the story towards the end of scene 2, adopting the motif of the Martian to suggest that partners in a relationship can remain unknown to each other. In the final scene Nick, in turn, picks up on Ruth's earlier story about the bear, but now he is using it not as an act of aggression but to reveal his own anxieties about masculinity and his inability to articulate his feelings. While the ending is ambivalent, Carroll finds in Ruth's rejection of Nick's story an essentially optimistic implication that the lovers may be able to develop an appropriate language. In finding the problems of language at the heart of a frustrating heterosexual relationship, both Carroll and Bigsby connect *The Woods* to *Sexual Perversity*.

Reunion (1976) and *Dark Pony* (1977)

A familiar argument about classic American drama holds that it is primarily concerned with the domestic sphere, almost by default: the Western movie or the 'great American novel' may be able to do justice to a history of constant westward expansion and Manifest Destiny, but direct engagement with that experience seems to be precluded from the stage almost by definition. Equally, it has been noted many times that Mamet is an exception: he certainly writes about the world of men, but usually men at work, in bars, in pool halls – anywhere, in fact, but in the home. That does not mean that he fails to address family relationships, merely that he writes about situations in which the family unit has already disintegrated, as these short plays bear out. *Reunion*, first performed in 1976, concerns the visit by Carol, a 24-year-old divorcee unhappily married for a second time, to the apartment of her father, Bernie, from whom she has been estranged for many years. Bigsby considers that with the passing of time, failure and desperation are no longer temporary difficulties for these characters but have settled into permanency. In a modification of his general view that in Mamet's plays stories are either evasions of the truth or lead worryingly towards a revelation of the truth they seek to avoid, Bigsby argues that in *Reunion* it does not matter whether the recollections of the past are accurate: rather, Bernie and Carol seek out a time in the past that offers safe territory, because that time is 'protected from knowledge of the betrayals that followed'.[6] No play offers safer ground for his view that the dialogues are little more than overlapping monologues, that the stories characters tell are largely bereft of anything other than a self-defensive value, and that Mamet's recurrent subject is the emotional distance between people caught in a land in which community and social institutions, not least the institution of marriage, have collapsed.

As usual, Carroll sees the play very differently. As in his discussion of *The Duck Variations*, he is sharp in drawing out the differences between the characters, and he notes here that Bernie possesses a certain working-class recognition that life holds no further promise for him and has come to accept his lot, whereas his daughter is now imbued with middle-class values and has traces of upward mobility, taking greater responsibility and looking for ways to improve her situation. Carroll also finds in Bernie's relative volubility and Carol's reticence an illustration of a recurrent Mamet situation: here, Carol is testing Bernie, forcing him to continue talking (and thereby prompting even more stumbling and fractured syntax), looking for signs that he can become the father he never was. And where Bigsby finds little more than repeated failures in the dialogue, Carroll sees the action building to a climax following a furious argument in which Carol forces Bernie to accept that she is entitled to a father. Despite Bernie's backsliding, and his final error in giving her a bracelet with the wrong birthdate inscribed on it, Carroll sees hopeful signs both that their relationship can be resurrected and that Bernie's journey has come to a satisfactory resolution.

In 1977 Mamet paired and preceded *Reunion* with a new ten-minute short, *Dark Pony*, another two-hander in which, on a drive home, a father tells his daughter the story of Rain Boy, a young Indian brave, who calls for his faithful horse Dark Pony to assist him whenever he finds himself in danger. Bigsby is always excellent at demolishing the idiocies of reviewers, some of whom saw the piece as merely comforting; in a country in which the historical treatment of the indigenous population amounts to nothing less than genocide, the magical interventions of the horse that saves them is surely heavily ironic. Moreover, when staged with *Reunion* the ironies multiply, for the obvious implication is that the characters are Bernie and Carol and that *Dark Pony* is an episode from their past. If so, the conjunction suggests that the father's attempts to protect his daughter from looming disaster were likewise doomed to failure. Only in the general comments about children's stories and fairy tales does Bigsby strike a questionable note: as ever, he sees their fictions as necessarily evasive, lies told in a doomed attempt to protect children from the horrors of adult life, without acknowledging the darkness that so often lies at their heart (as in many of the stories collected by the brothers Jacob Ludwig Grimm [1785–1865] and Wilhelm Karl Grimm [1786–1859]); as Bigsby recognises, the Grimms' versian of 'Babes in the Wood' imparts an atmosphere of foreboding to *The Woods*.

Bruce Barton contrasts the plays: the two characters in *Reunion* share no common cultural ground, and therefore their encounter is doomed to failure, whereas in *Dark Pony* they are joined together in space and time, and in the appreciation of the story. On the other hand, the latter piece is essentially passive – there is little dynamic interaction between teller and listener – accentuating its evanescent quality. For Barton, then, each explores in different ways the limits of successful performance, and he examines them in relation to *The Shawl*, the 'accomplishment' of which 'lies in its ability to combine the greater self-reflection of *Reunion* and *Dark Pony* with the always emergent physical engagement of Mamet's more eruptive works'.[7]

Three children's plays (1974–83)

The punning title of Thomas P. Adler's 'Mamet's *Three Children's Plays*: Where the Wilder Things Are'[8] connects the pieces Mamet wrote for younger audiences between 1974 and 1983 both to the classic children's book *Where the Wild Things Are* (1964) by Maurice Sendak (born 1928) and to Thornton Wilder (1897–1975), whose *Our Town* (1938) is one of Mamet's favourite plays. Adler proposes connections between Wilder and *The Uses of Enchantment: The Meaning and Importance of Fairy Tales* (1976) by the psychologist Bruno Bettelheim (1903–90), a book Mamet has frequently cited as a major influence: for all three writers, notes Adler, 'characterisation' and action should be divested of all but the most essential elements, to aid the audience or reader's identification with the protagonist and allow the story to do its work through the unconscious.

Adler connects to Wilder the metatheatrical qualities of the earliest of these plays, *The Poet and the Rent* (1974), and discusses the second, *The Revenge of the Space Pandas; or, Binky Rudich and the Two-Speed Clock* (1975) in terms of romantic comedy and a pattern of departure from and return to home that resonates throughout much of Mamet's work. By far the most interesting of the three children's plays is *The Frog Prince* (1983), which bears little resemblance to the Grimms' story of the same name. In their version, a beautiful princess loses her golden ball at the bottom of a well. She promises an ugly frog (in reality a bewitched prince) that she will share her bed with him if he retrieves it. He does so, and the princess's father insists that she keep her promise to the frog; repulsed, she hurls it against the wall, at which point he reverts to human form, and the couple are married. Adler explains Mamet's version as a kind of 'prequel' that accounts for the spell: a peasant woman cast it because the prince refused to give her some flowers he had picked for the princess. She comes to rule the kingdom as a dictator; the prince regains human form when a kindly milkmaid he has helped kisses him, and when he encounters the peasant women again he now gives her his flowers. Adler notes the dark quality to the play, accentuated by language and ideas more accessible to adults than children, and its disturbing moral: the prince had intended to place his flowers on the grave of a friend who has died in his service but is forced instead to surrender them to the peasant woman, suggesting that life is ultimately governed by forces that are unaccountably fickle and malign.

There is an almost communistic aspect to the children's plays that Adler also draws out. This is least apparent in the futuristic *Revenge of the Space Pandas*, in which, however, the decision to call a far-away planet 'Crestview' in order to attract investors anticipates the misleading titles given to the real estate sold in *Glengarry Glen Ross*. The slender plot of *The Poet and the Rent* hangs on the poet's difficulties in paying a grasping landlord, while several of the key events in *The Frog Prince* revolve around a character's attempts to secure private dominion over lands which, the play implies, should be regarded as free for the benefit of all. In these ways both Bigsby and Adler see the children's plays as lending support to their view of Mamet, at this stage of his career at least, as a social critic with quasi-Marxist leanings.

Squirrels (1974)

Squirrels is frequently and appropriately considered a first attempt at subject matter that Mamet would soon dramatise more effectively in *A Life in the Theatre*. It is a comedy about two writers: Art, the older, more pompous figure who is suffering writer's block concerning his story about squirrels, and Edmond, the younger man who hopes to learn the craft of writing from Art and is soon threatening to upstage his mentor, both by completing Art's work and by developing a relationship with the Cleaning Lady, who is another writer and Art's former lover. Carroll and Pascale Hubert-Liebler both consider *Squirrels* to be an undistinguished illustration of the theme of learning in Mamet's plays, but perhaps the most insightful critical observation on the play is Carroll's objection that, because it concerns writers who fuss grandiloquently over the need to find the precise word, it has an 'uncertain idiomatic allegiance'.[9] This unrealistic mixing of registers is something that would come to characterise Mamet's work from the mid-1980s onwards, leading most critics eventually to abandon the idea that he is a realistic writer. In this connection it is worth noting that when Mamet attended a production in 1990, he made up a new closing line – 'Or words to that effect' – that was used for the remaining performances. Toby Silverman Zinman takes this new line to represent her general view of the playwright, which is that it is not the content – '*what* Mamet has to say has been said before' – but the form of the words that matters.[10]

Unpublished plays: *Marranos* (1975) and *Lone Canoe* (1979)

Marranos was commissioned by the Bernard Horwich Jewish Community Center in Skokie, Illinois, in 1975. Aside from that production it remains unperformed and unpublished, for the simple reason that Mamet does not rate it highly. Students of the playwright's work are therefore indebted to Leslie Kane, who describes it in detail and makes an excellent case for seeing it as crucial both in Mamet's development and in understanding his later work.[11] *Marranos* was the first of Mamet's plays in which the ethnicity of the characters is of fundamental importance, the title referring to Jews who tried to escape persecution under the Spanish Inquisition. After a prologue, the first act begins with Dom H revealing to his 12-year-old grandson, Joao, the truth that the family is not Catholic, but Jewish. His father, Diogo, suspects they have been betrayed to the authorities, and makes preparations for escape. The second act brings the dreaded visitation of the villainous persecutor Fra Benedetto, whom Dom H and Diogo attempt to thwart by weaving a series of fictions that Kane compares to those of Bernie in *Sexual Perversity*, and to the competition between the two actors in *A Life in the Theatre*. Having apparently succeeded, the family is finally betrayed by the nursemaid, Gracia, revealed as having been the traitor all along and therefore, Kane notes, becoming the first in a line of deceptive women in Mamet's works. The family is arrested, and only Joao escapes. The play's two acts are framed by a prologue and epilogue presented by a latter-day nun, from whom the audience infers that Joao somehow ended up in South America, where his apparent descendants still recite some mangled Hebrew prayers.

The connections Kane makes between *Marranos* and Mamet's better-known works are more than just thematic. The grandfather's mentoring of Joao (who is close to the age of bar mitzvah), the family's forced concealment of the truth (Joao quickly learns to lie), the necessity for 'code-switching' that demands sudden changes of register, allow Kane to use this play as a kind of prologue to *Weasels and Wisemen* as a whole, for the dramatic situations in *Marranos* clearly place a specifically Jewish inflection on the teacher–pupil relationship and the recourse to acting and storytelling that recur throughout Mamet's plays. With this play in mind Kane's subsequent, related arguments for a Jewish dimension to the dynamics of language and the metadramatic aspects of Mamet's theatre as a whole become more convincing.

Lone Canoe, Mamet's first major commercial and artistic failure, tells the story of John Fairfax, an explorer from Victorian England, who has settled and married into a tribe of Indians following a calamitous voyage to the North during which his companions died. His fellow explorer,

Fredrick VanBrandt, who has been searching for Fairfax for years, finds him and urges him to return to London, where he is being blamed for the deaths. He agrees to return and clear his name, even shooting one of the Indians in his determination to escape with the wounded VanBrandt, only to discover that VanBrandt has lied; Fairfax is in fact revered in England while VanBrandt is blamed for the failure of previous attempts to rescue him. VanBrandt dies, and Fairfax is welcomed back to the tribe. Carroll crisply enumerates the problems with the play. The testing of the hero is at once too explicit and negated by circumstances over which Fairfax has no control, so the hero in fact has no free will to be tested. A similar irony pervades *Edmond*, which, however, is replete with 'paradoxes and dialectical ironies', in contrast to the 'banality which may be the result of a too-literal application of Bettelheim and Campbell' in *Lone Canoe*; the play also suffers from stiltedly portentous dialogue and an awkward mixing of modes, for example in the inclusion of several songs.[12] In this respect it resembles the children's plays, while also anticipating much of the later work that would baffle many critics by its mingling of different registers.

By the end of the 1970s Mamet had established himself alongside Sam Shepard as one of the two most important American playwrights of his generation. He was now about to eclipse his rival by becoming arguably the only major American dramatist to make a commercially and artistically successful transition to Hollywood.

CHAPTER FIVE

The Screenplays, 1981–9: *The Postman Always Rings Twice* (1981), *The Verdict* (1982), *The Untouchables* (1987), *We're No Angels* (1989)

Mamet has a lifelong fascination with cinema, and in the late 1970s wrote at least two unproduced screenplays, versions of *The Water Engine* and *Sexual Perversity in Chicago*. The stage version of the latter had caught the attention of Bob Rafelson, one of the directors who had brought about the 'Hollywood Renaissance' in the early 1970s. Rafelson hired Mamet to write the script for *The Postman Always Rings Twice*, kick-starting a parallel career as a screenwriter that would produce some of his most widely admired work.

The screenplay form has never really appealed to academic criticism. It is arguably too literary for film studies and too cinematic for textual analysis, and unlike the script for a stage play the writer generally has little contractual control over the material, which may be subject to rewriting on the whims of a director, producer or even actor. Mamet's disastrous experience with the adaptation of *Sexual Perversity* into *About Last Night...*, and to a lesser extent with *The Untouchables*, led him in future to insist on greater contractual control over the material. Many of his screenplays for other directors are adaptations, and while some (but not all) of the scripts he has directed himself have been published, of those he worked on for other directors only the relatively minor *We're No Angels* has been officially circulated, again contributing to a measure of critical neglect.

The Postman Always Rings Twice (1981)

Mamet's first commercial screenplay was an adaptation of a 1934 novel by James M. Cain (1892–1977) that had already been filmed three times: in a French version, *Le Dernier Tournant* (The Last Turn) (Pierre Chenal, 1939); in Italian, as *Ossessione* (Obsession) (Luchino Visconti, 1942); and, most famously, in a Hollywood version which shared the title of the novel (Tay Garnett, 1946). It tells the story of the murder of a Greek immigrant restaurant owner, Nick Papadakis, by his wife Cora and her lover, the drifter Frank Chambers, who dress up the killing as a motoring accident. A clever lawyer gets the charges against them dropped, only for Cora to die, ironically, in a real car crash. Rafelson and Mamet leave Frank grieving by the roadside, radically altering Cain's ending, in which Frank is wrongly accused of her murder and sentenced to death.

Gay Brewer identifies a number of additional changes: Frank is older and shorn of the romantic touches of his character in the book, and Mamet has added a craps game scene at a bus station and several passages of dialogue that are more characteristic of the screenwriter than the novelist.[1] Otherwise Brewer merely notes the obvious themes of crime and sex, and takes for granted Mamet's remarks in several interviews on the Aristotelian basis on which he constructed the screenplay. Bruce Barton's short chapter on screenwriting is not one of the better parts of his book either: he mistakenly asserts that the script is very faithful to Cain's novel, and overstates his case in proclaiming that in practice 'Mamet's films' – in general – are *entirely* consistent with the tradition of classical American film, which operates on an assumption . . . of narrative omniscience and transparency' (my emphasis).[2] Mamet's own comments on the screenplay, for example in Dan Yakir's profile for *Film Comment*,[3] are far more valuable, and he regards Cain's books in general as presenting variations on the same story of an interloper arriving in the kingdom and being seduced by the queen, with the king's tacit acceptance, so that Cain's stories 'are really about women'.[4]

The Verdict (1982)

Mamet's next filmed screenplay shows both an increasing ease with the medium and a more noticeably personal style. In comparison to *Postman*, *The Verdict* (1980) was a contemporary, previously unfilmed novel by Barry Reed (1927–2002), a little-known writer. Mamet himself pitched the idea to producers Richard Zanuck (born 1934) and David Brown (born 1916), and wrote a script that anticipates several of his later screenplays, such as those for *Homicide* and *Wag the Dog*, in transforming the ostensible source so radically that it almost defies Hollywood's customary distinction between adaptations and original material.

The Verdict has a complicated pre-production history, involving changes of director and actors, which has been detailed in several reliable sources.[5] Most important for the present discussion is that Sidney Lumet only agreed to direct on condition that the producers revert to the script as Mamet originally presented it, with one essential change: Mamet had not disclosed the verdict, a decision Lumet considered would be unacceptable to the audience, so the ending was rewritten. The film was a major critical success, garnering Mamet an Academy Award nomination for his script, in which Frank Galvin, an alcoholic, 'ambulance-chasing' lawyer, is given the chance to resurrect his career when he takes on a case against two doctors accused of criminal negligence in a routine operation that has left his client reduced to a vegetative state. Galvin refuses a proposed cash settlement and goes to trial, only to find his case steadily undermined by the powerful team of defence lawyers headed by Concannon, who has also paid for a spy, Laura, to infiltrate Galvin's team. Galvin is reduced to pleading with the jury to do what they know is right, and against the odds they find in his favour. As the film closes Galvin seems to have found the strength to end the affair with Laura, whose treachery he has uncovered.

Brewer provides useful detail on the adaptation, as to a lesser extent does Dennis Carroll. Mamet changed the names of certain characters, added or removed others, and altered the placement and emphasis of certain scenes: the opening sequence that establishes Galvin as an ambulance chaser was developed from a mere detail in the novel, and Mamet pushed the revelation of Laura's duplicity much further back in the story to heighten the effect of the betrayal. Brewer further notes that Mamet eliminated a storyline about anti-Semitism and instead focused the theme of bigotry, and therefore assimilation and social alienation, onto the Boston Irish community of which Galvin is a part. The resulting emphasis on Catholicism forms one strand of the film's wider concern with hierarchical institutions that purport to help ordinary people but fail to do so: the doctors play out the role of secular priests, while Brewer connects the lawyers to Mamet's long line of confidence men.

Carroll adeptly reveals the ambivalence running throughout the film: Laura, despite accepting the role given to her by Concannon, seems to want Galvin to expose her and to win the case; the jury's request to grant the plaintiff a higher sum than requested actually qualifies what might appear a clichéd happy ending by implicitly raising again the accusations of greed that have been levelled against Galvin before; and in the final moments the telephone continues to ring as Galvin hesitates over whether to take Laura's call. Carroll also distinguishes between screenplay and film by acknowledging the contributions of Lumet and cinematographer Andrej Bartkowiak (born 1950), noting for example the effect of the restricted palette of blues, reds and browns.

At first sight it is rather surprising that Carroll places *The Verdict* and *Edmond* together with various other plays in a chapter entitled 'Communion', but this is a broad category in Carroll's schema, in which communion can also be 'a lonelier and more trial-ridden process'.[6] What Carroll has in mind here is something broader still, the narrative paradigm outlined by Joseph Campbell in *The Hero with a Thousand Faces* (1949): 'A hero ventures forth from the world of common day into a region of supernatural wonder: fabulous forces are there encountered and a decisive victory is won: the hero comes back from this mysterious adventure with the power to bestow boons on his fellow man.'[7] That Mamet has acknowledged the influence of Campbell several times enables Carroll to outline a mythic structure to Mamet's work that the writer himself seems even more inclined to credit than the economic, social and historical contexts favoured by Bigsby, although there must be doubts about the discriminatory power of a paradigm that arguably reduces the history of Western storytelling to a 'monomyth'.

That, of course, is the attraction for the screenwriting manuals that in recent years have mined the Campbell motherlode quite shamelessly, and helps to account for the low esteem in which such tomes are generally held in academic circles. This is unfortunate, because the best of them provide serious studies of an otherwise neglected form. The most widely admired book in this field is probably *Adventures in the Screen Trade* (1983) by William Goldman (born 1931), which is not a manual but a memoir combined with Goldman's reflections on the craft of the screenwriter. His account of the production history of *The Verdict* was written as the film was being shot, and reveals Mamet as a fledgling screenwriter of unusual integrity, though his material concerning the script itself is largely confined to the rewritten ending.

Goldman values Mamet's work very highly, as do the authors of many subsequent manuals, most of which are clearly distinguished from conventional literary criticism in focusing overwhelmingly on structure but only marginally on language.[8] For example, Thomas Pope's chapter on *The Verdict* is subtitled 'Dialogue as Litany', yet he says nothing about dialogue and instead considers the screenplay 'a triumph of classic three-act theory', with the first act ending at the point where Galvin refuses the bishop's financial settlement and the third beginning when he gets the clue that will enable him to locate a crucial witness.[9] Pope observes that the only unclassical element in the second act is the revelation to the audience, but not to Galvin, that Laura is Concannon's spy; he argues, however, that Mamet could not have placed the scene elsewhere and importantly uses the irony 'to create sympathy for the character, not disdain'. This contributes to the success of the third act, because 'at second act breaks, it is the hero's ability to act where another would fail that is his defining characteristic'.[10]

The Verdict is one of the four films that Paul Lucey mines to illustrate all aspects of screenwriting in a 400-page manual. It is his main example of a 'character study'[11] – ironically, given Mamet's views on character – and, like Pope, he regards it as having a clearly defined three-act structure. He reproduces from Mamet's unpublished script a complete scene, in which Judge Sweeney tries in vain to orchestrate an out-of-court settlement between Galvin and Concannon. Again, Lucey's commentary is noteworthy not for textual analysis but for a sensitivity to structure and, in particular, an ability to evaluate the script in relation to criteria appropriate to commercial screenwriting. He concludes that *The Verdict* is 'a model of mainstream filmmaking that tells a complex story of law and personal redemption without theatrical excess or false emotion', rather than 'just another court case à la Perry Mason'.[12]

The Untouchables (1987)

Mamet followed his Oscar nomination for *The Verdict* by winning the Pulitzer Prize for *Glengarry Glen Ross*, after which he was a very hot ticket. By 1985 he was working on screenplays for two radically different films: *House of Games*, a low-budget picture he would direct himself, and *The Untouchables*, a studio blockbuster derived from the successful television series of the same title that ran from 1959 to 1963. According to producer Art Linson (born *c*.1942), Mamet's services were secured when the producer sat the writer down in a SoHo restaurant and said, 'Dave, don't you think that the best career move for somebody who just won the Pulitzer Prize would be to adapt an old television series like *The Untouchables* for a *shitload* of money?'[13] Mamet agreed, they ate lunch, and the first draft was written in four weeks.

In Mamet's version *The Untouchables* was a heavily fictionalised retelling of the Prohibition-era confrontation between Al Capone (Robert de Niro) and the eponymous heroes, headed by federal agent Elliot Ness (Kevin Costner). The film remains the most commercially successful of Mamet's career to date, and enhanced the reputations of all concerned, but offscreen there were difficulties that led to major changes in how he would subsequently work in cinema. Mamet was used to having complete authority over his own scripts in the theatre, and had already seen *Sexual Perversity in Chicago* taken out of his hands and cannibalised as *About Last Night. . .* (Edward Zwick, 1986). Meanwhile Linson had been having difficulties in persuading the studio to back the script. The main problem was that in Mamet's screenplays 'the characters do not always sound conversational in the way we are used to. I call it Mametese'.[14] Brewer similarly observes a 'stilted rhetoric' in some of Ness's speech, most strikingly in a line such as 'I have become what I beheld'.[15]

The problem the *Untouchables* executives had with the Mametese was sidelined when Brian De Palma signed up to direct, thus making a viable 'package', but both he and Linson were concerned that the role of Capone was too small, and that key moments in the plot development were obscure. Mamet would eventually add further scenes for

Capone, but refused to do additional rewrites after he began shooting *House of Games*, with producers who allowed him almost complete authorial control. Linson and De Palma discovered that no one could write Mamet like Mamet, and consequently *The Untouchables* contains important, wordless scenes created without the writer's consent: the episode at the opera where Capone learns of Malone's death, and De Palma's notorious slow-motion parody of the Odessa Steps sequence from *The Battleship Potemkin* (Sergei Eisenstein, 1925). Although Mamet would eventually re-establish a good partnership and friendship with Linson, each published his side of the argument: Mamet very quickly, in an article for *American Film* in 1987 (and probably also in *Speed-the-Plow* [1988], a ruthless satire on the mores of Hollywood producers), and Linson at more leisure in the first volume of his supremely readable memoirs, where he also quotes extensively from the unpublished screenplay. Between them, these pieces give a vivid picture of Mamet's approach to working in Hollywood.

For all these reasons *The Untouchables* has less integrity as a 'Mamet movie' than the groundbreaking and contemporaneous *House of Games*, and has received correspondingly little critical attention. Carroll's 1992 essay, which places Mamet's films and screenplays, from *The Untouchables* to *Homicide*, squarely in the same binary opposition of 'business' and 'communion' that animates much of his 1987 monograph, focuses on Malone's mentorship of Ness, the strength of the multi-ethnic grouping of the law enforcement officers as opposed to the homogeneity of Capone's gang, and the fact that the conclusion of the film 'implies that, in a society such as early 1930s Chicago, moral ends justify, indeed necessitate, immoral means'.[16]

Such a rigidly thematic approach makes little headway, and Brewer's section on *The Untouchables* in *David Mamet and Film* is much more useful, partly because it acknowledges the important differences between screenplay and film but also because the thematic generalisations about masculinity and rites of passage are subsumed within a less obvious, generic interpretation that notes this film's proximity to the Western. As in that seminally American form, *The Untouchables* explores the tensions between the feminised security of the home and violent, masculine action, but more significantly it treats history as myth: not only is the story, while ostensibly based on historical events, largely Mamet's invention (Ness and Capone never met, for example), but also an idealised past is played off against a corrupted present in such overtly Manichean terms that the previous age itself becomes an ideological fiction framing the contemporary culture's obsessions with violence and illegality. Accordingly Brewer compares *The Untouchables* to *The Water Engine*: each examines critically a quintessentially American story of the battle between good and evil, dramatises American progress via the processes of technological change, and reveals the transformation of event into ideological myth – both works take a particularly dim view of newspapermen – with an implied, self-reflexive comment on Mamet's own mediation of history as fable within an imagined Chicago of the 1930s. Partly as a result, the gloomy picture of endemic corruption and popular delusion is offset by a certain innocence: that the violence is precipitated by something as trivial as liquor seems almost quaint, and, as Brewer concludes, *The Untouchables* 'is finally a eulogy to elements of genre formulae and traditional American myth as storytelling devices'.[17]

In a later essay valuable for including substantial quotations from the unpublished screenplays, Brewer compares Mamet's scripts for *The Untouchables* and *Hoffa* (Danny DeVito, 1992), which again is largely set in a mythologised 1930s. Brewer suggests that the eponymous protagonist of the later film combines the 'old testament justice'[18] of Sean Connery's character, Malone, with the qualities of Capone, a violent and corrupt anti-hero who presents himself as a champion of the working man.

We're No Angels (1989)

The last of the screenplays considered in this chapter is the only one to have been published. Characteristically of the writer it bears only passing resemblance to its putative source, the 1955 picture of the same name starring Humphrey Bogart and directed by Michael Curtiz. There are also considerable divergences between the script and the film as directed by Neil Jordan, and, as Carroll observes (without going into detail), Mamet's version has much of the fable-like charm of *Things Change*, directed by Mamet a year before. In *We're No Angels*, two prisoners, Ned (Robert De Niro) and Jim (Sean Penn), escape from a brutal penitentiary, only to be mistaken for priests when they arrive at a small town on the Canadian border famed only for its statue of a weeping Virgin. The film plays on the obvious comic potential of the familiar story of disguised convicts on the run, before both men eventually find redemption: Jim by joining a monastery, and Ned by acquiring a family when he enters a relationship with a single mother, whose afflicted daughter is cured as if miraculously at the end.

The film is pleasant enough, although many reviewers felt the repeated gags on the same theme, combined with a surprisingly one-note, hammy performance from De Niro, ultimately made it stale and thin. It does not do justice to Mamet's richly textured screenplay, on which Brewer focuses exclusively in his discussion. He suggests that the screenplay continues the Western themes of *The Untouchables*, not only in the story of border-town criminals pitted against the law, but also in an Old Testament morality of an eye for an eye associated with Malone in the earlier film and with the savage prison warden in *We're No Angels*, a character Brewer describes as 'perhaps, the most purely evil character in all of Mamet'.[19] More ingenious, but less convincing, is Brewer's attempt to show that *We're No Angels* is a kind of dramatisation of 'The Bridge', the obscure novel that Karen tries to get a movie producer to film in *Speed-the-Plow* and which, as suggested in Chapter Ten, is finally too impenetrably prolix and fragmented to allow for any fully coherent interpretation. Nevertheless, this discussion of *We're No Angels* shows that the screenplay has depths that are not fully apparent in the film as released, and that Mamet was continuing to explore the kinds of metaphysical themes that had been apparent since *The Verdict* and that would shortly come to full prominence in 1991's *Homicide*.

Most noticeable in this respect is that, as Brewer observes, *We're No Angels* reprises a scene in Mamet's 1982 play *Edmond* in which two men cloistered together in a cell ruminate on the meaning of life. These two works bookend a decade in which Mamet had moved from promising young playwright to global celebrity in the worlds of theatre and film. Yet if *We're No Angels* has been largely dismissed as a relatively antiseptic entertainment, *Edmond* provided a visceral shock that continues to divide critics on almost every level.

CHAPTER SIX

Edmond (1982)

In the course of 23 rapid scenes, *Edmond*'s eponymous (anti)hero leaves the marriage that bores him and embarks on a rapid downward progress through the underside of urban America that will lead to murder, incarceration and rape. The play is set in New York, a city the playwright has compared to hell; the protagonist's surname is Burke, inviting ironic comparison to Edmund Burke (1729–97), the Irish-born British statesman renowned for his opposition to the French Revolution. Henry I. Schvey neatly summarises the implication: *Edmond* dramatises the breakdown of 'the partnership between the individual and the social order'[1] and the consequences of the untrammelled individualism graphically expressed by Teach in *American Buffalo*.

With the possible exception of *Oleanna*, none of Mamet's plays has divided critics so comprehensively, and in so many ways, as *Edmond*. Controversy surrounds its genre, mode, intertexts, structure, ending, moral framework, treatment of gender, contemporary significance, ideas about free will and determination, and even whether or not it is 'sick'. One explanation for this is that it combines a skeletal plot that leaves much to the imagination with individual scenes that can be quite shockingly graphic; another is that it is unclear what degree of seriousness to attach to the Fortune Teller's exposition at the beginning, or to the ending in which Edmond appears happy to accept a union with a prisoner who has just sodomised him. Accordingly it can seem that the characters are 'the playthings of form', except that it is hard to identify what this form is, in a work that can appear even to the most perceptive of critics to be 'a mystery without a solution'.[2]

Edmond's intertexts

Edmond has provoked a remarkable range of intertextual comparisons. The most frequently invoked possible source is *Woyzeck* (1837) by the German dramatist Georg Büchner (1813–37), which details the degradations of the protagonist in a downward spiral that culminates in the murder of his lover. Büchner died before completing the play, leaving it in a fragmentary state that allows for a vast range of critical conjecture about the nature and sequence of its events, and *Edmond* has a similar feeling of disconnection. An equally stark analogy, explored at some length by Jon Tuttle, is with *From Morn to Midnight* (1916), by the German dramatist Georg Kaiser (1878–1945), in which an unnamed cashier at a bank embarks on a similar journey, only to repent and attempt in vain to turn his fellow citizens against the lure of money. Bruce Barton, however, notes that in contrast to the Romantic, almost charismatic and evangelical Cashier, Edmond is immersed in a solipsistic desperation to escape the social forces that define him. More than one critic has compared *Edmond* to the expressionistic plays of Eugene O'Neill (1888–1953), while several have discussed the play in relation to Mamet's contemporaries: the dedication to fellow playwright Wallace Shawn (born 1943) prompts Robert Combs to compare it to Shawn's *Aunt Dan and Lemon* (1985), both being tragicomic plays whose protagonists think of themselves as innocents within a melodrama. Alisa Solomon considered it quite typical of several plays that premiered in New York in the same season, in simplifying complex moral questions and inviting the audience to empathise with a morally suspect protagonist.

More revealing of *Edmond*'s distinctiveness is that, more than with any other Mamet play, critics tend to make their comparisons with non-theatrical texts, while productions often incorporate multi-media elements. Combs finds in the story of a man leaving his wife to encounter the devil a parallel with a story by Nathaniel Hawthorne (1804–64), 'Young Goodman Brown' (1846); Bruce Barton finds resemblances to one of Mamet's favourite novels, *An American Tragedy* (1925), by Theodore Dreiser (1871–1945); while Daniel Dervin holds against the play the fact that part of the dramatic impetus, whereby the inhibited and fearful white male sees his fantasies lived out through the actions of black men, is reminiscent of 1950s texts by writers as diverse as Norman Mailer (born 1923), James Baldwin (1924–87) and Leslie Fiedler (1917–2003). Alain Piette notes how frequently *Edmond* has been discussed in terms of the visual arts: Anne Dean finds an analogy in the satirical sequence of paintings (and later engravings) depicting *The Rake's Progress* (1732–5) by William Hogarth (1697–1764); Dervin sees similarities to the protagonist, theme and episodic structure of the movie *Looking for Mr. Goodbar* (Richard Brooks, 1977); and a contemporary review compared it to the films of Martin Scorsese (born 1942). Piette himself suggests that it is reminiscent of the paintings of Edward Hopper (1882–1967).[3]

Dean also argues for a cinematic structure to the piece, a view that gains support from Gay Brewer's observation that traces of the plot bear comparison to *The Postman Always Rings Twice*: 'waitress, stranger, an ensuing and inevitable sexuality that leads to murder'.[4] Bruce Barton, by contrast, insists that it bears no relation to Mamet's work in film or his evolving aesthetics of screenwriting; instead, Edmond's concern about authenticity and performance, and the play's engagement with the transgressive capacity of theatre, root it in theatrical concerns. *Edmond* is almost unique in Mamet's canon in having prompted experimental staging, including the use of filmed and other pre-recorded material, and unusual performance spaces, in the Belgian productions considered by Piette and Johan Callens[5] – a fact that arguably contradicts rather than substantiates Barton's position.

Genre, form and mode

Of course, the particular works that a given critic will use for comparison (and those above are merely a sample) depend on what kind of play it is: and here there is no consensus at all. *Edmond* is clearly too stylised to be described as realistic in any simple sense, although some critics have seen in it a kind of modified realism. David Savran discusses it alongside *Sexual Perversity in Chicago* as an example of 'new realism', describing it as Mamet's 'most plot-driven' play, but one that makes the characters its 'dupes', and that denies the security of closure by substituting instead, in the closing dyad between Edmond and the Prisoner, 'a formal device, some theatrical equivalent to film's freeze frame – a sudden and violent suspension of the action'.[6] In comparing Mamet to Hopper, Alain Piette denies that either is a realist, yet implies that each deploys a realistic technique rooted in synecdoche whereby the spectator is presented with 'portions of . . . reality as if seen through a window whose frame allows us to perceive only a fragment of the total picture, forcing us to imagine the rest'. On the other hand, the realistic effect is undermined by the fact that Edmond is more articulate than most of Mamet's other characters, and accordingly Piette prefers to describe the play as 'new Romanticism of sorts', because Edmond is a larger-than-life protagonist living a marginal existence beyond the pale of respectable society.[7] Bigsby similarly suggests that Edmond's journey 'is a debased version of the [Byronic] romantic quest'.[8]

Realism also seems an unsuitable word because in his encounters with several characters Edmond searches for an explanation of his life. This suggests both expressionism and naturalism, and Richard Brucher accounts for the often unfavourable reviews by noting that the naturalistic expectation that the causes of present effects will be revealed is not satisfied; instead the play distances the spectator from Edmond by the use of irony and satire. Brucher sees the play less as a realistic tragedy than as a dark urban comedy informed by the ironic sensibility of Thorstein Veblen's critique of capitalism, and both he and Robert Combs compare it to Eugene O'Neill's *The Hairy Ape* (1922), arguing in each case that the play is not tragic but comic or tragicomic.

Combs further invokes O'Neill's *The Emperor Jones* (1916) in making the familiar suggestion that Edmond's story resembles the expressionistic play's journey into the depths of the protagonist.[9] Such arguments depend to some extent on accepting the linear structure and seeing the events as a projection of Edmond's conscious or unconscious desires. Piette, however, argues that the play is not structured as a journey but is in fact fragmented and episodic to such an extent that, with the exception of the framing scenes at the beginning and end, the episodes are self-contained and, with very few exceptions, do not display any dramatic progression from one to the next. For Piette this disconnection generates a frustration in the audience, comparable to Edmond's own, revolving around the question of whether it is even possible to make choices that determine one's existence.

Daniel Dervin is so disturbed by this method, which fails to provide or account for certain crucial 'transitions', that he concludes *Edmond* is 'a sick play'.[10] In a related argument, Alisa Solomon dismisses it as 'schmaltzified Brecht': it appears to use the dramatic methods of alienation, but in fact causes its audience to identify and become complicit with its protagonist, so that complex contemporary ethical and political issues are made 'familiar and complacent', because they are reduced finally to a matter of individual neurosis. The spectator, therefore, becomes a passive 'confessor without being distanced from the character'.[11]

Everyman

A remarkable number of critics, including Dervin, Dean, Dennis Carroll and Carla J. McDonough, have suggested that *Edmond* is a kind of morality play – or 'negative morality play'[12] – and/or that Edmond is an 'Everyman' figure. The implications are well illustrated in Jon Tuttle's analysis, in which he speaks of 'man's core malignity' and suggests that 'behavior that modern jurisprudence and Judeo-Christian morality deem barbaric is bred not by socioeconomics but rather in the bone'.[13] 'Everyman' therefore implies a trans-historical, trans-cultural 'human nature' of the kind we have already seen in Carroll's account of Joseph Campbell, and indeed for Carroll *Edmond* is the Mamet play that most 'clearly reveals the influence on him of *The Hero with a Thousand Faces*'.[14] In this interpretation, the beginning and middle scenes correspond to Campbell's stages of 'departure' and 'initiation' (although the same might be said of virtually any linear narrative). Edmond's monosyllabic and clichéd language at the beginning gives way to greater fluency and assertiveness as he leaves restrictive social conventions behind. Even at this stage, however, he is prone to illogical constructions, repetition and inability to complete a sentence, anticipating his reduction to almost total inarticulacy when he attempts to explain to the Chaplain why he murdered Glenna. The final scenes, in which Edmond first attempts to explain himself in a letter to the mother of a high-school sweetheart, and then enters into the relationship with the black prisoner, constitute, in Carroll's eyes, the final Campbellian stage of 'return', the most problematic aspect of the play for such an optimistic and redemptive reading. Carroll asserts that in writing the letter Edmond 'deeply examines' the past, that the relationship with his cell-mate is 'clearly an authentic one', and that the image of Edmond alone, after kissing the prisoner goodnight, is 'peaceful';[15] but it is hard not to note, with Bigsby, the irony that by the end of the play Edmond 'has simply reversed the roles of the first part of the play and is now more absolutely trapped in a smaller room than the one he had once sought to escape'.[16] Savran, perhaps wisely, has it both ways, seeing it as 'both real reconciliation and its demonic parody'.[17]

Dervin's insufferably patronising essay starts by assuming that Edmond is an Everyman figure but ends with the most obvious objection to this claim, which is that Everyman does not secretly want to be incarcerated and anally raped. Disturbed by the 'denial of human reality or personal history', the absence of clear motivation and the sudden transitions, Dervin concludes that Edmond is a masochist whose 'solution comprises his own idiosyncratic fate only'.[18] Both Brucher and Barton also reject the idea of Edmond as Everyman, for the simple and compelling reason that he is indisputably a white, middle-class man in an identifiable historical situation.

Seventies man

If Edmond is not an Everyman, he may well be 'a purely seventies figure'.[19] Bigsby helps to account for the notorious problems in interpreting the ending by noting that, in Edmond's world, language has become so devalued that even if Edmond were to offer a profound analysis of his situation, the terms in which he could do so are indistinguishable from the pseudo-philosophical terminology of personal liberation that surrounds him everywhere and that comes out of his own mouth as he embarks on his descent into mayhem. 'The language of the self-sufficient individual survives; the reality does not'.[20] This dichotomy is symptomatic of the collapse of the counter-culture of the 1960s in the America of the following decade, described in *The Culture of Narcissism* (1979) by Christopher Lasch (1932–94), in which the individual's sense of belonging has eroded to the point at which the hedonistic pursuit of personal pleasure and wealth can seem almost the only good. In view of the confusion occasioned by Mamet's refusal to dwell on causation in this play, it is worth quoting, with Bigsby, Lasch's remark that '[t]he new narcissist is haunted not by guilt but by anxiety'; in Mamet's world, governed by a perpetual fight to meet the demands of the present and the immediate future, guilt – a backward-looking emotion – has become, as Bigsby puts it, 'supererogatory'.[21]

Eighties man

While Bigsby takes *Edmond* to be rooted in what Lasch called the 'me' decade of the 1970s, Brucher exploits the presence of the fortune teller to suggest that this play is remarkably prescient when it comes to the social problems of America in the latter part of the 1980s and beyond, although this is the effect not so much of a supernatural revelation of the future as of an especially penetrating perception of the present. Comparing reactions to productions in 1982 and 1996, Brucher observes that the later audiences found the play less shocking, and asks whether this might be as a result of the public furore following the murder in 1989 of an African American youth in the New York district of Bensonhurst. He also places the play in a longer historical context: he acknowledges the ironic connections to Edmund Burke, but suggests that Mamet's protagonist has closer affinities with Veblen's predatory aristocrats.

In a refreshing antidote to the solemnity that characterises many critical discussions of this writer, Brucher argues that '*Edmond*, for all its nasty seriousness, may be another of Mamet's oblique comedies'.[22] One of the problems with identifying it with *Woyzeck*, for example, is that this pushes it close to the realms of tragedy, which invokes an empathetic and therefore potentially uncritical engagement with the suffering hero, whereas, as Brucher puts it pithily, 'resistance to tragic empathy keeps the social criticism alive'.[23] *Edmond* treats its hero ironically, as Brucher demonstrates very convincingly by comparing it to *The Hairy Ape*, another play usually regarded as naturalistic and tragic, yet which O'Neill explicitly subtitled a comedy. Edmond, like O'Neill's protagonist Yank, doesn't 'get it', and by definition this implies an ironic take on his actions. For example, his description of how he beat up the Pimp is a self-aggrandising fantasy, and he sentimentalises his meeting with Glenna, killing her (and blaming her for it) when she redefines their relationship in less flattering terms. By the end the audience has developed a critical perspective on Edmond's self-representations, so that while Brucher concedes an element of truth in Carroll's interpretation of the final scene, he notes that Edmond still seems incapable of accepting responsibility for killing Glenna, and that there is a marked element of parody (for example in the reference to *Hamlet*) that maintains the critical perspective Mamet has kept in play all along.

Gender

Carla J. McDonough starts her decidedly critical survey of masculinity in Mamet's drama with *Edmond*, prefaced by the writer's remarks on the breakdown of marriage, in which Mamet, in suggesting the importance to men of 'possession of a woman', expresses in McDonough's judgement a patriarchal and limited view of woman's roles in society and reduces her status to that of a marketplace commodity. Following the advice of a man in a bar who advises him to get laid, Edmond acts precisely as if women were indeed commodities: he tries to find a prostitute, and later kills Glenna because she refuses to accept his right to possess her. In sodomising Edmond, the Prisoner demonstrates that masculinity attempts to define itself through domination of another, who thereby becomes submissive and defined as feminine. McDonough here offers an explanation of why Edmond accepts the feminisation of which he appears terrified in earlier scenes, by suggesting (via the feminist theorist Luce Irigaray, born 1932) that until this point he has conformed with 'hom(m)o-sexual' desire, the system of social relations whereby men's relations with one another are played out through and displaced onto the commerce in women's bodies. As this system breaks down Edmond begins to recognise that the forced distinction between masculinity and femininity, the maintenance of which had previously seemed essential, is no longer sufficient to define his identity.

McDonough is understandably tentative in offering this explanation. It depends, for example, on the supposition that in the final scenes Edmond 'begin[s] truly to examine his past assumptions';[24] but Mamet's characters rarely revisit the past in this way, and it is difficult to accept that there is an irony-free authenticity in Edmond's closing ruminations in a scene that is as ambivalent as any in Mamet's work. For all the complications thrown up by the use of a term like 'hom(m)o-sexual', Alain Piette argues that McDonough's interpretation is too simple, because it is not only sexuality that is being redefined in this play. Instead, Edmond suffers from a general 'ontological confusion',[25] which is indicated by the scene with the Fortune Teller and continues to the very end, which McDonough rather glosses over in stating simply that in the final scene Edmond 'chat[s] amiably with the prisoner about the reason for their life on earth'.[26]

Barton similarly sees that there is more at stake here than just masculinity. At the end of the play Edmond sheds those things – race, gender, class, sexuality – that previously defined him, and adopts those roles he formerly hated or feared, notably in his liaison with the Prisoner. Barton also regards masculinity as inextricable from notions of performance and authenticity. In the central series of scenes, Edmond is repeatedly cast as the passive spectator at a series of commercialised deceptions.

What he wants is 'the possibility of emancipation through a performative mode of self-insistent physical action'[27] that has unpredictable and dangerous consequences for the self, and what he demands is authentic and 'organic' performance, a term Barton borrows from Mamet's views on acting and theatre. What drives Edmond to distraction and ultimately murder is that Glenna falsely proclaims herself to be an actress, although ironically in this scene Edmond is himself performing a masquerade, a 'mask of masculinity'.[28] In this characteristically ambivalent conjunction of masculinity and performance *Edmond* clearly anticipates Mamet's next play, *Glengarry Glen Ross*, a linguistic tour de force about corrupt real estate salesmen for which Mamet would receive the Pulitzer Prize in 1984, propelling him to international renown.

CHAPTER SEVEN

Glengarry Glen Ross (1983)

Glengarry Glen Ross premiered at the National Theatre in London in 1983, and within two years was the subject of a critical analysis by C. W. E. Bigsby that established the main lines followed by most subsequent commentators.[1] Bigsby places Glengarry within a history of American plays and novels about salesmen and confidence men, but in a major departure from Eugene O'Neill's The Iceman Cometh (1946), and from Death of a Salesman (1949) by Arthur Miller (1915–2005), Mamet shows the salesmen only at work: the putative distinction between their private lives and their occupations disappears, and the focus shifts to the language of selling. Bigsby captures the ambivalence whereby the apparent denunciation of American capitalism is balanced by admiration for the exuberance of the salesmen's dialogue and the creativity of their deceptions, so that there is potentially something even transcendent about the salesman's world that is analogous to artistic creation itself. Finally, Bigsby notes that the play is formally a hybrid, with an episodic first act but a second that has many of the qualities of the well-made play. He is puzzled by Mamet's interest in conventional forms, since the demand for plot proposes what Bigsby elsewhere in his study of the playwright sees as a false distinction between character and environment, while offering at the level of dramatic action the very illusions that the characters present to themselves in desperate attempts to evade the realities of their existence.

American ethics and nostalgia

Many subsequent critics develop Bigsby's recognition that the play dramatises both the corruption of American ideals and the suspicion that they never existed. Matthew C. Roudané argues that beneath the superficial postmodernity of some of Mamet's formal experiments he is a liberal humanist who dramatises the connection, explored by the French thinker Alexis de Tocqueville (1805–59) in Democracy in America

(1835), 'between the public self – the hurlyburly of those caught within a business-as-sacrament world – and the private self – the anguished characters' inner reality',[2] although in *Glengarry* the distinction has vanished and the inner self can only be inferred. In a later discussion of Mamet's plays in general (see the concluding chapter of this Guide), Roudané finds a similar tension, although the emphases are somewhat different and the specifically American contexts are examined in greater depth.[3]

Several essays in the 1996 collection *David Mamet's 'Glengarry Glen Ross': Text and Performance* examine how the question of ethics is refracted through nostalgia. Richard Brucher again brackets the play with *The Iceman Cometh* and *Death of a Salesman*, because all three evoke, only to travesty, a 'longing for an idyllic or idealistic past', in particular the idea of 'individualism associated with independent thinking and iconoclastic behavior' promulgated by Ralph Waldo Emerson (1803–82).[4] In *Glengarry* this emerges most clearly in Roma's pitch to Lingk, which, like Levene's sale to the Nyborgs and the 'D. Ray Morton' improvisation, is an example of 'pernicious nostalgia', the 'deliberately insincere or malicious appeal' to an alluring American ideology and, here, the correspondingly resonant, iconic images of railway carriages and home cooking. What differentiates Mamet from Miller, and perhaps O'Neill, is that his own position is hard to determine, and the audience thereby finds itself caught up in this pernicious nostalgia instead of recognising its own relationship to the morally devalued world of the play.

David Kennedy Sauer notes that Moss, Aaronow and Levene all invoke a golden age of selling, but from a careful analysis he infers that 'the whole prehistory of idyllic life at Glen Ross Farms is delusion':[5] there always was exploitation, and their language under pressure suggests they are not men but boys, fantasising about an ideal past to avoid thinking about the future. Sauer teases out these suppressed plots and stories, and argues that the sales contest is rigged from the beginning: Roma has been getting the best leads from Williamson, confirming that the other salesmen are locked into a system in which their hopes of achievement can only ever be a fantasy.

Steven Price similarly argues that the robbery represents the impotent child's desire to wreak revenge on Mitch and Murray, judgemental parental figures the salesmen secretly want to kill, and whose authority is ironically reinstated by the otherwise inexplicable theft of the telephones. He detects the language of murder throughout *Glengarry*, which conflates two kinds of detective story: the American 'hard-boiled' version and the 'classical' English whodunnit. This latter form erupts to trouble what is otherwise a distinctively American play: the expulsion of the lawbreaker purports to return the world to a state of innocence, a pastoral ideal associated with Thomas Jefferson (1743–1826, third President of the United States, 1801–9). This is conjured up by the names of the properties sold in the real-estate office, but remains a mirage in an urban play of pervasive criminality. Indeed, it is that American mythic ideal, rather than the land itself, which is commercially valuable; in this way the dominant ideology of free-market capitalism re-incorporates whatever appears to offer an escape from it. Mamet's presentation of American myth, then, 'is decidedly lacking in nostalgic illusion';[6] the myth was always corrupt, always a construction to justify the appropriation of power, property and wealth, so there is nothing incongruous in the salesman's self-perception as a latter-day cowboy or frontier pioneer for whom the land has now run out or been translated bathetically into real estate.

Elizabeth Klaver takes this kind of analysis still further by comparing *Glengarry* to *America* (1986), by the French postmodernist thinker Jean Baudrillard (1929–2007): 'land appears in the play only in the context of real estate contracts, leads, and the swirl of talk and theatricality of the salesmen', in 'a semiotic and performative universe' in which 'the value of real estate becomes relative to the system rather than to a world of actual things'.[7] Within this framework Klaver, too, sees a form of nostalgia. As she puts it neatly, alluding to the eighteenth-century French writer on America, J. Hector St. John de Crèvecoeur (1735–1813), '[i]n Crèvecoeur's day, the land could be stolen; in Mamet's day, only the leads'.[8]

Money and business ethics

As in *American Buffalo*, part of this nostalgia is bound up with representations of money. Linda Dorff distinguishes between the 'imaginary' or 'symbolic' money of cheques and credit cards circulating throughout *Glengarry*, and 'iconic' or 'real' money. This opposition is played out in the very title. Levene recalls selling Glen Ross Farms, 'in which "real" money is exchanged for "real" land', and the suppressed image is of the gold rush, of real money lying on the ground. By contrast, in the Glengarry Highlands sale in which the salesmen are currently engaged, real money is hard to locate, and instead 'credit cards or checks are exchanged for illusions'.[9] The older salesmen are associated with, and understand, real money but not 'postmodern Glengarry': they have been left behind by historical change.[10] The distinction between the two kinds of money erupts at particularly dramatic moments: when Levene produces real money in an attempt to bribe Williamson, it represents a scandalous disruption of business and signifies criminality, and when Williamson blows the 'D. Ray Morton' deception by revealing that

Lingk's cheque has already been cashed, thereby transforming imaginary money into real money, he 'reveals the criminal nature of the sale, disrupting Roma's play and unmasking him as a con artist'.[11]

A fascinatingly bizarre sideline is that, as David and Janice Sauer dryly observe, 'a whole debate which focuses mainly on *Glengarry Glen Ross* ... often finds a home in MBA [Master of Business Administration] programs'.[12] This debate takes the play as a serious case study of American business ethics, a term Hersh Zeifman, in an essay that predates any of these articles, describes as 'apparently oxymoronic'.[13] As with the screenwriting manuals that illuminate certain aspects of *The Verdict*, these business studies, while not criticism in any conventional sense, cast a usefully strange light on the play, especially given the widespread view that it is not as unambiguously disparaging of American capitalism as might at first appear. Moreover, as with *Oleanna*, those studies that solicit the empirical responses of actual spectators can provide solid support for a particular interpretation.

For example, Jason Berger and Cornelius B. Pratt showed *House of Games* and the film version of *Glengarry* to a group of students taking a course in business ethics. Although many reactions were banal, some respondents, notably men, admired Al Pacino's performance and even 'wanted to be like Ricky [Roma]'. The instructors express some dismay at this, concluding that 'there seems to be some misunderstanding among the students about the precise boundaries of ethical business communications'; indeed, 'their views of public relations were tantamount to world views', attributable to the fact that 'their conceptualization of corporate communications was still largely based on pervasive commonplace stereotypes' such as Mike and Roma.[14] Not only is this a reductive view of these characters, but more significantly Berger and Pratt evidently reject at source the one possibility that Mamet overtly affirms in remarking, of *American Buffalo*, that the reason why businessmen were offended was because they knew it was about them.

Eugene Garaventa more ambitiously frames the play between two antithetical views of business ethics: the 'theory of amorality', which holds that business need not conform to broader ethical frameworks because the selfish pursuit of economic advantage generates wealth that ultimately benefits both the business and society in general; and the 'theory of moral unity', which holds that in society there is only one ethical law to which business and other pursuits are equally accountable.[15] Although the salesmen operate according to the first theory, implicitly the play upholds the second. Garaventa asks several interesting questions that arise: should salesmen have equal access to the leads, should the firm take Levene's age and length of service into account, and what view should we take of Roma's actions in buying Lingk a drink without revealing his motives?

Race and ethnicity

Tony J. Stafford exhaustively surveys the various place names, noting the irony that while they connote pastoral beauty and geographical diversity, the salesmen remain rooted to the drab real-estate office. Their schemes to improve their position are therefore illusory, as is what Stafford appositely calls the 'promised land', a phrase that connects the twin subjects of his essay: not only do the names of the parcels of land indicate a fraud, but the names of the characters imply 'some latter-day reenactment of a Judeo-Christian struggle over and dispossession of the Jews from the Promised Land'. Stafford links the names Moss, Aaronow and Levene to Moses, Aaron and the tribe of Levi: 'Moses and Aaron...were charged by God with leading the Israelites to the Promised Land while the Levites were responsible for conducting the religious rituals',[16] and the name of Roma, the salesman destined to eclipse his older colleagues, suggests the coming of the Roman Empire and the dispossession of the Jews.

Stafford's astute and wholly convincing analysis informs Leslie Kane's discussion.[17] As so often, her insistence on reading aspects of the play in specifically Jewish terms can seem unwarranted; for example, it is hardly surprising that a play about business and sales contests should be replete with references to precise dollar amounts, so her attempt to show that it is instead rooted in the Book of Numbers looks forced. However, Kane convincingly builds on Stafford's argument for an ethnic dimension to the conflict between the management and the workforce. Other than Roma, the salesmen are Jewish, and in America salesmanship – either solitary or as a family concern – was one of the routes to advancement for Jews excluded from the collegiate and institutional hierarchies of big business, traditionally controlled by White Anglo-Saxon Protestants, of whom Williamson is evidently one. This subtextual drama is heightened when the salesmen identify themselves as slaves, and the management and the detective, Baylen, as the Gestapo. Meanwhile Roma possesses to a still greater extent his fellow salesmen's tenacity, wit, skill and capacity for invention, but he is closer to the authority figures of Mitch and Murray and their surrogate Williamson than they could ever be. Kane is exceptionally alert to the characteristically obscure details of the story: like Sauer, she infers that Williamson is in league with Roma and out to destroy Levene from the beginning, and she asks troubling questions throughout, such as why Levene is apparently staying in a hotel instead of at home, and what his failure to bring his wallet to the meeting with Williamson in the first scene suggests about his expectations for that meeting. Kane is also superb on the nuances of food and cooking, and in tracing the unspoken drama unfolding in the second act, as Baylen's investigation on the one hand and Levene's apparently successful sale to the Nyborgs on the other threaten radically to alter the sales contest, resulting in either criminal arrest or professional disaster for one or other of the salesmen. In examining such puzzling details Kane opens up all sorts of alternative readings.

Deborah R. Geis examines the issue of race and ethnicity from a wholly different perspective, taking as her starting-point a short story by Bharati Mukherjee (born 1940) in which an Indian woman experiences extreme discomfiture on hearing the audience's laughter at the characters' racist comments during a performance of Mamet's play. The salesmen construct the Poles and Indians as Other because their names signify weak leads, and therefore a potential failure for the salesmen, but Mukherjee's story indicates 'the complicity of the spectators in accepting, appreciating, and appropriating the characters' sexism and racism (however ironic Mamet's intention in having his characters say these lines in the first place: the balance of judgment is a delicate one)'.[18] This might indicate that the implied audience of the play is exclusive, an issue that also emerges in some disparaging readings of *Speed-the-Plow* and *Oleanna*, as we shall see.

Masculinity

As with his discussion of *American Buffalo*, Zeifman aims to explore the 'closed moral world' of *Glengarry*, and specifically the code of masculinity that presides over it. Zeifman sees these plays in similar terms, dominated as they are by machismo and a linguistic register that produces innumerable comic and oxymoronic constructions, because a plethora of homophobic and misogynistic insults are used interchangeably, and solely to signify lack of masculinity. Meanwhile the absent women, particularly the 'missing [Mrs] Lingk',[19] possess a power that indicates the failure of male attempts to exclude females and femininity. From this perspective the characters are clearly to be viewed critically, and Zeifman, alert to the charges of misogyny that could be levelled against Mamet – and soon would be, in spades – thinks that they are valid only in the sense that in some of his public statements he views women in essentialist, if positive, terms. Aside from this final claim, Carla J. McDonough broadly agrees, concluding that the salesmen are unable to break free of a system that works against them not because they enjoy the cutthroat competition but because they depend on the process by which it defines them as men. Where Zeifman, and certainly McDonough, are in error is in thinking that 'Mamet's dialogue seems to begin and end with sexual expletives'.[20] This is completely untrue of *The Duck Variations*, *The Water Engine*, *The Verdict*, *The Shawl* and *Things Change*, to name but a few examples of works produced prior to McDonough's essay, and even in those plays that seem best to support this assertion the dialogue is almost invariably marked by multiple registers.

A more discriminating approach is that of Robert Vorlicky, whose study of masculinity in the context of all-male American plays includes the most nuanced and perceptive study both of this aspect of Mamet's work and of the dialogue in *Glengarry*. The playwright has argued that the 'American dream' was constructed by and for the same white males who now regard themselves as its victims, and Vorlicky notes that his male characters assume the privileges of masculinity and perceive anyone who does not conform to that ideology, such as women or gay men, as Other. The resulting 'cooperative', 'social' dialogue does not differ in its predictable topics – masculinity, women, families, work, consumption – from that in 'the vast majority of the nearly one thousand published American male-cast plays'.[21] What distinguishes *Glengarry Glen Ross* even from *American Buffalo* is that the characters confine themselves to these culturally acceptable topics for the duration of the play – Lingk's statement that he lacks the power to negotiate is a shocking exception – so that access to their inner lives is denied. The social dialogue exposes the masculine ethos, yet is also cryptic, because the workplace hierarchy makes slippage between precision and ambiguity not just routine but essential.

Having identified the workings of this closed system, Vorlicky notes acutely that it impacts on the familiar debate about free will and determinism in Mamet's work and ideas, and that revolves in *Glengarry* around the figure of Aaronow. Freedom of choice is confined to staying in the system or leaving it; changing it from within is not an option, and in practice Mamet seem to deny also the possibility of changing it from outside, via 'social movements, including feminism'.[22] Consequently Mamet remains preoccupied by a patriarchal structure, including a language system, that appears unethical not only because it depends on subjugation of the Other, but also because it prohibits honest self-disclosure and communication between the men who have chosen to adhere to it. Each of the three scenes in Act 1 shows a pair of characters speaking metalinguistically – talking about talking – in ways that maintain dialogue while confounding precise meaning. Indeed, the ability to weave fictions is inseparable from the pursuit of power in this play, as is evident in the relative success of Roma and the weakness of Aaronow and Lingk. In Act 2 the presence of Williamson and Baylen in the offstage room further prohibits the salesmen from engaging in personal dialogue, not least because each of the onstage characters has a secret to maintain while wanting to acquire certain information from others. Accordingly, 'each strives to keep the dialogue social and not personal',[23] so that if Act 1 is characterised by 'metalinguistics', Act 2 is characterised by 'metatheatrics', focusing on the salesmen as performers. However, the real voice of power and authenticity is that of Jenny Lingk, mediated through her husband as if through a ventriloquist's dummy. Hers is one of the ideologies that survives in the play: in extracting Lingk from the deal she derives her power from law, yet she remains outside the patriarchal ethos that also persists in very differing inflections in the figures of Baylen (the embodiment of patriarchal law), Roma (who apparently believes he has the right to live beyond the law), and Williamson (whose position as a manager rather than a salesman allows him to preserve his authority).

Jeanne-Andrée Nelson argues that, in the absence of information about the personal histories of the characters, *Glengarry* cannot be seen as a study of corrupted innocence, since the history of that corruption is never shown. Instead, by way of a theoretical model derived from Sigmund Freud (1856–1939) and René Girard (born 1923), Nelson proposes that the characters are motivated by 'mimetic desire': a sense of lack or incompletion leads to the wish to mimic other characters who seem to possess 'narcissistic desire', the illusory but attractive appearance of self-sufficiency. The better salesmen operate by exploiting this dynamic of envy. In the first act, ironically, 'what seduces Lingk is the possibility of not being seduced ever again', and Roma attempts to repeat the trick in the second act when, in creating the character of 'D. Ray Morton' for Lingk's benefit, he and Levene demonstrate 'the lie of the narcissistic model fabricated by con artists'.[24] Less convincing is Nelson's suggestion that in the first scene Levene is trying a similar approach with Williamson; the office manager knows Levene is a loser whose performance signals desperation, so it is difficult to accept that at any point Levene 'is trying to posit himself as a desirable model for Williamson'.[25]

Language, dialogue and performance

Most of the other studies of the play's dialogue now look like footnotes to Vorlicky's analysis. Jeanette R. Malkin believes the only idiom of *Glengarry* is business jargon, a category that is less discriminating and flexible than Vorlicky's 'social dialogue', as becomes very clear when Malkin further proposes that all of the characters 'partake of the same inarticulate obscenities', as if 'jargon' and 'obscenity' were interchangeable terms. At a metaphorical level, this may of course be precisely what Mamet has in mind; but when Levene criticises Williamson for using a term like 'marshalling the leads', he clearly signals that this jargon phrase is of no use to a salesman and marks the speaker as an unmanly petty bureaucrat. Using a word derived from the theories of Benjamin Lee Whorf (1897–1941), Malkin argues that the 'patternment' of the language contributes to 'a sense of determinism' in Mamet's plays, and inevitably helps to produce 'a concept of success which is wholly materialistic and geared only toward personal gain'.[26]

Other theories challenge this deterministic view by presenting language as instrumental, a tool that can be exploited by the speaker to achieve desired effects. Foremost among these theories, perhaps, is the speech-act theory of J. L. Austin (1911–60), on whose *How to Do Things with Words* (1962) David Worster draws in 'How to Do Things with Salesmen'. Worster notes the self-referentiality of the constant talk about talk, and suggests that the salesmen are at least roughly aware of the distinction between felicitous and infelicitous speech acts: those that are felicitous demand the securing of uptake from the listener.[27] Worster does nice work in showing how the salesmen plant in their listeners' heads the idea that they must act immediately, and in showing how the power relationships in speech-act situations are repeatedly inscribed in sexual terms. Unlike Williamson and Mrs Lingk, however, the salesmen actually fail to secure their listeners' assent. To identify precisely why, one would have to invoke the kinds of ideological study that go beyond Worster's constraints, and his analysis is compromised to some degree by a deployment of speech-act theory that is sufficiently undiscriminating to lead to the very strange assertion, refuted by Vorlicky, that Aaronow's silence is a sign of power.

Two further essays each explore the interplay of two different kinds of language. Barry Goldensohn perceives a 'dialectical tension' between 'poetic' and 'realistic' speech, a tension that 'keeps us aware of pattern and significance without letting them dominate our sense of a real world',[28] while Jonathan S. Cullick examines the now customary dialectic between the 'discourse of community' and the 'discourse of competition'.[29] The former invites participation and response, and in *Glengarry* is associated with weakness, femininity and buying; the latter implies strength, masculinity and the 'closing' of both conversations and sales. Like Vorlicky, Cullick observes that success depends on the ability to keep the listener uncertain as to which mode is in play, as he demonstrates in convincing close readings of several of the play's most familiar passages and also in Williamson's concluding demolition of Levene, which shows that he is now on a par with the salesmen who have previously held him in such contempt.

Significant others

Glengarry is replete with references to characters who never appear. Writing in 1987, Philip C. Kolin suggests that Mitch and Murray may be invisible for reasons of verisimilitude: 'like so many bosses in America they make themselves hard to get at'.[30] Once feminist critics began to move the focus of attention away from business towards gender politics,

it was the numerous offstage women who began to receive greater attention, most extensively in an essay by Karen Blansfield, which observes
that their ability to disrupt the workings of the male world, and the fear
with which the men regard them, are signs of the power they actually
wield.[31]

Dorothy H. Jacobs surveys the absent women of *Glengarry*, several
of whom – the nurses on Jerry Graff's list, receptionists, the females
catalogued with disturbing contempt in Roma's pitch to Lingk – are
rarely mentioned in other commentaries on the play. The salesmen
think a woman's place is in the kitchen, as opposed to the jungle of
male business. In arguments reminiscent of those of McDonough, Vorlicky, Worster and David Radavich, Jacobs draws on feminist theory to
show how women are used as an object of not just sexual but also verbal
exchange between men, with the homosocial associations intensified by
the proximity of the discourses of salesmanship and sexual seduction.
Like Vorlicky, Jacobs notes that Jenny Lingk's voice emerges powerfully
through the mouth of her otherwise largely mute husband and 'modifies the phallocratic order. She breaks the silence and asserts the power
of the female voice'.[32] Jacobs's conclusions about Mamet are ambivalent: on the one hand the language can appear to celebrate an all-male
realm whose pleasures and values Mamet himself has often extolled, and
yet, as in Levene's hesitant lines about his daughter, the loss and influence of the opposite, ruthlessly marginalised feminine world is strikingly
evoked.

Play and film

In 1992 a film version of *Glengarry Glen Ross* was released, directed by
James Foley (born 1953) from Mamet's screenplay, featuring an all-star
cast and introducing a new character, Blake (Alec Baldwin), who has
been sent by Mitch and Murray to terrorise the salesmen with the new
sales contest. Robert I. Lublin argues that the two versions differ at a
fundamental level. The film's story is simpler: Blake shows that out-
landish success in the real estate game is perfectly possible, which helps
to explain why the salesmen continue to endure the humiliations of their
daily working lives. In the play, no one is successful in 'a society that has
gone into [economic] recession'.[33] Lublin ingeniously and convincingly
traces a narrative history of this malaise. Moss recalls a time when the
salesmen worked to build up a trusting relationship with their clients,
but at a certain point they began to rip off the customers, leading to a
dwindling client base, a fall in the value of the land, and an irreversible
decline towards the survival economy that has now forced Mitch and
Murray to reduce the workforce by initiating the sales contest. Hence

the characteristically ambivalent reactions of audiences towards characters who behave immorally, but for understandable and even admirable reasons: to stave off poverty, starvation and perhaps even, in the case of Levene's daughter, death. Lublin infers that, unlike in the movie version, Mitch and Murray themselves may be facing catastrophe as the real estate business in general enters recession. That Jerry Graff is willing to pay the salesmen to steal the leads from his rivals' firm suggests the very opposite of the economic success Moss attributes to him, while the loss of the leads may be enough to break Mitch and Murray's business. This is well argued, although some other critics such as Sauer give little credence to the salesmen's stories about the past. The question is not decidable.

Christopher Hudgins provides a very detailed account of the differences between the play and the film in arguing that the latter brings into stark relief certain thematic concerns that are implicit, but nevertheless readily discernible, in the stage version. Hudgins highlights four such themes: the critique of capitalism, 'the harsher elements of human nature', the importance of friendship, and the necessity of making ethical decisions in the face of the 'death consciousness' revealed in the aging Levene's predicament and in Roma's pitch to Lingk.[34] Not surprisingly, then, Hudgins sees the play in existential terms, with compassionate human relationships providing almost the only bastion against a cruel world stripped of other values. Like Lublin, he thinks this emerges most obviously in the film's added sequences showing Levene's concern for his daughter, and in Williamson's statement that he failed to cash Lingk's cheque because he stayed at home to play with his child, another detail absent from the play. Citing some of the speeches of Moss, Levene and Roma, Hudgins argues perceptively that Mamet often puts ethically laudable statements into the mouths of morally dubious characters, which further helps to explain why so many critics fail to perceive the 'positive' values affirmed in the play. This leads him to make the more problematic argument that Roma's friendship with Levene is genuine, and still more problematically that Roma also cares about Lingk's difficulties in his marriage, although Hudgins provides supporting evidence from the comments of Joe Mantegna (born 1947), who performed the role of Roma on stage, and by noting that the ending of the film, which 'is considerably softer' than that of the play, gives credence to the view that Roma thinks his friendship with Levene will persist.[35]

Hudgins's otherwise excellent essay highlights two difficulties that recur when critics fail to analyse the films in cinema-specific terms. First, he makes no distinction between the film and the screenplay, and indeed has simply transcribed the dialogue, which would not be a difficulty were it not that he frequently refers to the effects of editing, lighting, music and close-ups. These are rarely the province of the writer, and in the absence of the script Hudgins is on slippery ground in extrapolating from the film to broader statements about Mamet's thematic emphases in both the film and the stage versions. Second, like Gay Brewer and others, Hudgins accepts without question Mamet's statement that his work in cinema follows the example of the Russian film director Sergei Eisenstein (1898–1948), particularly in the use of 'uninflected cuts'. As we shall see in the later chapters on the films, Mamet's comments along these lines are always stimulating, but should be treated with extreme caution.

Indeed, by the mid-1980s it was becoming commonplace to regard Mamet himself as a kind of confidence trickster. Hints abound in *Glengarry Glen Ross* that the creative deceptions of the salesmen are akin to the work of the playwright and the actor, and the analogies are taken still further in Mamet's next, lesser-known, but equally magnificent play: *The Shawl*. We shall consider this, along with *Prairie du Chien*, in the next chapter.

CHAPTER EIGHT

Prairie du Chien (1978),
The Shawl (1985)

Prairie du Chien and *The Shawl* are short plays which were paired when Gregory Mosher (born 1949), Mamet's friend and collaborator at the Goodman Theatre in Chicago, decided to stage them for his first production on taking up the highly prestigious post of Director at the Lincoln Center in New York in 1985. *The Shawl* was a new piece, but *Prairie du Chien* had initially aired several years previously on National Public Radio.

Prairie du Chien (1978)

Set in a railway carriage on a night train travelling between Chicago and Duluth, the play revolves around two pairs of characters, who initially do not interact: two men (a voluble Dealer and the largely silent Gin Player) playing cards, and a Storyteller relating a kind of supernatural crime story to a Listener who is accompanied by his sleeping son. There is accordingly a structural relationship, if nothing more, between the two pairs. The play ends after the Gin Player violently accuses the Dealer of cheating, and fires a gun.

Dennis Carroll suggests that the play produces quite different effects depending on whether it is experienced as a radio or a stage play: in the former, one might infer that the murder story has somehow influenced the card players, but in the theatre, at least as directed by Mosher, the two groupings on stage remained quite separate.[1] Two later discussions, one of the stage play and one of the radio drama, do not entirely bear this out. Deborah R. Geis thinks that even on stage it is clear there is an ironic relationship between the terms used by the Dealer and the Storyteller's narrative; moreover, 'the two "confidence men" ... enter and exit the actual stage ... together, almost as if they were one character divided into two parts', although there is no way of confirming that either has been acting fraudulently.[2] Moreover, the two stories are embedded within a third, the train journey, while the play itself could be regarded as a confidence game, or indeed, in being both true and untrue at once, as resembling a dream, like that from which the sheriff in the Storyteller's tale cannot awaken. *Prairie du Chien* is therefore metadramatic in drawing attention to the problematic relationship of trust between the listener or audience and the speaker or play.

Ilkka Joki, who discusses it as a radio drama,[3] argues that although the Storyteller and the Listener are concerned to protect the boy from the story itself, the Listener wants to prepare his son for adult life, and therefore explains that fights can break out between men, though he does not reveal that the fight concerns money. Joki's analysis of speech genres takes a peculiar turn when he suggests that one point of the play is to remind adults of their responsibilities towards children, citing a radio show called *The Seven Words You Can't Say on Radio and Television* that aired one afternoon in 1973. Following the broadcast a parent complained that his son had been exposed to the comedian George Carlin (born 1937) reciting the words 'shit', 'piss', 'fuck', 'cunt', 'cocksucker', 'motherfucker', and 'tits'. It is not clear that this has anything to do with *Prairie du Chien*.

The Shawl (1985)

In this short, three-act play, lasting around 45 minutes, a woman named only as 'Miss A' seeks the advice of a clairvoyant, John, as to whether she should contest her late mother's will. John convinces her of his powers by apparently seeing events from her past, only to reveal afterwards to his lover, Charles, how the trick was done. Charles is impatient for John to get money from Miss A, and they stage a spectacular séance, only for Miss A to turn the tables on John and expose him as a fraud. In a series of twists, John first attempts to redeem himself with Miss A by telling her seemingly unknowable details about her mother's shawl, insists privately to Charles that this was another trick, and then finally, alone again with Miss A, tells her that he knows she burned the shawl five years ago, fully restoring her confidence in him and leaving the audience uncertain as to whether he has genuine powers or is just the latest in Mamet's succession of confidence men.

Bruce Barton's substantial analysis of *The Shawl* occupies a pivotal position in his account of Mamet's 'transition' from theatre to film. Throughout his book Barton is concerned to establish a fundamental distinction between Mamet's work in these two media. His principal argument is that as a film director Mamet makes the spectator the victim (or 'mark') of the film-as-confidence-game, but in his work for the theatre he attempts to establish an 'organic', communal relationship with the audience. *The Shawl* represents the fulfilment of this ideal of social spectatorship: Miss A, as John's onstage audience, effectively collaborates with him in constructing the scenario, so that each combines the roles of performer and spectator. Similarly, John's insistence on patiently explaining to Charles how to watch and observe, and his disregard for immediate financial reward, emphasise the active social role of spectatorship, into which the theatre audience is drawn when John shows Charles (and us) the trick 'from the back'. Charles refuses this role, however, and John's demystification of his art and denial of its power also represents a kind of internal rejection of the organic theatre that the play will nevertheless ultimately affirm.

This analysis is convincing, because Barton traces how *The Shawl* works as theatre. Other critics rather fruitlessly debate the question that the play leaves the audience contemplating at the end: whether, as John puts it in words that recall the Fortune Teller in Mamet's then-recent *Edmond*, there is really a hidden order in the world. For Philip C. Kolin, there is no doubt: *The Shawl* shows Mamet 'exorcis[ing] his audience's need for magic (or illusion) while paradoxically demonstrating their dependence on it', and the final act is a series of 'object lessons' in this regard, so that if we are still taken in by John's tricks we have 'fall[en] into the trap of . . . looking for a false explanation for the truth'.[4] Gay Brewer is more ambivalent but still sceptical, noting that in finally gaining Miss A's confidence John may well also gain financially. Henry I. Schvey, however, considers that 'the play is really about a man's growth and capacity for self-knowledge in the midst of corruption', and believes the ending 'confirms that the visionary experience has been real'.[5] Carroll agrees, but emphasises the relationships between the characters, and between them and the audience. He notes that after the third scene, the only one of the five to show all three characters together, John's allegiance shifts decisively from Charles to Miss A, and argues that by the end of the play their relationship is built on trust and mutual need, indicated by rhythms in the dialogue that suggest 'authenticity' and 'overlapping consonances of thought' developing between them.[6]

Kolin, Schvey and Carroll all come down on one side or another of a question that Mamet seems determined to keep in play. As Bigsby incisively puts it, what *The Shawl*, *The Duck Variations* and even *American Buffalo* finally reveal is an irony whereby 'the very faith which makes individuals vulnerable to exploitation and deceit is primary evidence of the survival of a sense of transcendent values for which otherwise [Mamet] can find no social correlative' – although by the time these words were published in 1992 Mamet had arguably found just such a correlative in Judaism.[7] Of greatest interest in this regard is the variety of interpretations of a scene which, on first viewing, is one of the least ambiguous of the play: the séance, which the audience knows beforehand is being staged by Charles and John in an attempt to con Miss A. This is indisputably inauthentic, in Carroll's terms, and yet Carroll appears seduced by its 'rich evocation of the lyricism and mystery of the unknown which the play celebrates'.[8] Geis's reading is more subtle, finding in John's monologue a 'doubleness' that characterises the play itself, since it 'privileges as a virtuoso solo the very mode of narrative that the characters' interactions have sought to deconstruct'.[9] Mamet's work in general 'ultimately throws into relief the ability of the theatrical work to "con," or persuade, its audience',[10] and the ending of *The Shawl* leaves us with 'a recognition of theatrical narrative's power to "conjure" images even in the face of scepticism about the possible fraudulence of such power'.[11]

Barton's analysis of the séance is particularly convincing in this respect. The irony of John's performance as the medium is that he is most in control of himself (in the sense that he is more or less following a script) at the very moment when he pretends to be possessed by a spirit. As Barton sees it, this is the culmination of a series of episodes in Mamet's plays, including Teach's assault on Bobby in *American Buffalo* and Edmond's murder of Glenna (a waitress who insists she is an actress), which are connected by a spectator's anger at being presented with a deceitful performance. Unlike the earlier plays, however, *The Shawl* is not transformed by a moment of physical violence; instead Miss A, for the first time in Mamet's work, fully takes on the responsibilities of critical spectatorship, while to a far greater degree than his predecessors John is self-aware, and thus able to reject his own dishonesty. In what follows, Mamet suggests the interdependence of performer and spectator. John persists in keeping his next appointment with Miss A without concern for the personal consequences, and like Stanislavsky's 'organic' actor, at this point he experiences a 'liberation into open and selfless spontaneity'.[12] Although John insists to Charles that this too is a sham, there is yet another reversal when Miss A returns. Here, she is assertive and John, the performer, is submissive and seemingly inarticulate, so that roles are reversed and the characters finally share a 'mutually supportive dynamic of personal performance'.[13]

Brewer sees *The Shawl* as a transitional piece between Mamet's recent plays, especially *Glengarry Glen Ross*, and his first film, *House of Games*. All three works are about confidence tricks, and in both *House of Games* and *The Shawl* Mamet's then wife Lindsay Crouse (born 1948) plays a repressed woman who seeks guidance from a man who pursues a dubious, quasi-psychological profession and claims to have access to secret information. Brewer and Barton both cite Crouse's statement that Mamet was consciously developing a greater interest in plot while writing *The Shawl*, a development that most critics, including Brewer, attribute to his extensive work for Hollywood during this period. Finally, in the figure of the confidence man, both works imply a self-reflexive comment on the work of the playwright or film-maker.

The differences, however, are more significant than the similarities. *House of Games* arguably represents the most significant development in Mamet's entire career, not only because it confirmed that cinema would henceforward consume at least as much of Mamet's attention as theatre, but also because, if *The Shawl* represents the culmination of his efforts to achieve a communal or 'organic' aesthetic in the theatre, *House of Games* is a hermetically sealed trap to catch the spectator.

CHAPTER NINE

House of Games (1987)

Mamet's experiences in Hollywood had brought frustrations as well as success, and by 1986 he had the opportunity cherished by many a screenwriter when the producer Michael Hausman gave him the chance to write and direct a low-budget film. Thereafter he would continue to write screenplays for other directors, but in doing so he would either retain substantial control over his scripts or work as a writer for hire on projects that carried, perhaps, lesser personal significance.

The first striking thing about *House of Games*, in light of Mamet's career to this point, is that the protagonist is a woman. Margaret Ford (Lindsay Crouse), a newly successful psychologist and author, becomes fascinated by a group of confidence men, in particular their apparent leader, Mike (Joe Mantegna), before realising too late that she has been their victim all along, at which point she wreaks the ultimate revenge. The film compelled a radical reinterpretation of Mamet's work as a whole, marrying epigrammatic and witty dialogue to an idiosyncratically austere style of acting and *mise-en-scène*; thereafter, few critics would describe his work in any medium as 'realistic'.

Psychoanalytical readings

William F. Van Wert's pioneering essay of 1990 contains some abstruse passages, but the general argument is clear enough, and indeed outlines the interpretive frame within which almost all worthwhile analyses of the film have worked, although his article is rarely mentioned in subsequent criticism. He notes that the audience, which initially identifies with Margaret's point of view, later comes to recognise that the film, or at least the confidence men, are really watching her. *House of Games* thereby compels a retrospective reinterpretation, yet there is no telling at what point the crooks selected her as their victim, and no way of knowing whether certain events, such as Mike's sexual tryst with Margaret, were planned or merely consequential. *House of Games*, then, is Mamet's 'master con ... with the spectator as mark'.[1]

Faced with a narrative that is incredible at the level of realism, Van Wert astutely seeks to explain most of it as a kind of dream or self-diagnosis of Margaret. For example, the suspiciously depopulated scene at the airport, where Mike is able to take Margaret into the baggage holding area without being challenged by airport security, is a kind of projection, a revenge drama played out in Margaret's mind, and represents the first stage of a self-treatment that is completed by her transformation in the final scene. This restores her to the social world, makes her comfortable in the company of women, and reconciles her compulsive kleptomania with self-forgiveness. The film, then, 'promotes psychoanalysis as a potent force for transformation'.[2] Richard Combs argues 'that the therapeutic process reaches [even] further back into the film, [and] is an alternative narrative to the con man's game – a feminine alternative to the masculine one. The "House of Games" ... is Dr Ford's invention, the staging ground for her therapy, "conceived" in the first part of the film where she is forever writing'.[3]

A plausible objection is that Van Wert incorrectly assumes that *House of Games* is sympathetic to psychoanalysis. Mamet has often commended Freud's *The Interpretation of Dreams* (1899), but principally as a description of the dream state as analogous to the process of artistic creation or the audience's understanding of culture; his view of psychoanalysis itself is deeply sceptical, and he has frequently ridiculed its claims to scientific rigour and therapeutic value. On the other hand, of course, *House of Games* itself may nevertheless wittingly or unwittingly 'promote psychoanalysis'. Van Wert favourably compares it to two films directed by Alfred Hitchcock (1899–1980), *Spellbound* (1945) and *Marnie* (1964), which contain spuriously optimistic transformations whereby the patient, whose symptoms are the product of the repression of a childhood trauma, is cured once the male analyst brings the forgotten incident back to mind. By contrast, Margaret may be an ineffective analyst, but Van Wert considers that 'her treatment of herself is much more realistic' than that to be found in Hitchcock and other classic Hollywood narratives',[4] at least in terms of the methodology of Jacques Lacan (1901–81), the psychoanalyst whose work would come to exert an overpowering influence on film theory, and on later interpretations of Mamet's film, as we shall soon see.

Unfortunately, Van Wert's essay is riddled with factual errors. He mishears dialogue with alarming frequency, and badly misrepresents entire scenes, as James Hyder points out in a stinging response printed in a later issue of the journal that published the original article.[5] In the crucial airport scene, Van Wert wrongly states that Mike's body falls onto a conveyor belt (in fact he collapses in a corner), that Margaret fails to collect her bag (instead she takes hers and leaves Mike's), and that Mike's last utterance – 'Thank you, sir, may I have another' – is nonsensical, whereas in fact it is a statement required of boys receiving corporal punishment at boarding school, and therefore works rather neatly as a closing taunt. This by no means exhausts the mistakes Hyder identifies, and although *Film Quarterly* appended Van Wert's response to Hyder's letter, in his attempted rebuttal he acknowledges only one howler and simply ignores several others. Neither the original essay nor the subsequent exchange with Hyder leaves the reader with much confidence in Van Wert's powers of observation, and much of what he says about the remainder of the film is open to similar objections. For instance, he claims that Billy Hahn is absent from the scene at Charlie's Tavern prior to Margaret's encounter with Mike at the airport; in fact, he is seen talking to the Vegas Man. Inexplicably, he asserts that Mamet provides no reaction shots of Margaret as she overhears Mike explaining how she was tricked, but there are several, including a long take in which a tear is actually seen to trickle down her cheek. Given that Van Wert's arguments about the film depend very largely on the transformations effected in the final three scenes at Charlie's Tavern, the airport and the restaurant, it is disturbing that several of his assertions concerning at least two of them are demonstrably false.

In identifying the inaccuracies, Hyder further charges that Van Wert has deployed an intimidating critical idiom that conceals the flaws in his reasoning. The essay is replete with references to Freud and, in particular, Lacan, as well as to Georges Bataille (1897–1962) and Michel Foucault. As such it bears many of the hallmarks of an essay written at the high point of critical theory in the late 1980s, with its attendant strengths – notably a determination to trace the workings of local linguistic signifiers within a larger psychoanalytical framework – and weaknesses, most obviously the commitment to a theoretical schema that, arguably, actually produces the text to which it supposedly offers a response. This is damagingly obvious when Van Wert mishears Mike's taunt about a dog returning to its own vomit as a dog returning to its *father*, and produces a piece of sheer sophistry to explain it.

Van Wert sought to defend some of his almost impenetrable reasoning by stating that the theoretical exposition had to be jettisoned at the editing stage. No such problem confronts Ann C. Hall, who devotes several pages of her essay on *House of Games* and *Speed-the-Plow* to an elucidation of relevant Lacanian theory. Everyone has a 'lack', and is incomplete; women are aware of this, but men falsely regard themselves as autonomous while actually seeking completion in something outside themselves – an Other, or what Lacan terms a *petit objet à*. This is most commonly supplied by a woman or, rather, a series of women, since men never correct their misreading of their lack. Women, meanwhile, have an 'ability to change', and they 'embody *jouissance*, a disruptive excess'. Margaret Ford, and Karen in *Speed-the-Plow*, possess these qualities and thereby challenge 'the power structures established in the plays' as well as 'the expectations of other characters and their audiences'. It is in this context that Hall makes the otherwise remarkable claim that Margaret and Karen 'embody this revolutionary femininity'.[6]

Hall is more adroit than Van Wert in handling the theoretical idiom, her close analysis of the film is less exciting but much more solid, and she is sharp on issues of gender. For example, at the beginning of the film Margaret's severely masculine appearance suggests that she is 'a woman pretending to be a man',[7] and Hall is equally good in reflecting on the male subculture of pool halls and confidence games. However, despite creating an apparently sound methodological foundation, Hall, who is an excellent critic of contemporary drama, never engages with Lacanian film theory, and she repeatedly refers to *House of Games* as a play, script or screenplay. It may be because she lacks a real theory of spectatorship and identification that she fails to come to any clear conclusion: on the one hand, Margaret appears to have confirmed Mike's analysis, but on the other hand, her stealing of the cigarette lighter is 'mysterious', and she is 'enigmatic', 'the sphinx'. It is not clear that on its own this constitutes quite the 'joyously subversive' conclusion Hall thinks it is.[8]

Hall also gives insufficient emphasis to the evidently ironic way in which Mamet, rather than just the characters, plays with very obvious Freudian symbols: guns, coins, cigarettes, cigars, keys, the knife, the cigarette lighter. Diane M. Borden, who remains committed to psychoanalytical interpretation, astutely argues that in *House of Games* this produces not closure but further mystery. The language of the con game and psychoanalysis both work in the same way, as a sign system that both offers and bars entry to a kind of secret society. It purports to be a problem-solving method, but actually increases the level of mystification, which is also present in the plot, and in the games played by the director. Most significantly 'though the "crime" may be resolved, the mystery not only remains, it is compounded'.[9] This phenomenon is rooted in the 'sublime', meaning here the simultaneous feelings of pleasure and fear engendered by the encounter with mystery, terror and horror, and specifically in Borden's analysis by the transgression of psychological and social boundaries. In both *House of Games* and Mamet's later film, *Homicide*, the protagonist experiences the sublime in falling in love with a figure who also represents an Other to which the hero wishes to subjugate him- or herself.

There is something classically deconstructive about this analysis: language refuses to remain stable but instead variously obscures meaning, generates unintended linguistic consequences, or becomes enmeshed with other discourses. For example, Borden detects the presence of a linguistic system based around advertising (the selling of books, cars and beer), notes that it is Margaret and not Mike who initiates the self-conscious gangster idiom spoken at the House of Games, and discusses some of the ways in which these apparently secret languages promise to unlock the unconscious yet fail ultimately to do so. Similarly, the meaning of the comically symbolic gun is not finally fixed, but instead is 'a free-floating phallic signifier' which 'beguiles and stymies', with the film finally suggesting that 'the signifier is never completely reducible to any one meaning'.[10]

House of Games and feminist film theory

By contrast, most of the overtly feminist discussions of *House of Games* confidently define the film's meanings quite precisely. The most valuable aspect of Bruce Barton's analysis is that he challenges at source Mamet's insistence that he is almost completely indebted to Eisenstein for a principle of montage whereby the juxtaposition of two shots creates a third, abstract idea in the mind of the audience. This claim has been accepted without qualification by most commentators, but Barton demonstrates that it is highly misleading. In the very first scene of *House of Games*, for example, a young woman holds out a book for Margaret to sign. There is not a juxtaposition of two shots here, but rather a 'juxtaposition of images within a single shot'.[11] More generally, unlike Eisenstein Mamet is primarily interested in plot, and consequently in the linkage rather than the collision of shots, making him much more like Eisenstein's compatriot and contemporary, Vsevolod Pudovkin (1893–1953), and closer to mainstream Hollywood practice.

Also helpful is Barton's discussion of suture, a complicated element in certain kinds of (particularly psychoanalytical) film theory derived from an interpretation of what is really going on in the standard Hollywood practice of shot/reverse shot editing. To oversimplify, according to this theory the first shot creates a potential anxiety in the spectator: from whose point of view am I seeing this? What is lurking in the offscreen space? The reverse shot reassuringly answers these questions, creating a reality effect by effacing the signs of cinematic production: instead of showing a camera or director, it suggests that the film is unfolding realistically and continuously in an illusory three-dimensional space that thereby, as it were, stitches the spectator into the *mise-en-scène*. As Barton observes, however, Mamet's films very often create the effect that events are being manipulated by an offscreen presence, and *House of Games* 'quietly foregrounds the overtly stylized and artificial environments (or *stagings*) that it captures', while playing on 'the audience's sense that a familiar and recognizable basis of experience is always (that is, perpetually) a single revelation away'.[12]

Elsewhere, Barton finds much in Mamet's style that is barely distinguishable from classical Hollywood cinema: he maintains narrative clarity to avoid audience confusion, there is a 'near seamless and often overtly authoritative continuity',[13] and Barton invokes the director's own statements to propose that Mamet is drawing the audience towards a single correct interpretation of the action. This proximity to conventional film-making, and the implications of a storyline in which a group of men takes an unwitting female victim for a ride, push Barton towards an overall view of the film that appears heavily influenced by a now-standard line on narrative and spectatorship derived from Laura Mulvey's overwhelmingly influential article 'Visual Pleasure and Narrative Cinema' (1975). Mulvey argues that the cinematic gaze, associated with voyeurism and penetration, is male, whereas the female is frequently the passive object of the gaze. This holds for *all* narrative cinema, although Mulvey's arguments have been qualified and modified by many feminist film theorists, such as Mary Ann Doane, Tania Modleski and indeed Mulvey herself.

Barton's remarkably unambiguous conclusions about *House of Games* are consonant with an unreconstructed Mulveyan line: the film seeks to contain the 'ideological excess' of the woman's femininity, and indeed Margaret 'ultimately fulfils a stereotypical male fantasy of subservience and expendability', so that in the final analysis 'the film valorizes a socially instituted dismissal of female significance'.[14] As always, Barton's analysis is also informed by his view that a particular kind of performance is central to Mamet's aesthetics. Mamet's 'is a world which values presence, participation, authenticity, and sincerity', and to a still greater degree than in the plays, these qualities are 'fundamentally male and inherently theatrical', while Margaret is 'doomed from the outset, as she is conceived as entirely female and categorically cinematic', aligning her with the 'passive and wilfully manipulated cinematic spectator'.[15] Implicit in the idea of containment and excess is another argument ultimately derived from feminist criticism and the abjection theory associated with Julia Kristeva (born 1941). This holds that the female is a leaky vessel, revealed here in Margaret's compulsive behaviour and propensity to verbal slips that reveal an otherwise hidden self she would prefer to keep out of sight.

Two earlier essays on the film arrive at similar conclusions concerning the ways in which the men (both Mamet and the male characters) valorise a masculine ideal that successfully contains – indeed, traps – the woman. Both Laura Kipnis and Marina deBellagente LaPalma (whose essay was published five years later but in apparent ignorance of Kipnis's work) make some of the same observations as Van Wert, Hall and Barton: at the beginning of the film Margaret appears asexual, only to be visibly transformed in the final scenes, and the film sets up a dichotomy between what Margaret thinks she sees and the ultimate recognition that these scenes have in fact been constructed for her to look at. *House of Games* is therefore manipulative in gender-specific ways, and Mamet's cinematic confidence game is a patriarchal construct with the woman (and, implicitly, women) as its victim(s).

For Kipnis, a dominant idea here is the notion of exchange. Margaret and the confidence men appear to be offering something to and gaining something from each other, but it is a tainted bargain: the men have concealed essential information from her, while Margaret's own profession, or at least competence, is thrown into question. They have been plotting her demise from the beginning, and because she is unwittingly caught in a structure written by others, she is 'split', and 'lacks self-identity'.[16] The film finally grants her an identity, but one conferred by men. Until the airport scene her relationship to Mike has resembled that of the patient to the analyst, whose function is to give voice to the patient's unconscious, so that the repetition compulsion can be broken. (Some years later, in *True and False*, Mamet would argue the precise opposite – such relationships exist so that their rituals can be repeated without end.) However, Mike possesses no interior self, no unconscious, and when Margaret finally recognises that he is driven solely by greed she shoots him, much as a patient might walk out on an unethical analyst. This is a moment of potential resistance, but in Kipnis's view Margaret's shooting of Mike does not represent the victory of the woman. On the contrary, at the airport Mike 'pronounce[s] the *truth* of Ford's *pathology* (the truth of the woman's *essence*)' (Kipnis's emphasis), and because by now Mike has been securely established as the film's 'epistemological hero', the audience recognises that he is simply right.[17] The final scene confirms his analysis: Margaret has finally accepted her femininity, but her theft of the lighter shows that all along she has been what he said she was, a compulsive thief.

Like Kipnis, LaPalma observes that Mamet's film resembles 1940s melodrama, but LaPalma is primarily interested in its relationship to a melodramatic sub-genre, the 'woman's film'. In the early scenes there are many signs (especially Freudian slips) that Margaret herself is suffering from repression, which, we subsequently learn, is bound up with her compulsion, including a compulsion to be a victim. In this way she resembles the heroines of 1940s woman's films such as *Now, Voyager* (Irving Rapper, 1942): she is emotionally sick and therefore a problem, the resolution or cure to which is provided by the man of science – often, in melodrama, a psychoanalyst. Mike fulfils this function in *House of Games*. For LaPalma, however, this is 'a false "woman's film"',[18] because it is motivated less by Margaret than by the confidence men, so that any potentially liberating or subversive function is replaced by a structure that positions Margaret not as the subject but as the object of the masculine gaze and male power.

Kipnis makes the very important point that, whereas the institutional validation of Margaret's authority is all too obvious, and she herself is an unconvincing practitioner of psychoanalysis, the sources of the confidence men's knowledge remain obscure. In other words, unlike Margaret they have no evident 'lack': the audience doesn't know when the plot against her was hatched, whether the whole stratagem was precisely planned from the beginning, or whether Mike is sometimes improvising in response to events. This obscurity increases his power and establishes the (working-class, masculine) confidence game as an unimpeachable epistemology that trumps the apparently analogous discipline of (bourgeois, feminine) psychiatry. Mamet works this trick so expertly that, as with patriarchy generally, what is actually a constructed world-view passes itself off as something almost natural. The spectator initially identifies with an inferior, feminised position before being manoeuvred 'into the position of a transvestite who ultimately renounces the female position and reclaims masculinity as the "correct" way of seeing' – represented by Mike, the 'master decoder' – once the failure of Margaret's reading becomes clear.[19] (The transvestite spectator is a necessary construct in arguments that seek to accommodate female spectatorship within the male cinematic gaze as theorised by Mulvey.)

The conclusion is unavoidable. Because the sources of this masculine knowledge remain unknown, for Kipnis 'the film works to produce and confirm this fantasy of perfect knowledge', and so, finally, 'it enforces the clutches of an unending transference, the legitimacy of paternal authority, and the grip of masculine power'.[20] Similarly, after noting that the confidence men display a casual violence towards and hatred of Margaret, LaPalma states that the film provides little 'to mitigate this hatred or suggest any other way of viewing her', so that Margaret becomes simply 'a vehicle of patriarchal values'.[21]

These are powerful arguments, but they are not unanswerable, and on at least two counts they appear self-contradictory. First, Kipnis's analysis suggests that there is something *specifically* culpable about Mamet's film, yet she appears committed to the Mulveyan claim that a gender-specific position underlies *all* narrative cinema. Second, and more importantly, she argues that 'Ford's interiority [or essence] becomes the film's primary concern',[22] and LaPalma agrees: the film 'traps the woman in an essentialist, ahistorical model' and 'is actually an analysis, a penetration of [Margaret]'.[23] Mamet is therefore guilty of a dangerous masculine presumption in exposing the 'essence' of the female character. Yet, on the other hand, he is accused of precisely the opposite: Kipnis asserts that at the start of the film Margaret is 'a different species entirely from any other cinematic heroine of recent memory',[24] while for LaPalma her Freudian slips appear to be 'only word games, not valid without individual lived content and factual information, which is precisely what is missing'.[25] If this is the case, then as Mamet repeatedly insists in general, and as Lindsay Crouse's performance as Margaret might be held to substantiate in particular, there *is* no 'character', and therefore there can be no essence to be penetrated. This would suggest that the ending is less closed than Barton, Kipnis and LaPalma think. It might also call into question a residual demand for realism that underlies these arguments, as when Kipnis expresses a certain scepticism at the ability of the confidence men to be able to predict Margaret's behaviour, or when LaPalma proposes that the film 'is arguably *realist*' (LaPalma's emphasis) in the sense that its depiction of the containment of feminine desire by male power 'is not an inaccurate description of social reality'.[26]

Semiotics, representation and the confidence game

In fact, as Kipnis points out, 'the con man is a phantasmatic figure of knowledge who would not himself withstand the microscrutiny devoted to the female',[27] which suggests that the film has very little to do with 'social reality'. As Michael Quinn puts it, Margaret is confronted by 'the problem of depth, of how many layers of playing a scam might involve, and how many of them she is supposed to see through', so that 'the problem of authentic action within it becomes the problem of which reality to affirm, which of the performances to accept as true'.[28] This problem has been convincingly theorised by Elizabeth Klaver, who believes that '[t]he film belongs more to postfeminism than to the genre of realism, the social problem play, or what LaPalma calls the "woman's film"'. Contrary to the hackneyed view that the artist works through fiction to reveal the truth, Klaver presents a metacinematic Mamet working as a confidence man. There is no reality to be unveiled; *House of Games* is an illustration of 'postmodern hyperrealism' in which '[t]he real (and realism) finally retreats so far back into a network of signs that it effectively disappears'.[29] Klaver convincingly demonstrates this by using Jean Baudrillard's theories of simulation in a way that suggests other critics have been playing the wrong language game in trying to answer such questions as when the plot against Margaret was hatched, and how much of it was improvised. For example, at Charlie's Tavern the confidence men reveal that the leaking gun in the poker scene is an example of 'realism', but Klaver notes that this in itself introduces two different possibilities: either the gun was supposed to pass as a real gun, in which case the plan was to con Margaret out of $6,000, or it introduces a further level of realism in which it was intended to leak, thereby collapsing the notional realism of the staged scene. Within the film's network of signs the demand for something to be exposed as finally, definitively 'real' seems almost nostalgic.

Steven Price questions criticism that analyses Margaret according to a psychoanalytical model. He argues that Margaret refuses to give up her identity because she doesn't have one, and disrupts the very methods of objectification and penetration that hostile critics see Mamet exploiting in the film. In particular, he challenges those readings that give a privileged status to the final scenes in which Margaret shoots Mike and then appears physically transformed at the end. Price objects that Margaret has undergone several changes of attire, and by implication of identity, in the course of the film, and that if anything her garish outfit and makeup in the final scene is the least convincing of all. This masquerade is one of the many ways in which she is a resistant force within the film, which not only sends up the 'object language' of psychoanalysis in its self-conscious use of Freudian symbols, but also questions the efficacy of the 'metalanguage' of psychoanalytical interpretation itself.[30]

Indeed, one of the most lucid and suggestive insights into *House of Games* comes from Roger Ebert, a popular newspaper and television reviewer whose interpretive paradigm in approaching Mamet's films comes not from psychoanalysis but from the world of stage illusion. This sufficiently explains why his comments have been uncited in mainstream academic criticism. Ebert compares Mamet to a magician deceiving his audience with a card trick and making up a story about the 'characters' (the King, the Queen) on the cards. This story, of course, has no realistic or psychological credibility, as the magician will concede in his tone of voice. This story 'is a diversion. The real story is, what's happening to the cards? What is he really doing while he's telling us he's doing something else?' Mamet directs his films '[l]ike a magician whose real cards are hidden', an analogy compounded by Mamet's tendency to deploy the same actors from film to film, 'just as a magician always starts with the same 52 cards'.[31] Ebert captures with brilliant clarity the consequences of accepting, as most critics finally believe we must, that a Mamet film does not describe a confidence game; it *is* a confidence game, with its audience as victim.

With his script for the blockbuster *The Untouchables*, and his move into direction with *House of Games*, Mamet had established himself as a major player in American film. With characteristic chutzpah, his next stage play would at once satirise the Hollywood that was so ready to fete him while pulling off the remarkable feat for a new, non-musical play of opening on Broadway. This was only partly due to Mamet's own prominent profile. The main reason was that *Speed-the-Plow* would, in the eyes of many, reprise the gulling of the female character in *House of Games*, but this time the victim would be perhaps the most famous woman on the planet: Madonna.

CHAPTER TEN

Speed-the-Plow (1988)

Mamet's new play was a send-up of both Hollywood producers and scriptwriters. The drama revolves around which of two competing scripts the newly promoted executive, Bobby Gould, will decide to film: the unabashedly commercial 'Doug Brown' screenplay promoted by his friend and associate Charlie Fox, or *The Bridge*, the obscurely 'authentic' novel about radiation championed by the temporary secretary, Karen, whom Gould is trying to get into bed. *Speed-the-Plow* is often compared to other works about Hollywood, and no fewer than five of the 18 essays in a 1997 collection about *Hollywood on Stage* discuss Mamet's play at some length. It was a runaway success, not only because it is a riot of brilliant one-liners and a satire on the Hollywood that had just provided Mamet with such acclaim, but also because it starred Madonna as Karen. Her performance received almost universally negative reviews, but later criticism implies that she may deliberately have been dealt an unwinnable hand.

The title phrase has medieval and religious connotations and means something like 'do your work well on earth and God will reward you', or more simply 'good luck', while also suggesting, in this context, a sexual pun. It is hardly surprising that both *Speed the Plough* (1800), by the English playwright Thomas Morton (1764–1838), and the quotation from *Pendennis* (1848–50), the novel by William Makepeace Thackeray (1811–63) with which Mamet prefaces the published edition, are likewise concerned with work, and Tony J. Stafford, who provides an illuminatingly full discussion of the title, has little success in establishing any further connection to Morton's play.[1]

Hollywood and the 'business trilogy'

Leslie Kane describes the early influx of Jewish money and talent into Hollywood, and, as she observes, Bobby Gould's namesake in *The Disappearance of the Jews* (1983) romanticises the Hollywood of the 1920s as a place in which Jews seized an opportunity to create their own community of wealth and power. (Bobby Gould is the name given to a series of connected Jewish characters in Mamet's work – see Chapters 12 and 13). Her suggestion that *Speed-the-Plow* represents a kind of historical conflation of the 1920s and 1980s receives little support from the text, however, and leads her to place less emphasis than most on the contemporary satire, and more on Fox and Gould's ethnicity. Although in places the chapter can accordingly look unbalanced, it is one of the most intriguing in her book. Kane thinks Mamet is parodying the caricatured 'stage Jew', and more importantly is tracing in Gould's adventures 'a parable of the wilderness: of being chosen, backsliding, being chastised, and renewing commitment'.[2] Indeed, the subject is nothing less than the threatened annihilation of the Jewish people, with Karen as its instrument.

Seen in this light, many of the qualities that some feminist critics regard as positive – Karen appears persuasive while being capable of transformation and crossing boundaries – become signifiers of a duplicitous, 'mythical trickster figure',[3] her witch-like powers enhanced through being effected at night. She seems to offer Gould the possibility of salvation, but she is, in effect, trying to convert him to Christianity, suggested also by the humourlessly apocalyptic and transformational quality of *The Bridge*, which Kane connects to the Book of Revelation and televangelism. At best, Karen is encouraging him towards a kind of assimilation that would erase his ethnicity, and from a Jewish perspective is therefore anything but benign. Kane reads Fox's references to the Baal Shem Tov and hiding the Afikomen as more or less explicit warnings to Gould about this, counselling him against committing an act of betrayal for the seductions of an outsider, which would violate a specifically Jewish ethical code of trust. In consequence Kane takes an unusually positive view of Fox, on whom the role of teacher (which has passed from character to character) finally falls, and who effects a kind of re-education of Gould. Kane sees the ejection of Karen and the reunion of the two men as a reaffirmation of a certain kind of faith at the end of a play that belongs in 'a rich tradition in American Jewish humor that takes aim against the merchandising of redemptive love'.[4]

Language

The Hollywood of *Speed-the-Plow* is a masculine workplace, and accordingly Ruby Cohn sees this play as the final part of Mamet's 'business trilogy' that also includes *American Buffalo* and *Glengarry Glen Ross*, in all of which 'Mamet implies that the foulest obscenity of all is the word "business"'.[5] Cohn rejects the naïve view that he records everyday

speech – his 'cunningly constructed run-on sentences are pure invention, never heard off the stage'[6] – and also disagrees with Mamet's
own early assertion that language determines behaviour.[7] For Cohn, the
opposite is true, and her essay examines how, for example, '[a] sense of
pressure compels Mamet's characters to omit prepositions, conjunctions,
or relative pronouns', which helps to explain the constant questioning
and 'interrogative rhythms'.[8] Cohn is sensitive to what Kane would later
term 'interior bilingualism', whereby Yiddish influences intrude noticeably. Slippages in the moral world of the plays, in which terms like
'right' and 'wrong' slither free from their ethical mooring, are expressed
in the grammatical and syntactic chaos: repetition and tautology, sudden
changes of tense, disagreement between subject and verb, floating pronouns, solecisms, and the 'semiotic slippage' in the use of obscenities.
Cohn implies that previous critics have nevertheless taken an uncritical
view of the language, and thinks that *Speed-the-Plow* shows Mamet's
'reach exceed[ing] his considerable grasp': his intention in creating
The Bridge, she believes, is 'to mock religious fundamentalism', and the
fact that some critics think the book is to be taken seriously indicates that
Mamet's linguistic powers have failed.[9] Wholly at odds with the excel-
lence of the rest of Cohn's essay, this argument is a groundless mixture of
impressionism and unsubstantiated assumptions about authorial intent.
Cohn, however, is only one of many whose doubts concerning *Speed-
the-Plow* in part result from an insistence on coming down on one side
of what the play sets up as an unresolved debate around Karen and
The Bridge.

Quite the opposite view, for example, is taken by Christopher C.
Hudgins, in an essay in the same collection which also groups this play
with *American Buffalo* and *Glengarry Glen Ross* and which, in conjunction
with Cohn's piece and a contemporaneous discussion by Toby Silverman
Zinman,[10] is one of a small cluster of articles at this time that represent
a marked advance in the understanding of Mamet's dialogue. Hudgins
thinks Mamet 'is comically evoking a religious vision', and that much of
the irony and humour in *Speed-the-Plow* comes from the deliberate presentation of serious material in comic terms. The most obvious example,
of course, is *The Bridge*, which is treated strictly comically at the beginning of the first act because it is presented through the purely venal eyes
of Fox and Gould. As the play progresses, however, Hudgins detects serious moral and religious ideas in the book, tempered by Mamet's dislike of
didacticism (hence the ironic treatment of the portentous style), before
the 'tremendous sadness' of Karen's defeat in Act 3.[11] Hudgins acknowledges that this argument requires him to adopt certain views that many
critics regard with scepticism, notably that Karen is not only a force for
good but also, particularly after the first Act, sincere, and that important
and laudable ideas are discernible in *The Bridge*.

Homosocial desire

Most critics point out that the relationship between Fox and Gould resembles the male camaraderie of the 'buddy movie', of which the Doug Brown script is a parody, and that they use the terminology of a homosexual liaison in describing their partnership. Given that this relationship is threatened by a woman who is expelled at the end in an apparent restoration of equilibrium, it is not surprising that two of the earliest critics to outline the 'homosocial' dimension to Mamet's work should turn their attention on this play.

David Radavich's relatively early (1991) and influential consideration of masculinity in several Mamet plays is sketchy, but astute in its consideration of the relationship between Fox and Gould. Radavich observes that very few of Mamet's previous plays had featured women at all; instead they dramatise tensions in all-male relationships between the desire for status and the desire for friendship. This brings with it the fear that this 'homosocial' desire will mutate into or become perceived as homosexual desire, and therefore necessitates a correspondingly vicious homophobic and misogynistic language, while business relationships, and capitalism generally, are often figured in terms of homosexual rape. *Speed-the-Plow* offers a more comic and affirmative representation of homosexuality (perhaps due to the tolerant environment of Hollywood) in the playful idiom in which the apparently straight men Fox and Gould discuss their relationship. This is threatened by Karen, and in consequence Fox in the third act is pushed towards making 'the baldest statement of homosocial desire for intense male friendship' in any of Mamet's works, while in this play, too, 'the perception of women as sexual "weakeners" or "corruptors" of men receives its most direct expression'.[12] Radavich concludes by positioning Mamet's work within a long tradition, identified by Leslie Fiedler, of male friendship in American literature: the innocence of that friendship has been lost, homosocial desire is now ambivalent, and such relationships have become inherently unstable due to competition between men and their inability to integrate such friendships into their relationships with women.

Carla J. McDonough notes that the hint of a mutually supportive male community that is seen in the relationship between Joe and Dale in *Lakeboat* has by now completely disappeared, and that the separation of spheres between business and leisure that Mamet also describes in essays is blurred out of existence in his plays. Instead, in *Speed-the-Plow* it is the men who demonstrate the 'invidious comparison, secrecy, and stealth' that Mamet attributes to women in *Some Freaks*.[13]

Feminist critiques

McDonough is surely right to argue that Karen's personality is simply eclipsed by that of Fox. However, Karen's treatment by the two men raises the contentious issue of Mamet's representation of women, which did not fully emerge as significant until after the appearance of *House of Games* and *Speed-the-Plow* and reached a climax with *Oleanna*. In all three of these works women come into direct conflict with men, and as we have already seen in the previous chapter, many critics argue that Mamet ultimately attempts to validate the male position. Accordingly, several essays adopt a strikingly aggressive attitude towards not just *Speed-the-Plow*, but Mamet himself. Marcia Blumberg, Jeanne-Andrée Nelson and Katherine H. Burkman all agree that *Speed-the-Plow* celebrates both Hollywood and the misogyny of Fox and Gould. Blumberg observes that '[t]he misogynistic, homophobic bent'[14] of Fox's third-act verbal annihilation of Gould has appeared in other Mamet plays, and also, she contends, in some of Mamet's essays, notably 'Decay: Some Thoughts for Actors', in *Writing in Restaurants*. It is true that this piece contains a reference to homosexuality that most people would probably regard as unfortunately phrased at best, but Blumberg's essay, which is not so much a work of criticism as a piece of polemical rhetoric, goes well beyond fair comment. Many might disagree with Mamet's suggestion in 'Decay' that the emergence of all kinds of disasters, including AIDS, signals that the contemporary world is experiencing a kind of collective Freudian death instinct, a desire to be at rest, and that nothing can be done to stop it; but Blumberg's conclusion that Mamet therefore 'homophobically sanctions the demise of a disproportionately affected gay community'[15] would be deeply offensive if it weren't so daft.

Burkman details some of the oft-noted resemblances between Mamet's play and Sam Shepard's *True West* (1980). She argues that in each case a play that nominally offers a critique of Hollywood in fact celebrates it, in part by failing to set up a credible opposition, so that ultimately these works become narcissistic. The false opposition in *Speed-the-Plow* is represented by Karen, who 'is just another kind of whore', and devoid of ambiguity, at least in the script.[16] Karen shares the same values as Fox and Gould, but her language is even more clichéd than theirs, so the audience regards her expulsion with relief. In the kind of unambiguous personal attack that also characterises Burkman's discussions of *Oleanna*, she concludes that Mamet 'identifies with the Hollywood moguls' misogyny and self-hate'.[17]

A similar but more complicated view emerges from Jeanne-Andrée Nelson's selective reading and interpretation of Mamet's statements about men, women and narrative, from which she concludes that he confuses the male mind with a universal consciousness, and thereby marginalises women. Nelson's strategy is to 'rescue' *Speed-the-Plow* by concentrating on the experience of the female reader. Like Burkman, she finds no room for ambiguity, yet she sees Karen in completely opposite terms, as an active female 'reader' who 'mirrors the interpretative effort of her female counterpart in the audience who refuses to participate in the misogynistic discourse of the patriarchal authority'.[18]

Nelson's methodology is seriously flawed, although this may in part be the effect of what seems to be a deliberate effort to read against the grain. She observes that the Fox–Gould story is linked to the Doug Brown script (and, at least implicitly, to what Nelson perceives as Mamet's world-view): they are masculine, focused on sexuality, and achieve victory through power, violence or sadism. Nelson's description of the two male plots actually identifies all kinds of differences between them, but she reflects neither on this nor on the seemingly obvious irony with which the play presents Fox, Gould and the Doug Brown film. Karen, meanwhile, is linked to *The Bridge*, and also to the female reader (or Nelson) in a second grouping that disrupts, in a positive and potentially fruitful way, the functioning of the first. Nelson does not give Mamet any credit for this, however, possibly because she appears unaware of his short story 'The Bridge' (published in 1985), which possesses many of the qualities of the novel of that name in *Speed-the-Plow*.[19] Arguing that the play is divided against itself is more sophisticated than the approach taken by Blumberg and Burkman, but Nelson's own analysis ought to indicate that, far from being a card-carrying masculinist who has somehow managed to create in Karen a paragon of feminist virtue, her creator could equally be regarded as a feminist writer.

This is the logical conclusion reached by Janet V. Haedicke, who rejects 'the Mamet-misogynist label' and sees in his work 'a feminist ethic', principally in the ways in which he dramatises gender as performance that transgresses, destabilises and transforms the 'illusion of fixed identity'.[20] Like Nelson, Haedicke sees that Karen's disruptive presence is bound up with her championing of *The Bridge*, and views this as a text that dissolves the linear logic and binary conception of gender that feminist theory tends to associate with patriarchy. For Haedicke, Karen 'embodies the intrinsic nature of ambivalence'; specifically, she 'transgresses boundaries in resisting the Hollywood-sanctified coding of women as Mother or Monster, Madonna or Whore'. In turning Gould against Karen in Act 3, Fox is forced to represent her once again in strictly binary terms, and in so doing 'aborts Gould's salvation'.[21]

Ann C. Hall is more ambivalent. She debates the effects of casting Madonna in the Broadway premiere, presciently notes a recurrent religiosity in both the imagery and the call-and-response structure of some of the dialogue, and, like Haedicke, uses post-structuralist theory to argue that the play resists the dualistic vision of women expressed by its male characters. Once again she recognises Karen as a disruptive force; indeed, as noted in the previous chapter, at one point she attributes to both Karen and Margaret Ford a 'revolutionary femininity' which challenges the patriarchal power that Fox and Gould retain for themselves and that both *Speed-the-Plow* and *House of Games* appear on the surface to champion.[22] As with her analysis of *House of Games*, however, Hall rather hedges her bets: on the one hand, she sees Karen, like Margaret, as an enigma; on the other hand, she assumes without much evidence that Karen is sincere, and that the play endorses the radiation book simply because it spends so much time discussing it.

Steven Price argues that the positions adopted by Nelson and Hall are self-contradictory.[23] They regard Karen favourably because she disrupts the plot's linear structure and resists the male characters' attempts to contain her within binary notions of identity and gender, yet on the other hand these critics seem to know all about her and regard her positions as fixed. Hall, for example, states that 'Karen is sincerely straightforward',[24] while Nelson insists that Karen quite simply 'is not' 'guilty of manipulation', and even purports to know what Karen is thinking offstage: when Karen reads to Gould some words from *The Bridge*, she 'is sure about the incorruptibility of their truth', and 'her voice duplicates the emotion she felt when she read alone'.[25] Price contends that instead of expecting the audience to favour one side over the other, Mamet's major works are characterised by a self-deconstructive strategy that resists any secure interpretive resolution. Psychoanalytical interpretations of the characters are flawed, not least because the mechanism of the confidence trick prohibits access to the conscious or unconscious minds of fictive constructs overtly lacking in deep psychology, while in performance *The Bridge* is so fragmented and dissonant that its meaning cannot be reconstructed.

Four years later, the controversy surrounding Mamet's representation of women would reach its height with *Oleanna*, and after that the gloves would be well and truly off. In the intervening period Mamet's own concerns would become more introspective, with his divorce from Lindsay Crouse, marriage to his second wife, Rebecca Pidgeon (born 1965), who played Karen in the London premiere of *Speed-the-Plow*, and an exploration, via the works considered in Chapters 12 and 13 of this guide, of the Jewish identity that had hitherto been seemingly marginal to his work. Perhaps because it directly engages with none of these public or private affairs, the film that Mamet produced after *Speed-the-Plow* has received comparatively little attention; yet *Things Change* is one of Mamet's best and most satisfying works.

CHAPTER ELEVEN

Things Change (1988)

Just as *The Shawl* stands out as a more quietly reflective piece than the other major plays of the 1980s, so Mamet's second film was a much simpler and more conventional affair than its predecessor, *House of Games*, or his third film, *Homicide*. In *Things Change* a gang of well-connected Chicago mobsters make an offer to an elderly and impoverished shoeshine man, Gino (Don Ameche): if he will take the rap for a murder one of the gang has committed, he will be financially rewarded on his release from jail. When he accepts, 'Mr Green' (Mike Nussbaum), the local Mafia boss, hands him a Sicilian coin as a symbol of their shared heritage, and he is entrusted for the three days preceding the trial to a minder, Jerry (Joe Mantegna), who is 'on probation' for poor performance. Jerry decides Gino deserves a more immediate reward, and he takes him to Lake Tahoe in Nevada, where he passes him off as 'Mr Johnson', supposedly a mobster VIP travelling incognito. The subterfuge threatens to unravel when Don Joseph Vincent (Robert Prosky) invites the mysterious Mr Johnson to his estate, where he is hosting a meeting of Godfathers. Gino convinces Don Vincent that he is genuine by showing him Green's Sicilian coin, and Don Vincent reciprocates by giving him a quarter that he can use to telephone should he ever need help. On returning to Chicago Jerry, who has tried and failed to persuade Gino to escape altogether, discovers that his real task is to kill him. Instead he assaults Frankie (J. J. Johnston), the mobster who has given him the order; Gino saves the day by calling Don Vincent, and the final shots reveal that it is now Frankie and not Gino who is to be the fall guy in court, while Jerry joins Gino at work in the shoeshine store.

Fairy tale and fable, myth and money

Mamet has described *Things Change* as 'a fable about frustrated ambition', a fable being 'a gentle myth that treats common human problems in an elevated way so that we can see them for what they are without being frightened by them'.[1] Dennis Carroll finds connections with Mamet's children's plays, while regarding the film as yet another illustration of his familiar theme of friendship versus business, with friendship here emerging victorious. At the centre of the film, of course, is the developing rapport between the two major characters, but as Carroll points out, 'what defeats the Mob and vindicates the redemptive power of Gino and Jerry's relationship' is the attachment forged between Gino and Don Vincent by an exchange of coins that ironically uses money to symbolise the enduring power of comradeship and ancient bonds.[2]

As such, *Things Change* is another illustration of the distinction between 'real' (or 'iconic') money and 'symbolic' money at the heart of *American Buffalo* and *Glengarry Glen Ross*. For Linda Dorff, the Sicilian coin represents 'a symbolic connection to a historical past' that 'is so powerful that iconic money becomes unnecessary', as Jerry and Gino discover on being told that the hotel will grant them whatever they want without accepting payment, or that a single phone call to Don Vincent can release them from enslavement and worse at the hands of the mob.[3] Gay Brewer suggests that '[t]he elaborate giving of coins . . . is a method of offering trust, demonstrating *Things Change* as another variation of confidence games',[4] although this seems strictly true only of Green and not of Gino or Don Vincent, while the film itself has none of the metacinematic confidence tricks that, for many, typify the 'Mamet movie'. More convincing is Brewer's suggestion that Gino's use of the coin to save himself and Jerry further connects *Things Change* to the 'fable or fairy tale', in many examples of which 'the granting of a wish accomplishes only restoration of original circumstances', since Gino is returned to the shoeshine store while the criminals remain in power.[5]

Close reading: Gay Brewer

Brewer's chapter on *Things Change* surveys the broadly positive reviews and draws on the actors' interviews circulated in the official production information pack. He sees a self-reflexive process here, whereby Mamet, the director-as-con-man, is also the Godfather on set, establishing a family atmosphere – the reappearance of several actors from *House of Games* and earlier stage productions confirms him as an ensemble director – that mirrors the Mafia families and, in particular, the theme of loyalty, in *Things Change*. In Brewer's eyes the first two films offer a conflated figure of the outcast, the deviant con man, the respected outlaw mobster, and the atavistic multi-skilled craftsman, which implicitly comments on Mamet's self-construction as a film artist.

Brewer's detailed commentary on the film itself contains several illuminating insights. He identifies the conspicuous display of leisure, rather than simple opulence, as the defining signifier of power, and traces this to the influence of Thorstein Veblen. The many lines in Italian contribute to the sense of an alternative, hidden order in the world that we have already noted in *Edmond* and *The Shawl*, and that will receive a more precise repetition in the use of Hebrew and Yiddish in *Homicide*. Gino is 'genuinely elusive',[6] and the uncertainty about whether he is fully aware of what is going on or is instead merely a simpleton, whose comments about shoes Don Vincent mistakenly takes for insightful metaphors about loyalty and power, prompts an apposite comparison to the novella *Being There* (1971), by Jerzy Kosinski (1933–91).

All of this is excellent; but it isn't much to show for 28 pages in a small font, and the same holds for Brewer's comparably lengthy chapters on *House of Games* and *Homicide*, the only other films Mamet had directed at the time Brewer was writing his book. It is easy enough to identify why there is so little beef in a monograph that is so diligently researched and fluently written: it is because Brewer is not a film expert. The comparison to *Being There*, for example, is well taken, but less illuminating than the recognition by the film critic Philip French that *Things Change* resembles not only the 1979 film version of Kosinski's tale, directed by Hal Ashby (1929–88), but still more strongly Ashby's *The Last Detail* (1973),[7] in which a hapless naval recruit is escorted to prison by two more experienced officers who take pity on him and decide to show him a good time en route. Nor, apparently, is Brewer well versed in film theory, since, like almost all critics who have come to Mamet's films from a literary or dramatic background, he accepts without comment Mamet's highly dubious assertion that his directorial style is almost wholly indebted to Eisenstein. Consequently Brewer finds himself in the curious position of repeatedly comparing Mamet to a confidence trickster while taking everything he says at face value. Perhaps partly as a result, his analysis is primarily thematic, and the themes aren't interesting: for example, '*Things Change* is in one respect a movie about the American Dream, about Old and New Worlds'.[8] Even when his discussion becomes more specific, as in tracing the atavistic code of honour or the relationship between language and power in the film, it often amounts to little more than elegant statements of the obvious, an effect heightened by the tendency to quote at length from the screenplay.

Ethics and ethnicity: Leslie Kane

Like much of the earlier criticism, such as the books by Anne Dean and Dennis Carroll, Brewer's study lacks a certain bite because it is does not pay sufficient attention to the possibility that an apparently uncontentious moral position – capitalism can have a corrosive effect on personal relationships, love and friendship are more important than business, and so on – is a great deal more complicated, and conceals significant ideological tensions within both Mamet's work and contemporary American culture. For Leslie Kane, as in a quite different way for the handful of critics who would soon launch the remarkable accusation that *Oleanna* aligned Mamet with right-wing neo-conservatism, the seemingly commonsense morality is contested and contestable ground. Kane devotes a chapter of *Weasels and Wisemen* to three of Mamet's film works: *Things Change*, *Homicide* and his screenplay for *The Edge*. In each of these she sees the theme of pedagogy or moral teaching, and a similar form, a quest story focusing on a pair of characters operating within a larger familial structure (a description that appears only marginally applicable to *Homicide*).

Within this slightly insipid framework, she soon begins to define her ideas more sharply. *Things Change* initially appears unpromising material for Kane, who proposes an archaeology of Mamet's philosophy and ethics rooted in Jewish moral teaching, but she smartly prefaces the discussion by noting Mamet's own observation that he and co-writer Shel Silverstein (1930–99) developed the idea for the film out of their memories of themselves as Chicagoans growing up in a city notorious for organised crime. Characteristically, this allows Kane to identify Jewish-specific foundations for themes and motifs such as the transmission of knowledge between generations, justice, memory, family and show business. To other eyes Mamet's dramatisation of this kind of material might appear trans-cultural, although in light of his growing interest in Judaism at around this time Kane's arguments are certainly worth entertaining. More convincing is the cumulative effect of details concerning nomenclature and social position. Kane suggests that the names of the characters who congregate at Green's mansion indicate 'a common Russian–Polish ethnicity'.[9] Gino, meanwhile, gains acceptance or success by means of disguise, but he is otherwise a marginal or outsider figure, and Kane suggests that when he and Jerry first wind up isolated at the Chicago hotel, they strike 'the quintessential pose of the Diaspora Jew'.[10] Elsewhere she, like Brewer, seems hard pressed to expand to sufficient length the analysis of this 'deceptively slight' film:[11] the waiting at the hotel, or on a country road, hardly warrants the comparison to *Waiting for Godot*, not least because, to take the latter example, the two men are sitting in a car at a crucial point in a linear narrative, suggesting more a parody of a road movie than a reference to absurdist drama. Kane is always worth reading as an antidote to received opinion, but the chapter on cinema is one of the less convincing parts of the book, not least because the game-playing analogy she pursues in discussing Mamet's direction is insufficiently developed, while she resembles Brewer in accepting unquestioningly his own comments about his approach to film.

Things disappear: Bruce Barton

This is not a charge that can be levelled at Bruce Barton. As noted in the chapter on *House of Games*, Barton shows that in practice Mamet owes far less to Eisenstein than to the more linear editing techniques of Pudovkin and, indeed, of the classical Hollywood cinema, and in this respect his analysis of Mamet's direction represents a significant advance. However, the contrast between the treatments of *Things Change* by Brewer and Barton, the only critics to have published books wholly or substantially on Mamet's films, is astonishing for a different reason. Brewer considers that the film, 'though co-written with Shel Silverstein, is pure Mamet',[12] but fails to analyse the specifically cinematic qualities that clearly indicate affinities between *House of Games* and *Homicide*, with *Things Change* a film apart. Barton, on the other hand, argues that because the screenplay is co-authored, *Things Change* is not a Mamet film (on which criterion Alfred Hitchcock never made a single picture), and therefore he does not write about this movie *at all*. This is exceptionally damaging to a book that explicitly presents itself as an account of 'Mamet's transition to film'. If the first and third films are transitional, it is difficult to see how the second could not be, but Barton ploughs on regardless, consequently introducing *Homicide*, not *Things Change*, as Mamet's 'second motion picture'.[13]

It is difficult not to think that Barton's problem lies less with the co-authorship of the script than with his claim that in *House of Games* and *Homicide* 'the still alien properties of film intersect with the conditions and conventions of theatrical practice'.[14] This would mean that his decision to omit *Things Change* has been taken on formal grounds; and indeed, whether or not one thinks of it as 'pure Mamet', it is a very different kind of film from *House of Games*, *Homicide*, or indeed *The Spanish Prisoner*, another film that Barton barely considers, although in this case it arguably lies outside the historical parameters of his study. In each of those three films the spectator is positioned as the mark of the film-as-confidence-game, an observation that does not apply to *Things Change*, which accordingly is structured and edited quite differently. Omitting it allows Barton to maintain an argument about consistency of form and development that would otherwise fall to pieces.

Not only is *Things Change* a small masterpiece, it also confirms that from the beginning Mamet was a far more versatile director than he is often given credit for, and was perfectly able to direct in a more conventional style if he chose. The highly distinctive direction of his other early films is therefore deliberate rather than the product of inexperience, incompetence or indifference ('something that he usually practices with his left hand'), as is sometimes claimed.[15] Without *Things Change* as a reference point, these things would not become apparent for many until the appearance in 1999 of *The Winslow Boy*, which needlessly surprised many reviewers who ought to have known better. *Things Change* has instead remained on the fringes of Mamet criticism because it looks anomalous, fitting comfortably neither into the cinematic sequence of *House of Games*, *Homicide* and *The Spanish Prisoner*, nor the 'Bobby Gould' sequence of *Speed-the-Plow*, *Bobby Gould in Hell* and *Homicide*. Moreover, *Speed-the-Plow* and *Things Change* are comedies, a mode to which, surprisingly, Mamet would not return until *The Spanish Prisoner* in 1997. Few would have predicted the altogether darker turn his work was now to take instead.

CHAPTER TWELVE

The 'Bobby Gould' Plays (c.1989)

Bobby Gould is not a recurrent character so much as a name given to different characters in different plays around whom similar concerns coalesce. Toby Silverman Zinman, who shrewdly observes that the apparent realism of much of Mamet's work in fact 'requires the elaborate parallel and simultaneous reading allegory demands', valuably if somewhat playfully attempts to pin Gould down more precisely. She rearranges the chronology of the plays to trace 'a gaudy and deeply outraged parody' of the *Divine Comedy* by the medieval Italian poet Dante Alighieri (1265–1321); she argues that they provide a king of Diabolical Comedy for our times, with Los Angeles, the City of Angels, as Inferno on earth, and follows what is perhaps a Gould figure through no fewer than six works in which he moves progressively towards a 'damnation [that] turns out to look a lot like earthly success'. She proposes that the young Bobby (no second name supplied) of *American Buffalo* (1975) matures into Robert, 'the unseen but motivating evil force' in *The Cryptogram* (1994, but dating from the late 1970s); Robert abandons his son and his wife, Donny, who again shares the name of a character in *American Buffalo*.[1] The first Bobby to be generally accepted as Bobby Gould emerges in *The Disappearance of the Jews* (1983), fantasising about what life must have been like for Jews in the Hollywood of the 1920s. Near the end of the play he casually says 'God *damn* me', and sure enough, in Zinman's story, Mamet writes *Bobby Gould in Hell* (1989), from which Gould is sent back to Hollywood to reappear in *Speed-the-Plow* (1988). Again he repeatedly if ironically prays to God, and Zinman takes his opening speech about being 'in the midst of the wilderness' as a clear invocation of Dante. In his final manifestation, as Bobby Gold in *Homicide*, 'Mamet seems to have created his most obvious surrogate'.[2] Zinman's piece was written prior to the staging of *The Old Neighborhood* trilogy in 1997, which places *The Disappearance of the Jews* alongside *Jolly* and *Deeny*, both written in 1989, and clearly identifies Bobby Gould as the same character in all three.

It is difficult to accept *American Buffalo* as a Bobby Gould play, and although *The Cryptogram* is undoubtedly closely connected to *The Old Neighborhood*, Robert seems a distant relative. The remaining plays, however, do form a distinct group, but one that is difficult to place chronologically. *The Disappearance of the Jews* has three distinct manifestations: performed in 1983, published as one of *Three Jewish Plays* in 1987, and integrated within *The Old Neighborhood* in 1997. In two of these it explicitly or implicitly forms part of a trilogy, and triggers associations with the other works, even though in *Three Jewish Plays* Gould does not appear in the companion pieces. Moreover, the Gould plays underwent not only a process of revision (Mamet had completed *The Old Neighborhood* in 1989 but reworked it prior to the 1997 premiere), but also of reconception, since it would appear that it was the work on *Speed-the-Plow* and *Homicide* that prompted the writing of several of these pieces and the revision of *The Disappearance of the Jews*. In 1989, then, Mamet was actively working on almost all of the 'Bobby Gould' works; hence the placement of the shorter pieces at this point in the Guide, with separate chapters on *Speed-the-Plow* and *Homicide*.

The above account draws heavily on Leslie Kane's work in *Weasels and Wisemen*, and one can only be grateful for her exemplary scholarship in tracing the history of these plays.[3] Kane's is by a distance the most important critical discussion of *The Old Neighborhood*, combining her customarily exhaustive explanation of Jewish ethical teachings, discriminating cross-references to other relevant texts in Mamet's canon, and an exceptionally detailed account of the autobiographical sources, drawn in part from her discussions with Mamet and several members of his family.

The Disappearance of the Jews (1983)

In its earlier incarnations *The Disappearance of the Jews* is divided into several short dialogues (which Mamet would later restructure to form one continuous piece), in which Bobby, a man in his thirties, sits reminiscing in a hotel room with his childhood friend, Joey. At the heart of their conversation lies the anxiety that their cultural identity, as men but particularly as Jews, is vanishing: Bobby, for example, has married a 'shiksa' (a gentile woman) and left the old neighbourhood. They attempt to construct an idealised image of their origins, as immigrants or as Jews in central Europe, but this remains a fantasy in their comic forgetfulness and their absurd imaginings of what life must have been like in the past.

In a thoughtful but risky discussion, Jeanne-Andrée Nelson resorts to the anthropological theories of René Girard to analyse their situation: faced with assimilation, their obvious strategy might be to construct or maintain cultural boundaries which, according to Girard, are initiated through the mechanism of scapegoating. The crucial moment for Nelson comes when Joey reveals his fantasy about killing his family: Joey accepts the guilt for this, whereas scapegoating is usually a means of allowing the persecutor to attach all blame to the victim. This, argues Nelson, indicates a specifically Judaic understanding of the scapegoating mechanism, but by a tragic irony it also means that the disappearance of the Jews is inevitable: quoting Joey's words, she suggests that '[t]he Jews are different because they will not "go kill things" and because they will not do so, they are marked for persecution. The difference will also cause their disappearance.'[4]

This is an exceedingly dangerous argument, since it risks homogenising Jewish thought and culture, and indeed implicitly if unintentionally suggests that Jews have been somehow complicit in their own victimisation: the very charge that Bobby's wife makes and that so appals Joey. Much more plausible, particularly in the light of *Homicide* (unavailable to Nelson, whose article was published in 1991), is Zinman's contention that 'Mamet has invented Jewish tough'.[5] Kane takes a more optimistic view than either Nelson or C. W. E. Bigsby, who sees in the title of *The Disappearance of the Jews* not only erasure through assimilation but the 'erosion of the self which stems from the denial of history and of the power of the individual to intervene in his own life'.[6] For Kane, they are engaged in an act of remembrance that is also 'an act of will', connected specifically to Jewish identity;[7] consequently her reading of the play qualifies the irony that Bigsby, equally characteristically, sees at its very heart. For example, she explains Joey's comic if morally appalling daydreams of sexual life on the shtetl (a small Jewish town or village in Eastern Europe) as an indication of the gulf between assimilated American Jews and 'a lost world known only . . . through fantasy and photographs',[8] while the humour is savagely undercut by the knowledge of the nocturnal terrors that were really visited on Jews in Europe. The comedy functions in part to show how Joey and Bobby are mentors to each other, with Bobby correcting Joey about the pogroms and Joey reminding Bobby that Jewish identity is transmitted through the maternal line. The two characters, then, are highly distinct, with Joey asserting a pride in Jewish tradition and identity ('postnostalgic' for 'an intact community', in Kane's resonant phrase),[9] and the quieter Bobby more respectful and empathetic.

Three Jewish Plays (1987)

The Disappearance of the Jews was published in 1987 alongside two very short pieces, *Goldberg Street* and *The Luftmensch*, as *Three Jewish Plays*.

The Luftmensch has received no serious attention, but *Goldberg Street*, in which a Jewish man tells stories of his youth to his daughter, and which Mamet prized sufficiently highly to give it titular pride of place in his 1985 collection *Goldberg Street: Short Plays and Monologues*, is highly regarded by both Zinman and Kane. Zinman briefly discusses it to illustrate her argument that almost all of Mamet's characters speak in Jewish rhythms and display aporia, 'the trope of doubt, the real or pretended inability to know what the subject under discussion is'.[10] Mamet has suggested that streets in America never have Jewish names, a comment that explains the title of a piece so 'utterly aporetic' that it is at once almost impenetrable and 'heartbreakingly moving'.[11] Kane, however, traces a much more detailed picture of this 'minimalist gem'.[12] The man recalls two events, both of which took place in the woods: soldiers hunting (presumably for Jews) in the Second World War, and an incident in which anti-Semitic members of his own platoon mocked him for his ability to use a compass. Combined with other references, for example to General Patton slapping a Jewish soldier, *Goldberg Street*, as Kane observes, connects the themes and reminiscences of *The Disappearance of the Jews* to the responsibilities of the parent as teacher dramatised more fully in *Jolly* in *The Old Neighborhood*.

Bobby Gould in Hell (1989)

One infers from *The Disappearance of the Jews* that Bobby left Chicago to forge a career in Hollywood, where we see a character of the same name in *Speed-the-Plow*. Following a performance of that play during its London premiere, a fragment of *Bobby Gould in Hell* was performed as a work in progress, suggesting that Gould is being punished for his behaviour as a Hollywood executive (Zinman less plausibly reverses this chronology). This short piece first alerted audiences to Gould as a serial character; the connection to the figure in *The Disappearance of the Jews* was less clear beforehand, since Mamet habitually recycles names that he gives to different characters, seen and unseen, in various plays. Shortly after the first production of this one-act play, Deborah R. Geis suggested presciently that it might presage 'an increasing preoccupation with the "trappings" of Renaissance drama',[13] a possibility realised when Mamet staged his version of *Faustus* in 2004. Indeed, *Bobby Gould in Hell* anticipates more generally the parody and pastiche that would come to characterise Mamet's work after the mid-1990s in such works as *Boston Marriage* (1999), *The Winslow Boy* (1999) and *The Voysey Inheritance* (2005). David Skeele argues that many of Mamet's plays, most obviously *Bobby Gould in Hell* but also *Sexual Perversity*, reveal him as a rather medieval moralist whose dramas draw on the tripartite characterisation of medieval morality plays, in which the Everyman figure is flanked and cajoled by polarised forces of Good and Evil.[14]

The Old Neighborhood (1989/1997)

This magnificent trilogy of short plays inscribes *The Disappearance of the Jews* within a larger structure in which it becomes the first of three meetings with relatives and old friends on Bobby Gould's return to Chicago. It demands much work from its audiences, since 'Mamet doesn't so much plot Bobby's story linearly as map it out on coordinates of character and place'.[15] After reminiscing with Joey, he visits his sister, the title character of the second play, *Jolly*, which confirms the suggestion in the first piece that Bobby's marriage to the casually anti-Semitic Laurie is falling apart. In three scenes, Jolly recounts, in what are largely monologues of unrelenting pain shot through with stories of bitter comedy and language of vivacious profanity, the life of emotional abuse that she and her brother suffered and continue to suffer at the hands of parents, step-parents and step-siblings. As Kane observes, *Jolly* is a remarkable play in the Mamet canon: linked to *The Cryptogram* as a rare portrait of a mother, Jolly is also very clearly a victim of patriarchal (as well as matriarchal) control, yet she is 'capable of balancing her disparate roles of wife, mother, daughter, and sister' while being 'literally and figuratively invested and involved in the life and future of her family'.[16] She also has a virtuoso's facility with the storytelling mode and vernacular obscenity equal to Mamet's most vividly masculine characters, and is routinely ignored by critics accusing the author of misogyny.

In the third and shortest piece, Bobby chats over coffee with Deeny, a lost love mentioned briefly in the first play, displaying the quietly monosyllabic persona that Kane regards as typical of the character throughout *The Old Neighborhood*. In the context of the preceding two plays, *Deeny* asks many questions that Mamet typically leaves unanswered: what do Bobby and Deeny hope to gain from their meeting, how profound was their relationship, and what will be its effect on Bobby, who as we now know is seeing her in a state of profound emotional distress?[17] The play preoccupies Howard Pearce, who has written no fewer than three articles on *The Old Neighborhood*, and has published widely on the playwright in several highly reputable journals. Nevertheless, it seems that Pearce is playing the wrong language game with Mamet. It is always troubling when a heavily theoretical or, in this case, philosophical framework produces textual readings that are banal, that other critics have arrived at independently of that framework, or that should have been revised in the light of previously published and readily available scholarship.

Pearce's work on *The Old Neighborhood* is open to all of these objections. A recent essay in *American Drama*, for example, devotes several pages to Edmund Husserl (1859–1938), Martin Heidegger (1889–1976), Hans-Georg Gadamer (1900–2002) and several more recent philosophers, all of which could be excised without damaging the material on Mamet. The most perceptive comments compare Mamet's work to Dante's *Divine Comedy*, ask whether or not Bobby Gould is the same character from play to play, and discuss whether or not *The Old Neighborhood* should be regarded as a single work. Yet Pearce has apparently read neither Zinman's article, which explores the Dantean analogy at length, nor Kane's book, which would have given him enough detail to comment more precisely on the Gould character and the trilological form; instead, his secondary material on Mamet is restricted to a single review from *The New York Times*. This has damaging consequences: Pearce states that the cruel figure who drives Jolly to distraction by controlling the estate is her brother, whereas it is essential to an understanding of the play to recognise that it is her stepfather.[18] Admittedly, *Jolly* is structured in such a way that the audience only gradually manages to piece together the family history, but an attentive reading should avoid the error, especially as Kane is always at hand as a reliable guide. What remains is the worthwhile observation that the title character of *Deeny* strengthens the association with Dante by providing a female 'guide' analogous to Dante's Beatrice; Zinman, writing before the appearance of *The Old Neighborhood*, could find no such figure in Gould's journey.[19] There is nothing more, and Pearce's other essays on Mamet are similarly flawed. (For his account of *The Cryptogram*, see Chapter 15.)

In the meantime, Mamet had taken the 'Bobby Gould' figure into entirely different territory, casting him as the confused protagonist of *Homicide*. This, Mamet's third and arguably most profound film, decisively places the growing preoccupation with American-Jewish existence at the centre of his concerns.

CHAPTER THIRTEEN

Homicide (1991)

In the film *Homicide*, Bobby Gould re-emerges as 'Bobby Gold', a secular Jewish detective who is reluctantly taken off the pursuit of a black fugitive, Randolph, to investigate the murder of an elderly Jewish shopkeeper, Mrs Klein. After her granddaughter overhears Gold deliver a shocking anti-Semitic tirade he is suddenly shamed into acknowledging his self-hatred, and thereafter he commits himself disastrously to helping a mysterious group of Jewish freedom fighters, for whom he commits an act of terrorism only for them to blackmail him as a result. Meanwhile his dereliction of duty leads to the death at Randolph's hands of his colleague and greatest friend, Sullivan.

Autobiographical and cultural contexts

Most unusually, Mamet conceded in the press information pack accompanying the film's London premiere that 'I wrote *Homicide* because I wanted to explore who I was and my Jewish roots'.[1] For those who had followed his career, this direct statement of autobiographical relevance was strikingly unexpected; John Lahr would still be trying to penetrate 'Fortress Mamet' several years later.[2] For many others, however, the film had a much wider significance. In a contemporary review, J. Hoberman asserted that this 'awful' and in places 'truly ridiculous' film 'proposes that there is an international Jewish conspiracy – or, rather, a counter-conspiracy – and what's more, it's a necessary one'.[3] As we shall see, this is a highly questionable reading, while Hoberman's further suggestion that the film 'is indifferent, if not hostile, to people of colour' seems offensively wide of the mark, as the climactic scene in which Gold attempts to comfort the stricken Randolph surely attests. Yet the concerns are readily explicable when one considers the truly poisonous intellectual and cultural atmosphere into which *Homicide* was released: Hoberman worries that the film 'is ready-made for exegesis by Professor Leonard Jeffries' (born 1937), a reference to a Professor of African American Studies who was openly proclaiming the existence of an ongoing Jewish conspiracy against black people. Discord between the African American and Jewish communities had been fuelled by several notorious incidents, such as the march led by future Democratic presidential candidate Al Sharpton (born 1954) through the largely Jewish quarter of Crown Heights in Brooklyn in 1991 in protest at an incident in which a black youth was killed by a car driven by a Hassidic Jew.

As Philip Hanson argues, this tension between Jewish and African Americans was but one symptom of a potential 'balkanization of America', as different ethnic groupings proclaim their separation from a centre that can no longer hold. In the same year as *Homicide* was released, 'The Cult of Ethnicity, Good and Bad', an essay by Arthur Schlesinger (1917–2007), described this disintegration of the American project of national identity into division and confusion. *Homicide*, then, is 'intensely of its historical moment', because it 'examines th[e] tension between American national identity and ethnic identity, a tension that had become *the* issue of the historical moment in America in 1991'.[4]

Ethics and ethnicity

Confronting nothing less than the social breakdown of America, an apocalyptic scenario evoked as much by the metaphysical crisis in the hero as the physical violence of a burning city, Bobby Gold – and Mamet – are faced with tough choices. And tough is what they choose, at least in the opinion of Hoberman and those critics who regard Mamet as buying into a testosterone-fuelled image of the 'tough Jew' who refuses to accept victimhood and rejects forgiveness, empathy and compassion as signs of a weakness that contributed to the centuries of persecution culminating in the Holocaust. Alain Piette suggests that the controversy arose partly because at a time of heightened tensions in the Middle East many Jewish commentators found in Mamet's work a 'detestable image' of a Jewish heritage centred on 'violence' and 'machismo',[5] what Warren Rosenberg calls an 'essentially conservative remasculinization process' bound up with a desire for history, order and belonging which were in the process of erasure by postmodernity.[6] Piette himself thinks the focus on ethnicity can be overstated, and in fact Mamet's best-known plays 'verge on the human and the universal'.[7]

Toby Silverman Zinman had earlier credited Mamet with inventing 'Jewish tough'. That may be true in the sense that 'he did it with language',[8] but the concept itself has a longer history. In Joel Streicker's summary of Paul Breines's *Tough Jews: Political Fantasies and the Moral Dilemma of American Jewry* (1990), this construction emerges in the wake of two crucial developments: an increasing loss of Jewish identity in America, partly as a result of intermarriage, and a parallel elevation of a particular kind of Jewish identity focused on remembering the Holocaust and commemorating Jewish resistance to it, alongside support for

Israel in the wake of its crushing victory in the Six Day War of 1967.[9] It is easy to see how Mamet, already a supremely masculinist writer in the eyes of many, could seem to be affirming this kind of male, hetero-sexual, violent Jewish image in *Homicide*: as most critics observe, there is a peculiar collusion between Gold, his police associates, the shadowy neo-Nazi organisation, and what both Hoberman and Streicker call the 'muscle Jews' in their collective misogyny and homophobia. Streicker, however, notes that *Homicide* shows the failure of this image: the muscle Jews form no productive connection with others, including Gold, with disastrous consequences. On the other hand, the film also rejects the assimilationist, secular model previously adopted by Gold and seen as the product of an internalised self-loathing. In short, as Ranen Omer puts it, Gold is 'a radically negative version of the abstract, assimilated Jew' – he seems completely baffled when he actually meets other Jews – yet the film will comprehensively destabilise his quest for an 'authentic identity'.[10]

This quest drives him to seek a sense of belonging in the ideological certainties of his new 'family', with Israel implicitly an ideal 'home', which could compensate Gold for his lack of any fulfilling family life. Streicker thinks this absence contributes to the marginalisation of women in the film, and may also help to explain the rise of the tough Jew as a response in the public sphere to the breakdown of the trad-itional Jewish family in America and the role of the mother within it. Streicker concludes that the ending of *Homicide* exposes militarism as a disproportionate response to American anti-Semitism, while the unrav-elling of the plot separates these events from the Holocaust and implies that any hope for the future lies in better race relations in America itself. Ultimately, however, the film offers no solution to the problem that solidarity with other groups seems necessarily to entail assimila-tion, while affirmations of Jewish identity (as seen also, in different form, in the religiously minded scholar Gold meets in the library) lead to separation. Streicker argues that this unsatisfactory situation remains in *Homicide* partly because the film only 'explore[s] a narrow though important range of ways of being Jewish in America'.[11]

Conversely, Omer notes that the Jewish secret society 'includes everything from aging Irgun commanders, to European refugees, to wealthy assimilationists to students of the Talmud and cabala, in short the gamut of Jewish experience in the twentieth century'.[12] Where Omer distinguishes different kinds of Jewish identity, and Streicker traces the ideological history of the tough Jew, Hanson demonstrates the existence of many different *interpretations* of ethnicity, arguing that it always involves the formation of boundaries by which some are included and others excluded, so that 'historically, the question of who is a Jew has itself not always been clear'.[13] Gold's mistake is to believe in the kind of essentialist, 'natural' ethnicity that the Kleins and Benjamin's group insist should transcend external loyalties, but which generates the problem it is supposed to overcome: while excluding personal identity, it merely creates different groups of outsiders depending on where the boundaries are drawn.

For example, there are several kinds of 'family': the police and the resistance group, but also Gold's friendship with Sullivan (which the latter jokes is a family relationship), as well as the families of Klein, Randolph and Wells (referred to in the screenplay and in many critical studies as the 'Grounder'), a man who is brought into the police station after murdering his wife and children. As Adam Zachary Newton puts it, *Homicide* 'groups and then regroups its characters after the fashion of a Venn diagram',[14] with the traits of each group intersecting with those of others. These groups 'present Robert Gold with a variety of values, out of which he will try to construct his identity',[15] and the Jewish organisation offers 'tribal identity'.[16] Hanson therefore places *Homicide* in the context of the ongoing debate about pluralism (by which in theory everyone may become assimilated, and which has to some extent protected American Jews from persecution) and multiculturalism (the assertion of difference). To the extent that the film takes a position, it rejects both of these views and instead values family and 'organically shaped personal relationships'.[17] In the final moments, Gold is given the opportunity to see that the Grounder has indeed shown him the nature of evil: it lies in destroying these intimate, personal bonds.

Conspiracy theories

A problem with the otherwise impressive essays of Streicker and Hanson is that after their detailed exposition of *Homicide*'s engagement with seemingly intractable social, ethical and historical questions, their concluding appeals for better race or personal relations are so unexceptionable as to seem almost banal. One reason for this is that in focusing on thematic issues, they rather skate over some highly problematic questions concerning the plot. Every critic points out the signs of conspiracy, but most either ignore it to focus on theme or write as if it were not, finally, a difficulty. Streicker, for example, confidently enumerates the membership of Benjamin's organisation, yet it is hard to know how extensive it is: does it involve the Kleins, or the scholar at the library? Kane notes that Gold is led from the library to 212 Humboldt Street 'as surely as if he had received a calling card',[18] which establishes that the Jewish group is happy to work by deception, yet she accepts without question Chava's statement that the Andersen store is a front for a neo-Nazi organisation. As Richard Combs notes, the Nazi paraphernalia 'is very neatly laid out', a possible explanation being 'that the scene looks so stagy because [Gold] is being set up'.[19] Alain Piette remarks that they are 'probably not Jewish activists at all', but does not explore the implications other than to remark that the typically unsentimental conclusion saves the film from becoming sheer melodrama.[20] Omer suggests that the police force and the Jewish group both 'seem to be part of a master con-game, a world of "rigged" appearances or perhaps an eternal enigma'.[21] In light of all this, Hoberman's assumption that the film proposes the necessity of a Jewish 'counter-conspiracy' looks dubious in the extreme.

Two critics in particular, however, have taken a close look at the conspiracy and how it functions within the film. William Van Wert is almost as confused and error-prone on *Homicide* as he is in his earlier interpretation of *House of Games*, yet the overall shape of his argument in 'Conspiracy Theory in Mamet' is compelling. He notes that the coincidences are too extensive and convenient to be credible, and under scrutiny the narrative simply falls to pieces. It is therefore a mistake to look for realistic explanations; instead, as he astutely observes, 'conspiracy operates as a phantasmagorical space, and events spiral the way they might in dreams', to the point where 'conspiracy is the only connection between events'.[22] This is intimately bound up with the narrative method of the film, whereby 'each new event [is] a deflection that makes us forgetful of what came before' and 'obscures the usual cause–effect relationship, makes events more autonomous vis-à-vis other events and allows for a freer play with temporality and point of view'.[23] All of this is quite excellent, but elsewhere Van Wert, while attributing to the protagonist a profound yet inexplicable lucidity, finds mysteries where there are none. For example, he cannot explain Gold's final banishment from the homicide department, even though Gold has failed to solve the murder case while acting with such irresponsible disloyalty that Sullivan gets killed.

Like Van Wert, Newton argues that the film is full of floating signifiers. These include Gold's lost and unfired gun, but are mostly textual: the 'Grofaz' paper, the address of 212, the list of Jewish gun-runners, and the racist flyer associated with Andersen. These contribute to a 'wildly overdetermined nexus of overlapping conspiracies which may or may not be real', and in which many of the events seem highly improbable.[24] Via a process analogous but not identical to Van Wert's 'deflections', but which leads to a much more disparaging analysis, Newton thinks that nothing is revealed and everything is open-ended, because '*everything* in the film appears gratuitous, a constant sliding from one thing to another'.[25] Most damagingly, the black characters are portrayed crudely and there is no logical connection between the Jewish Gold and the black Randolph. Newton concludes that '[e]ither *Homicide* is postmodern reflexivity made so superfine as to be ultimately tendentious, or it is just out of control'.[26]

Literary and linguistic analyses

Drawing on Zinman's essay, which argues that in *American Buffalo* 'the absence of meaning *is* the meaning',[27] Omer finds that *Homicide* is every bit as replete with rhetorical questions as the earlier play. This, the presence of multiple and (to Gold) secret languages, and the fact that the plot hinges on the single word 'Grofaz(t)', implies that language is simultaneously 'all we really have' and yet is 'as undependable as anything else'. Consequently, just as Zinman compares Mamet to Beckett and Hemingway, so Omer places him alongside Walter Benjamin (1892–1940) and Franz Kafka (1881–1924) as 'a radical skeptic of both language and absolutist identities'. Omer draws extensively on Kane's discussion of *Marranos* (see Chapter 4), but doubts her 'optimistic reading of Mamet's ethnicity' whereby 'the past is recovered and one's identity reclaimed'; instead, whatever Mamet's intentions, there is a 'universality [to] Bobby Gold's existential crisis, which may ultimately be non-denominational', and consequently the only substantial Jewish identity remains that of 'victimhood'.[28]

Whether or not one agrees with this conclusion, Omer's qualifications may be applied equally to Kane's later reading of *Homicide*, which combines a typically scholarly analysis of the linguistic and numerological signs in the screenplay with a rather literal interpretation of the action. Kane argues that the theme of betrayal must be placed within specifically Jewish contexts of diaspora, homelessness and belonging. Like Van Wert, she observes the detective story's reference to the Oëdipal myth when Gold becomes the object of his own investigation, and this is combined with another kind of quest narrative, namely 'Kabbalah, Jewish mysticism'.[29] Yet the uncertain motivations and membership of the Jewish organisation make this film hazardous territory for the confident binding of textual allusion to ethical imperatives at which Kane so excels, and her typically optimistic assertion that in the closing shot Gold is 'just beginning his search for clues to his Jewish identity' is curious in light of all that has gone before.[30]

Cinematic analyses

Laurence Roth argues that Omer and Newton (and one might add Kane) approach the film from a literary rather than a cinematic standpoint that places too much emphasis on language. For Roth, this misrepresents how the audience understands the film, and his own discussion examines cinema-specific qualities such as editing and point of view. In a careful analysis of the opening sequence, in which the FBI mount their failed assault on Randolph's apartment, Roth argues that the shifting points of view finally force spectators to choose, but only one way: we identify with the authorities, and spectatorship becomes a form of collaboration. Gold, like the other authority figures, initially wears a suit and tie, but as he investigates the candy store killing his uniform starts to fall apart. This is the first sign of conflicted loyalties that will seemingly be decisively resolved at the Kleins' apartment when the camera, as much as Mrs Klein's granddaughter, forces him to confront the shame of his internalised anti-Semitism. On pursuing the case from this new, Jewish perspective, however, Gold finds not 'authenticity' but 'an anti-detective story', which Roth appropriately compares to the short story 'Death and the Compass' (1942) by Jorge Luis Borges (1899–1986). The resemblances lie not simply in the plot; instead, 'like other anti-detective stories, *Homicide* is responding to the chaos of the contemporary world, a chaos that . . . is both metaphysical and quite physical'.[31] This leads to an intriguing reading of the final recognition scene between Wells and Gold: the detective has previously ignored the killer, but now sees that his metaphysical and ideological preoccupations have made him indifferent to the terrible reality of murder. This is the payoff for getting the audience to share Gold's point of view: as Wells is led to the cells we recognise that 'how one views a murder locks one into a perspective that is like a cage or like manacles'.[32]

Bruce Barton, who is equally concerned to analyse Mamet's films from a cinematic point of view, advances two significant arguments about *Homicide*. First, he distinguishes its narrative and *mise-en-scène* from those of *House of Games*. In the earlier film every action appears preplanned, to the point where 'it becomes increasingly difficult and ultimately impossible to identify a verifiably consequential action', whereas in *Homicide* 'all actions are seen as wildly consequential' (Barton's emphasis).[33] The second argument is an important point concerning perception and framing: 'Gold is doomed to making decisions based upon what is revealed within the frame of what is made visible to him. Yet what quickly becomes clear is that anything approaching actual, comprehensive meaning inevitably lies beyond that circumscribed vision'.[34] This gives a very good cinematic explanation of why the effects of the conspiracy theory are felt very tangibly while the nature and extent of that conspiracy remain a mystery. The discussion is rather let down, however, by too narrow a focus. Wells is not mentioned at all, for example, so the chapter consequently represents very well the strengths and weaknesses of Barton's book, in which a sustained attention to important technical and affective properties of theatre and cinema goes hand in hand with a damagingly selective approach to the material.

Homicide was a contentious film, but compared to what was to follow it treats its incendiary material with kid gloves. If there is any truth in the suggestion that in this film Mamet was 'laying claim ... to the Jewish cultural heritage',[35] the controversy was magnified because, as Piette observes, it was soon to be followed by *Oleanna*, possibly the most notorious and socially divisive play in the history of American drama.

CHAPTER FOURTEEN

Oleanna (1992)

Oleanna is undoubtedly the most widely discussed American play of the 1990s, with only *Angels in America* (1990–3), by Tony Kushner (born 1956), attracting a remotely similar degree of attention. There the comparisons end; critics have occasionally been led to propose that there must be something wrong with Kushner's play because everybody seemed to like it, but *Oleanna* was socially and critically divisive from the outset. The explosive drama about a female student who visits the office of her male professor for advice in Act 1, accuses him of making sexual advances in Act 2, and is physically assaulted by him at the end of the play, provoked correspondingly ferocious responses from its audiences and critics.

Richard Badenhausen remarks that *Oleanna* was 'held almost hostage by the cultural circumstances surrounding the play's debut in 1992'.[1] If so, many have seen it as a willing hostage, provocatively testing ideological fault lines in America that were every bit as divisive as the problem of race relations Mamet had recently invoked in *Homicide*. A strengthening neo-conservative movement on the political right had deployed the term 'political correctness' to identify what it cast as left-wing, multi-culturalist attempts to inhibit free speech, particularly on university campuses. Meanwhile, in the autumn of 1991, some six months before the premiere of *Oleanna*, the Senate hearings on the proposed appointment of the black judge Clarence Thomas (born 1948) to the Supreme Court had become blanketed in an ideological fog in which both issues of sexual harassment and racism seemed to be involved. Thomas stood accused by lawyer Anita Hill (born 1956) of a history of harassment; he denied the charge, and transformed the issue into one of alleged racism against him (although Hill was also black). A common allegation was that, like Carol in Mamet's play, she was being directed by a shadowy special-interest group.

Almost all serious discussion of *Oleanna* revolves, to a greater or lesser extent, around a problem that everyone notices: Carol undergoes a sudden, unexplained, and realistically incredible shift from stumbling inarticulacy in the first act to confident assertion in the second. This is widely seen as evidence that Mamet weights the dice against the woman, whose sudden transformation could make her appear devious or unhinged. Mamet has always claimed that the drama is even-handed, but in practice most people have sided with John, seeming to feel that his climactic explosion of violence against a defenceless woman is somehow justified. Accordingly many have argued that the play is misogynistic, with Carla J. McDonough charitably noting 'the difficulty of speaking fairly from two sides of an argument in which the speaker himself is already immersed'.[2]

A 'postmodern' play?

A more favourable view holds that it is a mistake to look for realism, conventional dramatic form or rounded characters in *Oleanna*; instead, the real focus is on the ways that institutional conventions construct language and power relations that are open to abuse by either party. The play is full of 'gaps', so that 'much dispute hovers over not only the meaning of the episodes in *Oleanna* but about literally what events actually take place'.[3] This method has certainly provoked much confusion: for example, Katherine H. Burkman thinks that *Oleanna* 'leaves some essentials untold', yet also 'plays upon our prejudices without leaving anything essential out'.[4] Similarly, Harry J. Elam, Jr's contention that the play 'creates a situation in which misogynistic treatment of women can be condoned and even justified in the name of academic freedom and integrity' follows and, arguably, flatly contradicts his observation in the same paragraph that in calling Carol a 'bitch' John is probably contravening '[l]aws protecting against hate speech'.[5] Unlike Elam, those who defend *Oleanna* invariably recognise that it presents a distinctly critical view of John, which may or may not be accompanied by the argument that Carol is a more sympathetic figure than has generally been acknowledged.

Sandra Tomc's discussion of 'truth' in *Oleanna* unwittingly provides a strong case for doubting its realism. Tomc regards the play as almost defiantly 'nonpostmodernist',[6] and takes its subject to be sexual harassment, which almost by definition cannot be empirically observed. She demonstrates this by surveying contemporary performance art, novels about virtual reality and cyberspace, and media and critical responses to the Clarence Thomas hearings. *Oleanna* stands out as different in this context because, in staging the encounter between John and Carol, Mamet leaves 'no room for ambiguity...the possibility of stable "truths" can be taken for granted'.[7] Tomc cites in support not only the events of the play but also Mamet's oft-repeated claim that the theatre is a forum in which the playwright and the society commit to the celebration of truth. Therefore, although Tomc thinks that *Oleanna* 'shocks with its political simplicity' and displays an 'inattention to the possibility of nuanced or multiple readings', 'its belligerent claims to truth-telling, its propagandistic plot, [and] its stalwart refusal of an erotics or politics of indeterminacy' at least makes it possible for a play that, in these terms, is highly orthodox and reactionary, paradoxically to take up the controversialist stance that seems to be lost to performance art.[8] This final point is moot, but the rest is nonsense: the endless critical controversy surrounding what actually happens in *Oleanna* refutes Tomc's assertions, and when Mamet talks about 'truth' in the comments she cites he is arguing on an abstract moral plane, not proposing theatre as a substitute for the polygraph test.

Similarly, Carol's sudden transformation is symptomatic of Mamet's general refusal, in Thomas E. Porter's terms, to provide anything as unified as 'character' or 'identity' in either her or John.[9] Accordingly, Badenhausen regards the play as 'Brechtian', while both Porter and David Sauer consider it 'postmodern'. Much as the literary theorist Stanley Fish (born 1938) proposes that differing interpretations of texts are the product of the different 'interpretive communities' to which critics belong, for Sauer '*Oleanna* is not about John and Carol, the characters, so much as it is about how we read John and Carol'.[10] The play is an illustration of 'postmodern realism': it is indeterminate, offering no real clues to spectator or actor as to how to interpret Carol's behaviour. It thereby denies the deep character, the truth wrapped in an enigma, of both Method acting and modernism. Sauer tellingly cites the pivotal moment when Carol is on the verge of telling John a secret, only to be interrupted when he takes a telephone call. The secret is never mentioned again, and as Sauer astutely observes, 'there is no evidence that Mamet had anything more in mind to explain Carol's secret. Actor, Audience, and Author are all left with only the text, and no subtext, to interpret'.[11] In this respect the violent debate surrounding *Oleanna* is a reflection of John and Carol's mutual incomprehension. Sauer's case is convincing, although Mamet's play lacks the self-reflexivity that one might expect of a truly postmodern work, and the 'gaps' may be knowingly strategic on its author's part, deliberately prompting the questions other critics attempt to answer.

Subtexts

Thomas H. Goggans, for example, does try to explain Carol's behaviour, by tracing a subtext that reveals her to be not a villain but a victim of childhood sexual abuse. This, he suggests, is the secret she was about to reveal to John, and is in her mind when she tells him that students have made sacrifices and overcome sexual prejudices and other humiliations. John's insinuations in the first act that he and Carol can break the rules so long as they don't tell anyone can indeed sound like a 'molester's rap', and her insecurities may have been heightened by recollections of past situations in which 'she obeys the demands of a male authority figure and yet cannot "satisfy" him'.[12] In this way Goggans fills in the deep character and backstory that Mamet characteristically leaves implicit, if not completely blank. This interpretation cannot be proved one way or the other, of course, but it is very coherent, and has the particular advantage of explaining Carol's sudden change in the second act: she has learned the 'pugnacious style which goes hand in hand with the rhetoric of abuse', and finds support and meaning in 'the ideological rigidity of the Group'.[13]

For Leslie Kane it is John, and not Carol, who possesses sub-textual depth. Kane believes the pedagogic context is less American higher education than Jewish ethical precepts concerning 'education of character',[14] and she offers some typically resourceful interpretations to support this view. John says he is a pedant 'by birth'; Mamet has elsewhere ascribed his self-proclaimed pedantry to the history of Talmudic scholarship. When John tells Carol he is trying to 'save' her the word strikes most commentators as patronising and self-serving, but Kane suggests that he is speaking from a Jewish 'ethical responsibility' to save her from 'humiliation'.[15] Some of the localised readings are at the outer limits of ingenuity, requiring almost literally a leap of faith (Kane sees in John's statistics on college entrance figures a covert – and, for anyone else, undetectable – reference to a split between Orthodox and Reform Jews in the United States), and much of the evidence for his ethnicity is 'inferred' and 'implicit'.[16]

Unlike Kane's similar approach to other works, here the often subtle and inspired readings are in the service of a truly incendiary argument. She proposes that in challenging John's behaviour, Carol is raising the 'character issue' in ways that have historically been used to discriminate against Jews as 'perverted and perverting', 'deceiv[ing], corrupt[ing], and lust[ing] after women', to the point that 'Jewishness itself stands accused'.[17] The chapter is unique and quite brilliant; it is also the point in Kane's book where the evidence is thinnest where it needs to be most convincing, and this reading, which in many ways polarises the characters beyond anything in the most vituperative feminist critiques, pushes the play into the realms of melodrama.

Political correctness and higher education

Critics who examine the play in relation to the contemporary crisis in American higher education often mention the then-recent appearance of several books detailing the neo-conservative critique of 'political correctness', such as *The Closing of the American Mind* (1987) by Allan Bloom

(1930–92) and *Tenured Radicals: How Politics Has Corrupted Our Higher Education* (1990) by Roger Kimball (born 1953). The failure to note that the 'political correctness movement' itself is something of a construct of the political right is a serious weakness of Roger Bechtel's essay, which otherwise provides a usefully solid defence of the play. Bechtel insists that John and Carol are not realistically credible characters but instead products of institutional language that defines and limits John as much as Carol: his is wilfully obscure, hers is rigid and totalitarian, but language always has power, always performs actions, and always has effects. As we have seen, in *American Buffalo* Donny's attempted distinction between talk and action proves false; Bechtel argues that the same applies to *Oleanna*. Taking Carol to be representative of the 'political correctness movement', Bechtel suggests that while she may feel injured by the language of others, she too causes injury not only to John's public language but to his private speech when she instructs him not to call his wife 'baby', and it is John's resulting feeling of complete impotence that occasions his violence. Bechtel concludes that 'whenever one tries to control the language of another' there are 'disastrous consequences'.[18]

Marc Silverstein is much more disparaging, and argues that the audience applause greeting the assault on Carol expresses the ideological concerns of a middle class that feels its economic position and cultural institutions to be under threat. He therefore aligns *Oleanna* with the politics of the New Right, which was gaining ascendancy at this time partly by shifting the analysis of the late-capitalist 'legitimation crisis' (in Jürgen Habermas's phrase) from economics and politics to culture. The neo-conservatives saw the university as a site for disseminating ideas of a common culture (a phrase which obscures a very specific cultural agenda), demonising as 'politically correct' those who affirmed a multiculturalism that regards positively differences of class, race and gender. While acknowledging that Mamet's earlier plays hardly place him within the ranks of the New Right, Silverstein proposes that *Oleanna* stages just such a 'cultural imaginary'. In particular, it depoliticises the serious ideological underpinnings of feminist thought by reducing them to the question of power. For example, Carol's 'group' wants to ban John's book, in a kind of parody of the feminist attempt to modify the predominantly male canon of authors studied on university syllabi, and criticising him for calling his wife 'baby' is the last straw because it implicitly attacks the sanctity of the family. Conversely, Silverstein provocatively aligns John's second-act manoeuvre, in which he tries to get Carol to agree that they share a 'common humanity', with the common culture of the New Right.

Silverstein is undoubtedly right that interpretations of the play were influenced by this context. Burkman likewise proposes that 'Mamet's appeal in his drama is to just such a common culture',[19] and Porter also believes the play engages with 'postmodern difference and divisiveness in contemporary American culture' by probing away at the fault line between the liberal proponents of cultural difference and the conservative defence of foundational principles, although Porter does not refer to Silverstein's essay and regards the play more favourably.[20] However, as we saw in the chapter on *Homicide*, at this precise moment Mamet was predominantly engaged in addressing specifically Jewish rather than 'common' cultural concerns, so he was hardly likely to be perceived at this time as either a woolly or an uncompromisingly right-wing proponent of common values in any simple sense. Moreover, Silverstein remarks that for Mamet 'education is a good in itself';[21] this is the precise opposite of the case, both in Mamet's public pronouncements and, it would seem, in *Oleanna*. Silverstein's arguments are fascinating, but ultimately they collapse liberal humanism and neo-conservatism into one – exactly the kind of 'demonization and terroristic exclusion of those who identify themselves in terms of difference' for which he castigates Mamet.[22]

Sexual harassment and misogyny

Several years after the controversy surrounding the early productions of *Oleanna* had died down, Stanton B. Garner and Richard C. Raymond separately conducted empirical experiments with their students which confirmed, for these focus groups at least, that sexual harassment, rather than either pedagogy or political correctness, was the dominant concern, although they noted that the issues are related.[23] Male and female respondents alike were almost unanimous in considering John the more sympathetic character, and in regarding Carol with sometimes unrestrained hatred. Garner's students also routinely commented on Carol's physical appearance and clothing, and not at all on John's: in adopting a kind of physical uniform that corresponded to an ideological uniformity imposed by her 'group', she appeared to be lacking in human feeling.

This effect was most pronounced in the Mamet-directed premiere in May 1992 in Cambridge, Massachusetts, when Carol was transformed from sexless frump in the first act to a figure wearing a quasi-Maoist outfit in the third. Later productions have generally sought to lessen the impact of the costume changes, and during the New York rehearsals Mamet removed a passage after the fight in which Carol insists that John read out her list of charges against him; consequently, the published text ends with the fight followed by Carol's enigmatic words 'yes. That's right'.[24] Most have considered that the Cambridge ending, in which John is humiliated, further weights the audience's sympathies in his favour, although Harold Pinter reverted to this ending, against Mamet's wishes, when he directed the British premiere in 1993. Ira Nadel convincingly argues that this well-received production at least partly achieved Pinter's aim of showing that Carol has a calm, revolutionary authority that seeks to challenge a male system.[25]

Burkman considers that the tarnishing of Anita Hill's name during the Clarence Thomas hearings finds 'a frightening parallel' in *Oleanna*, which presents a similarly 'flat, stereotypical portrait of a woman out to destroy a man', backed by powerful left-wing interests.[26] It is crucial to note here that Burkman does not regard Carol (unlike Hill) as an innocent; on the contrary, 'she is rather playing a socially constructed role of the innocent', for example by 'almost demanding' that John act in a 'personal' way towards her and then querying his motives when he does.[27] The insidious undermining of Carol is symptomatic of this 'misogynist and misanthropic play', which deliberately, it would seem, loses the focus on sexual harassment by attacking political correctness, which in turn 'becomes the means to a more general attack on feminism', apparently the play's real target.[28] Elsewhere Burkman has stated in still more unequivocal terms, and also apropos of *Oleanna*, that 'Mamet gets caught in his male characters' web of misogyny because he identifies with their hate of women and of themselves'.[29]

Carla J. McDonough similarly considers that the play manoeuvres the audience into recognising 'that the sexual harassment charges are bogus and that political correctness is to blame',[30] not least because the version of feminism that Mamet has Carol espouse is unpalatable. John's assault on Carol thereby becomes explicable and defensible, unlike her destruction of John, and so the play, which gives 'a simplistic reading of gender misunderstandings',[31] confirms the fear of women and femininity that McDonough detects throughout Mamet's work.

More recently, Kellie Bean has dismissed the 'backlash' against the early consensus that the piece is concerned with 'sexual harassment' and 'gender politics',[32] although she cites only Christine MacLeod's article (below) and does not do justice to its arguments. Bean derives from Silverstein the twin views that *Oleanna* is itself a 'backlash story' against 'political correctness' in American universities, and that John's humanism conceals what is actually a defence of his own privileged status.[33] She enumerates the familiar charges that John is hypocritical, patriarchal and violent, while noting that the play constructs Carol as villain, even though, in an obvious contradiction, Bean suddenly and hyperbolically presents her as victim: 'Carol dares to challenge her professor's authority', and thereby 'leads herself to the slaughter'.[34] The play takes a simplistically binary view of gender, adopts the conservative form of realism, and Carol's final words – 'yes. That's right' – signify the author's approval of what has happened to her; in short, 'David Mamet disguises a vicious misogynist fantasy in a weak argument against political correctness'.[35]

Pedagogy, language and power

A serious problem with studies such as Bean's that regard the play as an attack on feminism and/or political correctness is that they tend to see the characters in melodramatic terms. This has been the case from the very beginning: in a highly influential review of the 1992 New York production that followed the Cambridge premiere, the eminent professor Elaine Showalter charged that Mamet makes 'his female protagonist a dishonest, androgynous zealot, and his male protagonist a devoted husband and father who defends freedom of thought'.[36]

Yet John has very obvious failings, which are emphasised by those later and more supportive commentators who regard this as a 'play of pedagogy'.[37] Some such reorientation is called for in light of the fact that, according to Badenhausen, not one of the early reviews even mentioned teaching.[38] Verna Foster puts it simply: unlike Mamet's earlier studies of the teacher–pupil relationship, *Oleanna*, while not a realistic play, presents 'a *literal* teacher and a *literal* student'; therefore, it is not 'a metaphor' but instead is '*about* education' (Foster's emphasis). Within this context it is not, however, simply about who is right or wrong. As Foster incisively comments, 'the primary issue in *Oleanna* is not evidentiary – whom to believe'; instead, the play is about power.[39]

In realistic terms John is clearly a bad tutor, teaching 'not knowledge . . . not values . . . not clarity of expression . . . [but] obfuscation, intimidation, and misreading'.[40] Mamet takes a dim view of schools, universities, critics and academics generally, so there is no need to look for a precise referent, although Badenhausen, who thinks John is not wholly unrecognisable as a contemporary academic, may have in mind elements of the critical theory prominent in humanities departments since 1968. Michael Mangan compares John's ideas to the radical educational theories of the 1960s and 1970s, citing as examples *Deschooling Society* (1973) by Ivan Illich (1926–2002), and *How Children Fail* (1969) by John Holt (1923–85).[41] As Porter notes, much of the play's irony derives from John's inability to see himself as others do, but equally remarkable is that Showalter, Elam and others apparently do not recognise that both Mamet and his audiences may see through him and draw the appropriate conclusions. Badenhausen even suggests that Showalter's failure to perceive a sympathetic side to Carol constitutes a misreading that unwittingly mimics John's, while conversely 'Carol is a careful reader who gets better at that vocation as the play progresses'.[42]

For Jean Jacques Weber, the problem in *Oleanna* arises largely because John and Carol have radically different 'schemata', or pre-existing assumptions, concerning education.[43] Carol has legitimate expectations that John will help her, and so follows a 'power of' model: she assumes that the lecturer can impart his superior knowledge, and that the student will understand so long as she follows his instructions. John, however, ostensibly follows a 'power to' model, which asks the students to think for themselves. In practice, of course, he does not do this, and his professed schema is unwittingly confrontational because it challenges some of Carol's preconceptions about his powers as a teacher. After Act 1 Carol adopts a third, 'power over' model: the institution exerts power over the students, and she does not challenge this model but instead embraces it by appropriating power for herself. Within this model, free speech is inevitably destroyed.

Steven Ryan arrives at similar conclusions by a different route.[44] He takes a rigorously logical approach by dissecting the drama according to Mamet's stated principles of writing, most importantly the subordination of all other elements to the Stanislavskian 'through-line', which according to Ryan here concerns the power relations between the characters. He detects two principal reasons why the through-line is obscured, leading to the confusion and violent responses of audiences. First, in Act 1 the characters make little explicit reference to their power relationship, so that its subsequent emergence in Carol's turning of the tables in Act 2 comes as a shock and occasions accusations of inconsistent characterisation. Some commentators have sought to explain this by suggesting that her behaviour in the first act is just a performance, and that from the very beginning she and her group have plotted John's demise. Ryan counters that, while many of her charges against academia are valid, her third-act accusations of rape are incoherent, suggesting that she has only recently become acquainted with the 'group' and has not fully understood its ideology. Instead, like Weber, Ryan argues that her violent rejection of John is occasioned by her need for certainty; John, however, is eminently fallible, and when reading his book fails to enlighten her, she transfers her feelings of guilt and inadequacy to him. Secondly, the play's 'secondary themes' are so strong that the ending became a problem for the playwright, and in Ryan's view Mamet's preferred ending repeatedly shifts the audience's sympathies between the characters.

Many other critics agree that the confrontation between John and Carol is never resolved; instead, each turns catastrophically for support to something resembling Weber's 'power over' model. Foster unusually thinks that Carol recognises from the outset the sexual implications of the power relationship, which she proceeds to exploit after failing in her initial desire simply to be told what to do to succeed. In fact, 'there is no way in which either teacher or student can shake off their assigned roles',[45] and attempts to do so, as when John behaves in a more 'personal' way, lead to disaster. Foster compares Mamet's play to *The Lesson* (1951), by Eugène Ionesco (1909–94), as does Craig Stewart Walker, who thinks each play is rooted in arguments propounded by the philosopher Friedrich Nietzsche (1844–1900) against reason, order and transcendent human morality: '[t]here is only the will to power imposed upon chaos', and Mamet's university is a systemic, 'material domination of the students'.[46] Accordingly Walker reads Carol's sudden transformation not realistically but as a projection of this central idea that meaning inheres not in shared values but in the imposition of power. Walker's argument is a little underdeveloped, but captures the sense of impotent desperation that grips each of the characters.

Christine MacLeod gives the best, most carefully nuanced, and most influential reading of the power relationship in the pedagogical context. Like Badenhausen, she points out that those who attack the play as misogynistic, and those who defend it as an exposé of a totalitarian strain of political correctness, are united in perceiving Carol as a villain. For MacLeod, as for many critics writing after the initial storm of controversy had subsided, 'the gender difference...is not the crux of the matter'.[47] (For Bean, of course, it is, and she takes issue with MacLeod's reorientation on precisely these grounds.) Focusing on the allegations of sexual harassment obscures the real nature of the dynamic, which revolves around questions of institutional status in a play concerned with the mechanisms of 'power, hierarchy and the control of language',[48] the manipulation of which Carol learns from John. For example, her 'group' mirrors the Tenure Committee; John's arbitrary decision to 'say' that Carol has an 'A' grade is mirrored in her decision to 'say' that his behaviour was sexually oriented; and in the first act John appears to believe that his speech brings facts into being, which is precisely what Carol does when she later accuses him of rape. Carol, then, uses gender as a tactical weapon; 'her abuse of power' is 'demonstrably *un*fair' (MacLeod's emphasis), mirroring 'the power that men have traditionally held over women' but whose 'operations and assumptions only become truly visible when seen in an unfamiliar light'.[49] Again, however, MacLeod does not wish to reduce the play to a drama about 'sexual politics'; instead, it is 'part of the writer's overall critique of a capitalist system based on competitive individualism',[50] metaphorically raises the spectre of any kind of postcolonialist revolt in which the oppressed succeed by appropriating the weapons of the oppressor, and – in a perhaps over-optimistic conclusion – 'looks to the freedom of an alternative social formation, beyond the enslaving categories and patterns of competitive binarism'.[51]

For Kenneth Womack, *Oleanna* is a 'fairly unsubtle' satire on the institution of higher education, as well as the 'political correctness' and 'rampant intellectualism' that prohibit empathetic relationships and a nuanced approach to contentious issues.[52] Womack suggests that the play addresses the broader ethical questions surrounding education: is the educator's role to disseminate information or to teach students how to learn for themselves? Are students there to acquire knowledge or simply to perform their allotted role within the educational hierarchy? Like Kane, Womack invokes the philosopher Emmanuel Levinas (1906– 95) and his concept of 'alterity' – the ethical obligations incurred in recognising not just our empathetic relation to others but their 'face', the irreducible difference of their consciousness. Womack suggests that John and Carol both recognise these moral imperatives to some extent, but partly due to the nature of the educational institution and its relation-ships, they are finally too self-absorbed to act in accordance with them.

The film adaptation

Surprisingly, Womack's analysis is drawn substantially from Mamet's film of 1994, but does not explore in detail the difference between the cinema and stage versions. Indeed, there has been hardly any substan-tial criticism of the movie, which disappeared almost unseen on first release, although it has since been made available on DVD. The princi-pal changes concern several short scenes, largely without dialogue, that open out the action, especially between acts. Before the second act John is shown alone in the new house after a party; he then smartens up in a public washroom before the second meeting with Carol in his office. Before Act 3 a dishevelled John is shown in his hotel room working on the complaint, and Carol photocopies the apology for him to sign and arranges for a poster to be made commenting on staff – student relations; we then see the poster pinned up in the college. In these and other ways the film moves towards providing the 'stable truths' that Tomc problem-atically detects in the stage version, and the movie suffers further from losing the claustrophobic tension experienced in theatrical performance. The most substantial and useful commentary on the film and its rela-tion to the play is probably that conducted by Daniel Rosenthal in the student edition of the text.[53]

In the aftermath of *Oleanna*, few Mamet works were immune from accu-sations of misogyny. The writer himself seemed more interested in the concerns suggested by the 'Bobby Gould' pieces, and his next play, *The Cryptogram*, would apparently take the autobiographical strain a good deal further. That even this play, however, revised from a draft com-pleted many years before, would again prompt the occasional furious denunciation is a good indication of the extent to which the reception of Mamet's work was becoming framed by his controversial intervention in the ongoing gender wars of the 1990s.

CHAPTER FIFTEEN

The Cryptogram (1994)

Leslie Kane records that Mamet had been working since the late 1970s on a play called *Donny March*, which would become *The Cryptogram*. Like *The Old Neighborhood*, it details an unhappy family not unlike that of the playwright's childhood. Set in 1959, the ten-year-old John, plagued by sleeplessness, is about two years younger than Mamet would have been in that year, and Kane sees similarities between John's mother, Donny, and Mamet's own mother, Lenore. The father, Robert, is absent, and we discover at the end of the first act that he is leaving Donny; Mamet has occasionally discussed the traumatic effect of his parents' divorce. The third character, a homosexual man called Del, knew about Robert's infidelity without telling Donny; thus the play details multiple betrayals, among which, in most readings of the play, is Donny's failure to provide emotional security for her troubled son.

Autobiography and ethnicity

Throughout *Weasels and Wisemen*, Leslie Kane associates certain recurrent images, including the photographs and knives which, together with a blanket, figure prominently in *The Cryptogram*, with a specifically Judaic approach to remembering. As ever, this argument is open to objection at the level of specifics. Kane insists that Donny is Jewish despite conceding that the play contains no particular suggestion of this; indeed, she points out that Donny is if anything the opposite of the most common Jewish mother stereotypes. More convincing is her description of Donny as 'distracted and well-intentioned, protective and disloyal, comforting and crushed by pain, rendering her [Mamet's] most complex woman [character], a mother betrayed into betraying her own son'.[1] When considered alongside Jolly in *The Old Neighborhood*, and the mothers and grandmothers of the film *Homicide* and the short story *Passover*, Donny gives Kane ample evidence that in the 1990s Mamet demonstrated his 'mastery' in the creation of such female characters.[2]

Kane also says Del is Jewish, but again there is little evidence for this, so it is hard to agree that 'Mamet's configuring of the Jewish male as homosexual offers a plethora of interpretations consistent with the alterity and secrecy intrinsic in this play'.[3] As usual, however, Kane's interpretative frame prompts some fascinating suggestions. For example, the play explores figures marginalised within a patriarchal culture – children, women, homosexuals and (accepting the autobiographical context if not necessarily Kane's arguments) Jewish Americans – who bring broader cultural associations to the play's interest in other, more obvious secrets surrounding infidelity, betrayal and the relations of parents to their children. Kane convincingly argues that the frequent recourse to alternative languages to avoid revealing something to the children in many Jewish homes generally, and in Mamet's childhood home specifically, gives further resonance to the idea that this is a house of secrets, although 'things [still] get through'.[4] John's sleeplessness she illuminatingly relates, via Emmanuel Levinas, to the idea that ethical responsibility demands constant wakefulness, while her extensive scholarship enables her to make a productive comparison to Mamet's unpublished *Marranos*, showing how and why *The Cryptogram* is the better play.

She carefully reconstructs much of what can be known about the characters' past history, and traces some of the workings of the play's several 'embedded narratives' concerning the blanket, the photograph, and, in particular, the story about the Three Misfortunes that so troubles John. As Kane notes, this is 'a variant of the classic fairy tale of the three caskets, the third typically releasing disaster'.[5] Fairy tales commonly commence with the real or apparent death of a parent; hence John's anxiety about the story suggests that he at least subliminally understands from the beginning that his father will not return. Many reviewers assume that as the play ends John, standing on the stairs holding a knife, is about to commit suicide; Kane, however, startlingly yet quite convincingly connects it to the Old Testament story (Genesis 28: 11–19) of Jacob's dream of a ladder to heaven. With characteristic optimism, she finds in these final moments 'a mystical, metaphysical interpretation'[6] quite at odds with the readings of many other critics. Later, Kane would propose more straightforwardly that, '[v]irtually and metaphorically empowered to survive, he not only listens to himself, but to a Higher Voice that does not lure him to his death'.[7]

The Cryptogram and American domestic realism

It has been widely observed that, at least prior to this play and *The Old Neighborhood*, Mamet conspicuously avoided writing in the dominant form of American drama, usually described as middle-class domestic realism. Both Janet V. Haedicke and Martin Schaub contend that in *The*

Cryptogram Mamet engages with this mode – for example in the apparently autobiographical references and the disharmonious family – only to subvert it. For Schaub this is apparent even in the set: the living room is a place of 'utter dislocation', the family members having either left or begun preparations to do so.[8] John's fractured and bewildering speech in the second act shows that, for him, 'things that are customarily held to carry meanings – books, buildings, the globe, history, thought – are collapsing'. Schaub contends, however, that John finds a substitute reality in the sounds and meanings of words, and rightly questions Del's claim that words have only the meanings their speaker assigns to them. Part of the purpose of the play is to establish meanings, however problematic, so one can see why Schaub suggests that *The Cryptogram* develops '(post)postmodern lines of thought', although the discussion of postmodernism itself is both unnecessary and rather brusque, while the suggestion that John achieves a sense of communion in his 'magic world' looks like mystification.[9]

For Janet V. Haedicke, *The Cryptogram* is subversive because the playwright who had consistently conflated the economic, theatrical and familial realms, in *American Buffalo* for example, now 'exposes the mythologized, politically capitalized Family as a system providing a prototype for the economic system'.[10] The triangle of a mother, a child and a gay man parodies both the American nuclear family and the Oedipal triangle, while the dramatic structure undermines domestic realism because the protagonist is divided into three, the linear search for truth is subverted, no goal is finally attained, and the mother figure exposes the illusory nature of the quest. Each of the onstage figures struggles to assert a self-identity in relation to the absent father; moreover, each tries to fix an identity for the others, most obviously in Donny's reduction of Del to a 'fairy' or a 'faggot'. In an argument that here resembles Kane's, Haedicke traces these struggles for definition in the cryptic language, the fixation on objects such as the blanket and the knife, and each character's habitual watchfulness, a tendency which, as Haedicke observes, Mamet has elsewhere attached to the Jew, and which she herself attaches to the homosexual and the woman, 'similarly scripted in a masculinist economy as sexual and social outsiders'.[11] Haedicke sees the dualism of conventionally prescribed roles breaking down in the final act, most notably in the figure of Donny: just as her name transgresses conventional boundaries of masculine and feminine, so she resists the mother/monster binarism that threatens to engulf her. Reviewers almost invariably empathise with John and assume that the final moments indicate his imminent suicide, but, again very like Kane, Haedicke notes that John is poised on the stair landing – that is, on a threshold – and that, while in the immediately preceding confrontation with him Donny has 'invalidated her object position within' the Oedipal narrative, she has also 'provid[ed] for her son instead the possibility of transformation through the telling of his own story'.[12]

Meaning and mystification

Howard Pearce also explores transitions and threshold states: John's constant movement between upstairs and downstairs, between sleeping and waking, between past and present, between fiction and reality, between mental states recuperable realistically and those that suggest a kind of transcendence, between ideas of life as a play or a dream. The comparison to Pinter's *Moonlight* (1993) is apt, but Pearce's relentlessly philosophical bent is heavy going, repetitive, and sometimes vapid and questionable at the same time, as when he remarks that 'Del's attempts to touch Donny as well as John express a need for community',[13] as if the play did not problematise the very notion of community or play off different kinds of community against one another.

Thomas P. Adler places his account of the play alongside a pithy and reliable summary of Mamet's brilliant but typically elusive *Three Uses of the Knife* (1998), a study of dramatic composition.[14] This book expands upon Mamet's oft-stated view that the purpose of drama is not to provide rational solutions to human problems, still less to soothe its fears through pandering to melodramatic constructions of good and evil, but instead to deliver an Aristotelian catharsis by rendering the apparently incomprehensible into a structure of meaning and resolution. *The Cryptogram* provides an excellent case study: first, because it is precisely the interplay of incomprehensibility and meaning that preoccupies most of its critics; and second, because the meaning of the knife and other signifiers is contested ground. Adler notes that knives figure prominently in a range of texts that immediately precede and follow *Three Uses of the Knife*, including *The Cryptogram*, in which it fails to conform to a single meaning. For Del, the knife initially signifies a homoerotic attraction to Robert, revealed also in his penchant for wearing Robert's clothes, befriending his wife, and offering him his bed for a tryst with a woman. Later, however, Del reads the knife as a bribe, and finally, when he discovers that it was merely shop-bought, it loses meaning altogether – a betrayal for which Del exacts a kind of impotent revenge in handing it to John. For John, by the end of the play, it is the last object left that is associated with his father, and while Adler concedes that Mamet leaves the ending open, he connects Del's actions in giving the knife to the boy with suicide and with the deaths of children in *Miss Julie* (1888), by August Strindberg (1849–1912); *Hedda Gabler* (1890), by Henrik Ibsen (1828–1906); and *'night, Mother* (1983), by Marsha Norman (born 1947).

Perhaps the most remarkable essay on *The Cryptogram* is that of Linda Dorff. This provides a kind of uncanny mirror of Mamet's play, for just as she detects beneath the mystifications of its language a truly abhorrent view of women and gay men, so the theoretical edifice of her essay is built on a startlingly crude view of how the play works. Dorff agrees that it *appears* to deconstruct male mythology through exposing the father as a serial traitor to his wife, son and friend. Moreover, she acknowledges that the torrent of 'misogynistic and homophobic invective' that often erupts from the mouth of Mamet's male characters in general, when faced with loss of power, exposes the character's weakness.[15] The usual argument is that at such moments 'Mamet's plays', to quote the title of one of the earliest pieces ever published on the playwright, 'shed [the] masculinity myth'.[16]

Whether or not this was ever the case, Dorff detects a definite shift in *Oleanna* and *The Cryptogram*, which are 'attempted defenses of the belief systems with which Mamet's men identify'. Just as the male character's invective is unleashed in an attempt to 'deny his own castration' (loss of authority), so 'Mamet shrouds his *allegiance to* and *belief in* male mythology in mysticism' (Dorff's emphasis), so that *The Cryptogram* merely '*masquerades* as a drama of Others' (my emphasis). In reality its cryptic language, and the mysterious significations of the objects associated with Robert, cover the father in a nostalgic, romantic shroud while maintaining his position as offstage, controlling patriarch, so that the play 'becomes a sort of hymn to the phallic (symbolic) order'.[17] In an analysis that presents itself as ultra-sophisticated while contradicting everything you thought you knew about distinguishing the character from the tale and the tale from the teller, Dorff thinks the authorial voice of the playwright sounds loud and clear. She concludes that the language of Donny's homophobic verbal assault on Del, like that of Del's self-loathing, 'does not seem to be spoken by the voices of a woman and a gay man, but rather by the voice of a heterosexual male ... speaking from behind Mamet's wizard-curtain, manifest[ing] a basic belief in male mythology that reinscribes the woman as "cunt" and gay man as "fairy"'.[18] Once one strips away Dorff's own wizard-curtain of Jean Baudrillard, Jacques Lacan, Jill Dolan, Kaja Silverman and convoluted reasoning, it is hard not to conclude that she is stating, quite simply, that David Mamet thinks all women are cunts.

Such views had, by the mid-1990s, become surprisingly commonplace. Moreover, Mamet's work in this decade had been marked by a serious exploration of Judaic values, a number of bleak and possibly autobiographical pieces about childhood, and some extremely controversial interventions in the most divisive issues facing America. The light touch and comic mode that had previously characterised much of his best work seemed a distant memory. In this context the appearance in 1997 of the film *The Spanish Prisoner*, a superb 'light thriller' that was something of a homage to Hitchcock, was a delightful surprise.

CHAPTER SIXTEEN

The Spanish Prisoner (1997), The Edge (1997), Wag the Dog (1997)

Although it is generally held that in the 1990s Mamet largely sacrificed his theatrical work for the lures of Hollywood, in fact he produced several important plays, while the only Mamet-directed film to emerge between 1991 and 1997 was the very low-key adaptation of *Oleanna*. He was certainly in demand as a screenwriter and 'script doctor', however, and 1997 was to be a triumphant year both in the theatre, with *The Old Neighborhood*, and in the cinema, where *The Spanish Prisoner* proved to be one of the most accessible and satisfying of his movies, while two additional films confirmed his status as the hottest screenwriter in Hollywood.

The Spanish Prisoner (1997)

Like *House of Games*, Mamet's new film was an entertaining cinematic confidence game, this time concerning the efforts of a group of tricksters, headed by Jimmy Dell (Steve Martin), to steal an economically important but undefined piece of intellectual property, 'the Process', from its inventor Joe Ross (Campbell Scott). The spring 1999 issue of the screenwriting journal *Scenario* is something of a special issue on *The Spanish Prisoner*, with no fewer than three items published in the wake of Mamet's then latest film. Most importantly, it contains a draft version of the screenplay that differs significantly both from the film and from the version published in book form alongside *The Winslow Boy*. It also reproduces Mamet's responses to a series of written questions, notable chiefly as an illustration of his infinite capacity for the deadpan evasion of straight answers. The third item, by Jonathan Rosenbaum, compares *House of Games* and *The Spanish Prisoner* to Hitchcock's movies, and suggests that while the former has connections to *Rear Window* (1954), *Vertigo* (1958) and *Marnie* (1964), the latter resembles *The Thirty-Nine Steps* (1935) and *North by Northwest* (1959): 'Mamet–Hitchcock Lite', as Rosenbaum puts it.[1]

In a related discussion, Mike Digou argues that the coin in *American Buffalo*, the 'leads' in *Glengarry Glen Ross*, and the bribe paid to Gino in *Things Change*, as well as the 'Process' in *The Spanish Prisoner*,[2] are examples of the Hitchcockian MacGuffin: a plot device such as stolen plans, or a valuable suitcase, that sets events in motion and that the characters unquestioningly accept as significant, but which the director and audience may recognise as little more than a pretext for the story. This collapses a lot of important distinctions, and neither Rosenbaum nor Digou finally gets much mileage out of the Hitchcock connection, which Leslie Kane effortlessly explores by way not only of the confidence trick specifically but also game playing generally, prompted perhaps by the tennis-playing motif in *The Spanish Prisoner* which, as she points out, recalls Hitchcock's *Strangers on a Train* (1955). She very crisply defines a narrative method whereby 'focus is directed toward the acquisition of/or [sic] disclosure of facts on the one hand and caveats concerning security on the other'.[3] However, instead of following up this promising beginning with a detailed analysis of how this method propels the fiendishly brilliant plot, Kane opts for a synopsis and commentary that draws extensive if uncritical parallels with Mamet's stated directorial methods, which admittedly works much better when, as here, his remarks concern the gulling of the audience rather than the appropriation of Eisenstein.

Several critics follow Kane in connecting *The Spanish Prisoner* to *House of Games*, often in rather unexpected ways. Jeffrey O. McIntire-Strasburg explains that Ross's simultaneous satisfaction in his own integrity and anxiety about whether he is really successful make him the perfect 'mark'.[4] McIntire-Strasburg views the well-worn association of Mamet's confidence men with teachers through the lens of the pedagogical theories of Paulo Freire (1921–97), according to which the mentor becomes a depositor of knowledge into the empty vessel of the pupil. This model has been invoked before, in two essays on *Oleanna*,[5] and more interesting is the discriminating discussion of how the confidence games actually work. The con men are not autonomous: they depend on outside help. In *The Spanish Prisoner* a variety of figures such as love interest Susan (Rebecca Pidgeon) and the boss of Ross's company, Klein (Ben Gazzara), are drafted in as additional mentors to prevent Ross from seeing through Dell, but outsiders can also aid the criminals unwittingly: Ross's friend George Lang (Ricky Jay), like Maria in *House of Games*, unintentionally drives the protagonist further into the clutches of the villains.

Todd F. Davis and Kenneth Womack arrive at similar conclusions as to why Ross is an ideal victim in their account of ethics in *House of Games*, *The Spanish Prisoner* and *State and Main*. Drawing from the same well as Womack's earlier essay on *Oleanna* (see Chapter 14 of this Guide), they explore these films by way of the philosophy of Emmanuel Levinas, specifically the responsibilities demanded by the 'ethical imperative' of alterity – the imaginative act of entering into the life of another person that leads to 'the possibility for renewal and redemption' and to 'the possibility of being "altered" '.[6] Davis and Womack identify different kinds of Otherness in each of the three films. In *House of Games*, Mike is Margaret's 'Dialectical Other', revealing those aspects of her being that she would prefer not to recognise, and killing him is an act of negating the self-knowledge that would have given her the chance to develop an integrated personality. The Hollywood crew in *State and Main* represent to the idealistic screenwriter Joe White the 'Alien Other' that remains irreducibly outside the self, but with which he eventually comes to terms and thereby 'enjoys a genuinely altered relationship with the ethically conflicted others' in an act of self-forgiveness on Mamet's part for working in Hollywood.[7] In *The Spanish Prisoner* Klein, Dell and Susan constitute a 'negative reference group', each offering something that speaks to Ross's desires and thereby setting him up for the 'long con' that will make him 'so enticed by [the group's] wealth and privilege that his ethical perceptions seem murky'.[8] At the end of the film he refuses to help Susan and retreats to his former self, an interiorised existence which, like Margaret's at the end of *House of Games*, refuses alterity. The major drawback of this approach becomes apparent in the remarkable claim that Mamet makes 'concerted efforts in his screenplays to create round characters',[9] which hardly squares with either Mamet's published statements or the screenplays and films themselves, with the arguable exception of early scripts such as *The Verdict*. Psychological interpretations of Mamet's films, especially those that take on an ethical dimension, always risk being trumped by Roger Ebert's analogy of the pack of cards (see Chapter 9 of this Guide).

Much the most ambitious approach to *The Spanish Prisoner* to date is Temenuga Trifonova's identification of the film not as a homage to an old master but as a highly contemporary movie, one of a number of films made in the late 1990s that develop important innovations in the treatment of cinematic time and point of view, including *The Matrix* (Andy and Larry Wachowski, 1999), *Fight Club* (David Fincher, 1999), *The Sixth Sense* (M. Night Shyamalan, 1999), *Memento* (Christopher Nolan, 2000) and *Run, Lola, Run* (Tom Tykwer, 2000). This produces one of the most insightful accounts yet of the 'Mamet movie' in general. For example, Trifonova brilliantly identifies a paradox concerning the oft-remarked retrospective analysis conducted by the viewer on recognising the existence of the confidence game: far from emerging as a master con, it becomes more and more difficult to accept its reality. As she puts it, '[t]here is so much pressure to explain how every single detail was part of the plan, to make it fit into a strict causal relationship with every other detail in the story, that the more strongly the film insists that events were planned, the harder it is to reduce them to such a plan'.[10]

Much like Elizabeth Klaver's Baudrillardian analysis of *House of Games*, Trifonova argues that such films work according to a contemporary cinematic logic that erases commonsense distinctions between the 'real' and the 'unreal', the accidental and the planned ('or even [the] *destined*'), and instead unfolds as a 'virtual' and purely cinematic construction.[11] Trifonova's article challenges at source all attempts to trace an ethical system, rounded characters or weighty themes in films whose significance arguably lies in their remarkable and still under-recognised innovations in exploiting the medium of cinema.

The Edge (1997)

Aside from the screenplays for the films Mamet has directed himself, little of his later writing for film has been extensively analysed, although he is routinely noted as one of Hollywood's top screenwriters. An exception is his original screenplay for the adventure thriller *The Edge* (Lee Tamahori, 1997), in which a plane carrying Charles Morse (Anthony Hopkins), a bookishly intellectual millionaire, and Robert Green (Alec Baldwin), a photographer and younger rival for the affections of Charles's beautiful young wife (Elle Macpherson), crashes in the Alaskan wilderness. Charles and Bob struggle alternately to survive and to destroy each other, leading reviewers to comment almost as frequently on this model Mametian relationship between men as on their encounter with a giant bear, whose performance was universally praised.

The Edge is unique among the films not directed by Mamet in being 'written by' him, in the specific Hollywood sense that the same writer is responsible for both the original story and the screenplay developed from it. This may help to account for its high reputation among Mamet scholars: it appears to reveal clearly the distinction between Mamet as a creative artist and the studios as the purveyors of crass commercial product. Originally called *Bookworm*, which perhaps describes its creator as well as the protagonist, the studio insisted on changing the name, eventually deciding on the apparently meaningless title under which it was finally released. Claire Magaha, partly via the much-travelled path of Joseph Campbell, picks up on this tension in a rather crude reading whereby Charles's experiences in the wilderness represent an 'allegory of self', an internal battle between 'true and false, natural and artificial', between authentic, enlightened spirituality and the 'postmodern' values of 'materialism and artifice'. Authenticity wins. This wouldn't be so bad were it not that this noticeably unresearched thought-piece is couched throughout in the language of New Age psychobabble, and that it constructs an offensively simplistic opposition between 'the enlightened or analytical spectator' like Magaha, and the 'mass audience' or 'postmodern viewership' that just doesn't understand things at quite the same level.[12]

Leslie Kane characteristically considers *The Edge* 'an intrinsically Jewish story'[13] about persecution, survival and the testing of faith, supporting her argument with extensive quotation from the unpublished screenplay and teasing out some surprising implications, some convincing, others ingenious, from details in the script and the film. For example, the action takes place in the north, a region with various symbolic Jewish associations with evil, wealth and the ending of exile, which resonate throughout the film. This kind of poetic, associative logic extends also to the characters: Green, who is identified as Jewish, possesses many of the same attributes of the stereotypical villain Kane detects in the Jewish characters of *Speed-the-Plow* and *Glengarry*, while Morse, who is not Jewish and in most respects functions as Green's antithesis, nevertheless 'may be viewed as a mythic Jew whose ethnicity is implicit rather than explicit'. This looks like having it both ways – after insisting that Green's ethnicity is central, Kane also proposes that the film simply concerns 'the ongoing battle between our "lower" and "higher" nature'[14] – but it is logical that a Jewish writer exploring such basic dichotomies and ethical questions would also frame them through a more culturally specific experience, so that a Jewish world-view may emerge through the exploration of characters whose ethnicity is undetermined and even irrelevant. In any case, Kane does her usual smart work in tracing the significations of such familiar Mametic signifiers as knives, photographs, watches and books.

One of these, the knife, is examined by Thomas P. Adler, who argues that the character of Morse conflates two figures widely found in Mamet's work – the man of action and the intellectual – as in the ineffectual, bookish Del and the unseen outdoorsman husband of Mamet's then-recent stage play *The Cryptogram*. Adler observes that the relationship between Morse and Green illustrates the 'homosocial desire' theorised by Eve Kosofsky Sedgwick (born 1950) in terms used before by David Radavich and others in discussing Mamet's work. The most direct connection with *The Cryptogram* is the birthday gift of a knife that Bob gives to Charles. Adler suggests that because the knife in the course of the screenplay is used to sustain life, rather than for the acts of aggression that it signifies in the play, it implies here a movement towards 'forgiveness and compassion'.[15]

Adler regards the ending remarkably highly, and compares its 'intensity' to that of Shakespeare's *King Lear* (*c.* 1606), while considering that it 'pierces to the heart as almost nothing else in Mamet's work does'.[16] Kane likewise remarks that in this screenplay Mamet is on 'top form',[17] while Magaha thinks that if you can interpret the film as well as she can, it will become 'an instrument of personal enlightenment'.[18] Given these extraordinary valuations it seems only proper to indicate how and why Mamet came to write the script. Art Linson, the producer whose relationship with Mamet had survived *The Untouchables*, needed to come up with a hit movie to relieve the pressure from his superiors, so he contacted Mamet proposing an adventure movie featuring 'two guys'. Linson was otherwise bereft of ideas, at which point Mamet immediately suggested it could be about 'two guys and a bear'.[19] On completion of the deal, he rapidly developed a script that draws as much on the conventions of the action-adventure genre as on the arguably more personal concerns of his own plays and films, while the responses of reviewers suggest that much of the appeal of the completed movie lies in the spectacular visual effect of the landscape (and the bear). Linson wanted more from Mamet than just a script: he wanted a big name associated with a sellable idea to get the film greenlighted, and at that time, as one of his associates allegedly put it, '[i]f Mamet were drooling all over his shoes and said, "I want to write about the art of grilling squid," you woulda ended up with a deal'.[20]

Wag the Dog (1997)

In the same year Mamet was one of the prime movers behind what became one of the most celebrated films of the decade, *Wag the Dog* (Barry Levinson, 1997), the screenplay for which was nominated for an Academy Award. To distract attention from a compromising sexual affair, the President of the United States declares a war on Albania that is a pure media invention. What gave the film legs, to the point where its title has become a byword for political and media manipulation, is that it was released in America just before the Monica Lewinsky scandal, followed suspiciously quickly by a missile strike on a Sudanese factory, emerged to dog the remainder of Bill Clinton's presidential career.

The accepted view of Mamet's role is summarised by Michele Ronnick, who observes that most of the major characters in the script and film, including the Hollywood director Motss (Dustin Hoffman), the spin-doctor Brean (Robert de Niro) and the deranged William 'Old Shoe' Schumann (Woody Harrelson), the figure around whom Motss and Brean spin the war fantasy, are not present in the source novel, Larry Beinhart's *American Hero* (1993). Moreover, as Ronnick delicately puts it, 'Hilary Henkin [born 1962] has been given screen credit for *Wag the Dog*, but most sources minimize her contribution'.[21] Tom Stempel's detailed account of the production history, however, casts some doubt on the implication that Mamet should have been credited with sole authorship.[22] Henkin was brought in to write the screenplay after the rights were bought by de Niro's company, Tribeca, but Barry Levinson disliked her draft and recruited Mamet, who saw neither the novel nor

Henkin's script. Stempel, however, argues that substantial material from both of these sources can be found, albeit transformed, in the final version, probably via Levinson in his consultations with Mamet. Stempel also compares Mamet's drafts of October and December 1996, along with some revised pages written in January 1997 when the film was in production; the December draft eliminates several short scenes and at Levinson's suggestion changes the sex of Ames, the President's assistant, from male to female (the part was played by Anne Heche (born 1969) in the movie). Extracts from the October version, along with a short discussion of some of the differences from Beinhart's novel, appear in a short article in *Creative Screenwriting*.[23]

The Spanish Prisoner was the last of the three 'Mamet movies' (the others are *House of Games* and *Homicide*) that are best understood as a confidence game, with the spectator as victim. Thereafter he has experimented with different forms; all these later movies are interesting, but none has received the same degree of critical attention as his earlier films.

CHAPTER SEVENTEEN

The Winslow Boy (1999) and after: *State and Main* (2000), *Heist* (2001), *Spartan* (2004), *Boston Marriage* (1999)

M amet followed the successes of 1997 with another superb film, *The Winslow Boy*, in 1999. Much of the work thereafter, however, has been characterised by looser structures and a seemingly wilful obscurity or controversial subject matter, possibly in keeping with the new roles he adopted as columnist for the *Guardian* and blogger for the online *Huffington Post*. Only with the television series *The Unit* (2006–present), devised and sometimes written and directed by Mamet, and currently in its third season, has he returned to popular acclaim.

The Winslow Boy (1999)

Many of the first reviews of *The Winslow Boy* expressed surprised that Mamet should adapt for film what many described as the 'war horse' drama of 1946 by the English playwright Terence Rattigan (1911–77). Why would this modern American poet of the obscene be interested in a well-made play, set on the eve of the First World War, in which a middle-class English father fights for justice for the son who has been expelled from a naval college for allegedly stealing a postal order, takes on the legal and political establishment, and wins? More perceptive reviewers noted that the struggle to maintain moral values in the face of superior power, the themes of loyalty and deception, and the fascination with extremes of emotion played out with emotionless sangfroid were quintessential Mamet subjects, and in general the critical response was positive, even if the box-office returns were disappointing.

Irene Morra's discussion of *The Winslow Boy* is an essay of two halves, the first examining authorship, to which we shall return, and the second performing the related and extremely valuable service of clarifying exactly what it was that Mamet adapted. Some qualifications are necessary: contrary to her assertion, it was in fact commonplace for reviewers to remark on the existence of the previous 1948 film adaptation directed by Anthony Asquith (1902–68), for which Rattigan co-wrote the screenplay; but what they did not do was recognise that Mamet demonstrably draws on this film, as well as on the stage play, in creating his own version. Nor does Mamet himself acknowledge it, so Morra's charge of appropriation is well founded in this instance. She concludes that Mamet 'need[s] to position his film in relation to a *theatrical*, rather than a cinematic precedent', partly, it seems, because the cinematic audience would approach an American director adapting a very English stage play with 'relative critical leniency'.[1] This looks like an implausibly convoluted thing for Mamet to do, but more seriously fails to recognise just how much Mamet there still is in the screenplay: in interleaving the two previous versions, in making tiny alterations to innumerable individual lines, and in supplying completely new material that is more extensive than one would guess from Morra's account.

She gives a comparative analysis of all three versions, noting that Asquith's film 'opens out' the action to such an extent that it fully ties the Winslow case to the wider social and national interest. Mamet's version has far fewer scenes outside the Winslow home, and in this respect is closer to Rattigan's play, which is confined entirely to the drawing room; Morra concludes that Mamet is more interested in the private significance of these events for the individuals concerned than in the national debate they bring about. She makes the further, important point that the potential for intimacy between the barrister Sir Robert Morton (Jeremy Northam) and Arthur's daughter Catherine (Rebecca Pidgeon) is suggested from an early stage, which throws Sir Robert's motives into doubt. The romantic relationship is much less prominent in Asquith's version and absent from the stage play.

Mamet, like some reviewers, suggests the film is a testament to Edwardian values without noting that Rattigan's work was already a pastiche of Edwardiana. Morra argues with justification that the stage play is 'a commentary upon, if not a reinvention of, an Edwardian dramatic tradition',[2] and in her reading at least implicitly casts an un-Edwardian, critical eye on Arthur's willingness to sacrifice almost everything to pursue the case. Mamet, on the other hand, glosses over such tensions, constructing a kind of mythic Edwardian drama of manners that allows him to develop the love story as a competitor to that concerning the pursuit of justice. Morra's account of Mamet's film, and indeed Mamet, is contestable in almost every detail, but it performs a great service in clearing away some of the fog surrounding the adaptation, albeit at the cost of blowing in a few misty strands of its own.

Her view of the film's Edwardian setting differs significantly from that of Ira Nadel, who compares Mamet's screenplay to Pinter's adaptation of the novel *The French Lieutenant's Woman* (1969) by John Fowles (1926–2005), for the 1981 film version directed by Karel Reisz (1926–2002). Nadel argues that while Mamet and Pinter hardly ever show either crime or punishment in their plays, their screenplays frequently do. Each is drawn to the idea of lying as a moral crime that violates a social order that then seeks to restore itself, and 'the Victorian and Edwardian periods shared [these writers'] own outrage against deceit while acknowledging its existence',[3] a view Nadel supports by means of a brief historical survey of nineteenth-century attitudes to lying. He suggests that the Victorian social ideal, revolving around hierarchies of class, gender, society and morality, survives into the Edwardian period of *The Winslow Boy*, in which the greatest punishment is shame; hence Mamet's particular interest in the point at which the pursuit of justice threatens to become merely selfish. Nadel also notes that although right is seen to be done and the family is victorious, any sense of guilt attaches merely to the institutions of the government and the Admiralty, who must only admit their error; 'there is no suggestion that the Admiralty will ever change its ways'.[4]

While Nadel suggests that the adaptation offers a historical frame within which to judge modern values, Morra sees it as a contemporary cultural artefact bound up with Mamet's current standing as an author. She argues that his ascription of almost sole authorship to Rattigan in his preface to the published screenplay is contradicted by marketing and screen credits that appear to show Mamet himself appropriating that status, but her argument does not sufficiently distinguish between the author 'Mamet' as a cultural product of the commercial decisions of studios, marketing departments and the like, and Mamet's own self-fashioning of a persona. More sophisticated is the recent work of Yannis Tzioumakis on Mamet and 'industrial auteurism'.[5]

Recent films: *State and Main* (2000), *Heist* (2001) and *Spartan* (2004)

Tzioumakis does not analyse the films themselves but their trailers, looking for signs of how Mamet is constructed as author by distributors seeking to maximise the marketing potential of the films. He identifies three stages, in the first of which, from 1987 to 1992, Mamet's name was rarely used prominently in the marketing of a film and his construction as an auteur was unstable. This is because at the same time as David Mamet, the screenwriter of *The Untouchables*, was becoming a significant player in Hollywood, a second David Mamet was the writer-director of three commercially unsuccessful films, and was becoming peripheral. Ironically, however, the association with Madonna in *Speed-the-Plow* gave him a reputation as a knowing Hollywood insider, as well as celebrity status enhanced by the controversy surrounding *Oleanna* in 1992 and the hype surrounding the all-star adaptation of *Glengarry Glen Ross* in the same year. In the second stage, from *The Spanish Prisoner* through to *State and Main*, his status becomes clearer: he was associated with the art-house circuit and 'American independent cinema', worked with independent distributors, ceased writing for the majors (with the exception of *The Edge*), and acquired what was in effect a brand name used in targeting a small but loyal market eager to see 'a David Mamet film'.

Tzioumakis proposes that a third stage may be identified, beginning in 2001 when Mamet, having established through this 'brand name' a new 'position of power', 'attempted to reestablish his ties with mainstream Hollywood' through working on *Hannibal* (Ridley Scott, 2001) for MGM and Universal, and directing *Heist* for Warner Bros. Crucial to this argument is that Mamet's name remained on the credits for *Hannibal* as co-writer, even though Steven Zaillian (born 1953) eventually wrote a completely different screenplay and Mamet's was not used. Tzioumakis speculates that Mamet retained the association with *Hannibal* in his efforts to secure the funding for *Heist*, which in turn was intended as part of a strategy whereby he would become 'a relatively solid brand name who can deliver a large audience for a studio-financed film',[6] although given the commercial failure of both *Heist* and Mamet's next film, *Spartan*, this stage would appear to be short-lived. Tzioumakis's major article offers a perspective completely different from the theme-based discussions of Mamet's films by theatre critics, or indeed the stylistic analysis of the few academic writers who have attempted a serious study of Mamet's directorial technique. He arguably extrapolates too much from the trailers, but nevertheless establishes a more subtle and discriminating basis for the analysis of Mamet and film authorship than has hitherto been attempted.

A further extra-textual context in which to consider Mamet's current status concerns the nature of the material that is being published on the films. Bruce Barton's book appeared in 2005, yet confines itself to films released in 1987 and 1991; relatively little has been written on *The Spanish Prisoner* or *The Winslow Boy*; and to date nothing at all of substance has been printed in scholarly books or journals on the films from *State and Main* onwards. Other than the inevitable newspaper reviews, popular film magazines and the internet, the only regular forum for the discussion of these films and screenplays has been the journal *Creative Screenwriting*, which often contains relatively substantial articles on Mamet's scripts. This publication is primarily an instructional tool for aspiring writers, however, so the focus tends to be on how he addresses problems commonly found in the screenwriting process, although it is also valuable for its regular inclusion of substantial excerpts from often unpublished screenplays. (For a discussion of screenwriting manuals in general, see Chapter 5 of this Guide.)

The critical neglect of Mamet's recent films goes hand in hand with disappointing box-office returns and genuinely mixed reviews in the mainstream and electronic press, an extensive reading of which gives some indication of why these movies have not proved popular. *State and Main*, an often delightful satire on Hollywood, is a good deal less vicious than *Speed-the-Plow*, while *Heist* was routinely criticised for its unconvincing action sequences, despite what was, for a Mamet film, a substantial budget. Moreover, the narrative is often difficult to follow, a problem that many also found with his most recent film, *Spartan*, an action-adventure movie in which the daughter of the President of the United States is kidnapped and sold to a white slavery ring in the Middle East. Many reviewers found this preposterous, even offensive, although others relished what is surely a satire on American foreign policy. Mamet's difficulties in securing a larger cinema audience may instead be due to finding himself in a vicious circle not unlike the one that traps Levene in *Glengarry Glen Ross*: he can't climb higher because they're giving him dreck. As Tzioumakis shows, his films have not opened on enough screens to garner substantial box-office takings, but in the absence of those takings any subsequent movie is unlikely to be aggressively marketed and distributed – or even made.

Boston Marriage (1999) and other recent plays

Yet another explanation for the lack of popular or critical acclaim for these films becomes more readily apparent when they are considered in conjunction with the recent stage plays, which include *Boston Marriage* (1999), *Faustus* (2004), *Romance* (2005) and *The Voysey Inheritance* (2005), a reworking of the 1905 play by the English dramatist Harley Granville-Barker (1877–1946). Two principal modes are discernible in these works, both of which have tended to dominate Mamet's output since the late 1990s. The first is political satire: *Romance* is an outrageous, uneven, but intermittently brilliant send-up of political attitudes towards the Middle East, and in this respect has much in common not only with *Spartan* but with much of the material Mamet has produced as a columnist for the *Guardian* in Britain between 2003 and 2005 and as a blogger for the online *Huffington Post* thereafter. The second is parody and pastiche: *Romance* is a deliberate travesty of a courtroom drama; *Faustus* offers an almost impenetrable gloss on a story with many notable theatrical antecedents, most pertinently that of the Elizabethan playwright Christopher Marlowe (1564–93); *The Voysey Inheritance* repeats the trick of *The Winslow Boy* by substantially reworking a well-known work of Edwardian or mock-Edwardian theatre that engages issues of class, money and scandal; and Maurice Charney accurately describes *Boston Marriage* as 'a parody of Restoration comedy of manners' via *The Importance of Being Earnest* (1895) by Oscar Wilde (1854–1900).[7] (The title is a euphemism for a lesbian relationship, and the cast, uniquely for a Mamet play, is composed of three women.)

As with the recent films, almost no scholarly studies have yet appeared on these plays, save for a small amount of material on *Boston Marriage*. In her article on *The Winslow Boy*, Morra notes Mamet's claim that his enthusiasm for Rattigan's play was sparked when he took on the task of reworking *Dangerous Corner* (1932), by the English playwright J. B. Priestley (1894–1984), for an off-Broadway production; the Rattigan adaptation was then followed by the self-proclaimed 'comedy of manners' *Boston Marriage*. Morra argues that Mamet's work in general, and the works produced at roughly the same time as *The Winslow Boy* in particular, can be seen as both American and modern on the one hand, and English and 'traditionalist' on the other. Rattigan's play itself has no such divided loyalties: it is 'essentially British in structure, theme, and intended audience', so in adapting it Mamet was presented with 'a greater challenge in contextualizing his enthusiasms for "outdated" British theatre within his cultural environment'.[8]

That environment – the intended audience – Morra takes, from Mamet's commentary on the DVD, to be almost exclusively American, and in many ways identical to the audience for his plays. It is not at all clear what Mamet's purpose in some of his recent work is, but with the possible exception of *The Unit* (2006–present), there is little to suggest he has been unduly concerned either about pleasing an audience, or about 'the potential validity of such a form to American drama' when working on *Boston Marriage*.[9] Few can have taken much pleasure from that play, *Faustus*, or the novel *Wilson* (2000), all of which are essentially one-joke affairs in which a parody of a familiar form (respectively the comedy of manners, the Elizabethan tragedy and the academic treatise) is conducted at some length. The question of whether *Boston Marriage* is actually a self-parody is 'unanswerable ... because all of *Boston Marriage* seems parodic in tone', and Charney rightly suggests that 'arch' would be the more appropriate word.[10] Janet V. Haedicke drily remarks that this play 'evokes speculation as to the direction of Mamet's future drama',[11] just as Christopher Bigsby remarked that '*Wilson* is not so much a stage in his career as time out from it'.[12] In a conclusion that might stand for almost all of Mamet's recent work, Charney speculates that Mamet 'is deliberately pushing the envelope and seeing how far he can go without audience and readers rising up in protest'.[13]

Conclusion

The work in theatre and film by no means exhausts Mamet's achievements; as long ago as 1993, Ilkka Joki noted that he 'has worked with *all* the dramatic media'.[1] One of these, television, has recently become much more significant in his career, and since Joki's book appeared Mamet has also published three novels.

Novels

The persona behind the sometimes baffling novels appears very different from that of either the playwright or the film director, and is seemingly marked by wilful difficulty and modernist solipsism. Christopher Bigsby could find little previous criticism to draw on in his survey of the novels for the 2004 *Cambridge Companion to David Mamet*, and at times appears to be struggling to make headway himself. He admires *The Village* (1994) for its accumulation of small and seemingly disconnected details that builds a picture of lives shored up against despair, for the rhythms of the language, and for the ways in which significant events are merely hinted at. He also commends *The Old Religion* (1998), a novel based on a real event, for a highly ambitious method of characterisation whereby Leo Frank (1884–1915), an innocent Jew wrongly convicted of murder, is delineated through the things he has chosen not to be, just as the novel itself is best defined in terms of what it is not. (Even Bigsby, however, seems stuck for anything to say about *Wilson* (2000), an interminable parody of misplaced scholarship.)

Thomas P. Adler dissects the logic of Frank's interior monologue: Abraham did not kill his son, yet the Christian God did, for love of the world – therefore it is this love that leads to murder. Frank elaborates a taxonomy of persecution – religious, racial, ethnic, sexist – leading him to conclude that it is America itself that is flawed, so he should question his loyalty to it. Adler briefly considers some additional recent adaptations of the real-life case, and notes that the story of Frank's posthumous castration by a lynch mob is Mamet's invention. This, the fact that Frank is murdered by having his throat cut, and the testimony at his trial concerning circumcision, all indicate to Adler a fascination with the image of the knife that provides the connective tissue between this novel and Mamet's brilliant study of dramatic writing, *Three Uses of the Knife*. Each of these texts indicates that the pursuit of meaning is a value in itself, whereas the unhindered application of pure reason leads to evil. Adler is superbly incisive in tracing the critique of reason in a range of Mamet's works, in observing the unsettling effects of this position in 'a post-Enlightenment age', and in suggesting that when, in *Three Uses of the Knife*, Mamet affirms the need to 'perceive the pattern wrought by our character', he is advancing 'what, from O'Neill onward in the drama, has become a peculiarly American formulation of the intersection of free will and determinism'.[2]

Ilkka Joki compares *The Village* to Thornton Wilder's *Our Town* and to the autobiographical narrative *Walden, or, A Life in the Woods* (1854), by Henry David Thoreau (1817–62). Joki focuses on the narrator of *The Village*, observing certain cinematic qualities but also noting how the narrator shifts between omniscience and identification with the voice of particular characters. As in his earlier book-length study, which explores Mamet's work via the theories of Mikhail Bakhtin, Joki is here interested in the intermingling of 'monologic' and 'dialogic', 'high' and 'low' ('demotic') utterances, in what Bakhtin terms 'dialogised polyphony', the exploitation of which Joki sees as one of the strengths of the novel.[3]

Television scripts

Joki has also addressed Mamet's work for television. The few published studies in this field to date share a common emphasis on the 'through-line' of a range of scripts published in Mamet's 1990 collection, *Five Television Plays*. Joki briefly discusses the unproduced *The Museum of Science and Industry Story* in relation to *The Water Engine*, which shares some similar material, before focusing on *A Wasted Weekend*, Mamet's script for a 1987 episode of the long-running police series *Hill Street Blues*.[4] The published script differs from the televised version in omitting a storyline about one of the female characters; Joki notes that this makes the published version more of a masculine affair, and strengthens the through-line, although Steve Ryan elicited a letter from Mamet in which he stated that he did not know why the two versions differ. Ryan thinks all three major storylines are connected by a through-line that defines a police officer's duty, especially in life-threatening situations.[5]

Franz Wieselhuber examines two further unproduced teleplays from the same collection, *A Waitress in Yellowstone* and *We Will Take You There, Episode One: A Hudson's Bay Start*. In the preface to *Five Television Plays*, and elsewhere, Mamet complains about the venal motives and artistic ignorance of television executives. Wieselhuber posits that an alternative explanation for Mamet's failure to break into television might be the quality and nature of Mamet's scripts, and has no difficulty in demonstrating that *A Waitress in Yellowstone* is unviable, although he notes greater potential in *We Will Take You There*. What may finally have dissuaded the executives, Wieselhuber speculates, 'could well be this uncompromising insistence on the truth of the through-line and the strange quality of dialogue it occasionally produces'.[6] The subsequent success of *The Unit* renders some of these arguments obsolete.

Summary: the works and the personae

A conference organised by Johan Callens in Brussels in 2008 takes as its theme the interdisciplinarity and multi-media aspects of Mamet's work, and gives a sound indication that this, rather than the purist notions of drama and film for which he has often been noted, is likely to be the focus of much future scholarship. Indeed, many of the early views of Mamet have by now been almost completely reversed, partly because the study of American drama in general has become more theorised, partly because the American 'culture wars' of the 1990s have made earlier assumptions about common culture highly problematic, and partly because his own work has changed markedly in nature since the late 1980s.

Although in the 1990s literary criticism subjected every major author to an often tediously predictable analysis of race, class and especially gender, in Mamet's case much of the work along these lines has been genuinely insightful and highly productive in challenging received opinion. There will always be those for whom he is tainted by misogyny, and others for whom the charge is unwarranted, especially when applied to Mamet personally; but a more discriminating approach has come through examining masculinity in relation to Jewish identity, and in particular '[t]he tension between the universalized and the specifically ethnic need to remasculinize'.[7] It is perhaps because Mamet's own position has been a developing one, in public at least, that Leslie Kane's arguments for a specifically Jewish world-view underlying virtually all of his work, including *American Buffalo* and other early plays, have not received widespread assent. However, the 'identity politics' has become more pronounced in his recent blogs for *The Huffington Post* and in *The Wicked Son: Anti-Semitism, Self-Hatred, and the Jews* (2006), in which Mamet goes still further than previously in rejecting the assimilationist ('self-loathing') model and in the unequivocal defence of Israel. One reviewer dismissed *The Wicked Son* as an 'incendiary rant',[8] which does not do justice to its arguments, but in suggesting that 'the embrace of "tribal" identity may prove disabling' to Mamet's artistry the reviewer gives voice to an increasingly widespread concern about the inaccessibility of much of Mamet's recent work prior to *The Unit*.

While there is considerable uncertainty about where Mamet is heading, a significant degree of consensus has emerged about where he has been, despite the polarised views of gender. The best criticism of the last ten to fifteen years is fairly consistent in perceiving a particular dynamic: on the one hand, the author's voice can appear to sound with conviction, appealing to foundational and largely unequivocal (if contestable) first principles, initially within a broad context of American individualism and then within a narrowing set of masculine and Judaic values; on the other hand, these principles are difficult to extricate from the ironic, postmodern recycling of images, while any attempt to identify a monologic authorial voice becomes problematic in the light of the fascination with pastiche, institutional language and the effects of different media.

This tension is found in studies of all of the major aspects of Mamet's work. In *Oleanna* Mamet either dismisses the relativism of 'political correctness' in the name of common values, or suggests that all values are inextricable from institutional contexts. Warren Rosenberg assumes that in *Homicide* Mamet remains drawn to the ethic of the 'tough Jew', and that 'Gold acts like a schlemiel [a stupid, awkward or unlucky person] not . . . as a result of his choosing identity politics, but, for Mamet, because he neglects to choose it soon enough';[9] but there are many who retain the 'liberal' interpretation of the film that Rosenberg rejects. Linda Dorff thinks the voice of the male author rings loud and clear in *The Cryptogram*, while others point to the same play as evidence that Mamet can create realistically convincing female characters. Callens's analysis of the 'double logic of remediation' in *The Water Engine* traces the play of media as simultaneously opaque, jamming access to any unproblematic notion of the real, and as revealing underneath a nostalgic longing for transparency. Several studies of *American Buffalo* show that the play dramatises the desire for the security of 'real' money in a world in which the circulation of currency destroys it. And those who assumed Mamet was a mainstream liberal humanist now need to take account of his increasingly clearly defined position, much like that of his friend, the prominent Harvard lawyer Alan Dershowitz (born 1938), as a Jew with uncompromising views on assimilation and the defence of Israel.

A similar dynamic can be seen in the potential or actual discrepancies between the public personae projected in Mamet's essays and interviews, on the one hand, and his work in theatre and film, on the other. Many who discern a particular ideological position within a given work, and selectively excavate Mamet's public pronouncements for supporting evidence, too hastily elide these differences. By contrast, until recently the few critics who had attempted an analysis of the ideology of his work in general had tended to see him, albeit tentatively, as a kind of American postmodernist, and carefully distinguished the work from the persona. Richard Brucher's essay on 'pernicious nostalgia' in *Glengarry Glen Ross* (Chapter 7), for example, persistently invokes Emersonian ideals – dangerously, as Brucher concedes, firstly because the degree of 'sincerity' even in Mamet's essays is open to question, and secondly because it can play into the hands of a nostalgia for lost American ideals that Mamet will frequently invoke and debunk at the same time. Yet as both Brucher and Matthew C. Roudané explain, something similar is found in Arthur Miller's work as well. Miller saw the 'American Dream' of human perfectibility as an ever-present ironic backdrop against which the failure of his characters is measured, and Roudané connects this to American ideas of Nature that also influence Mamet. Roudané's summary of this tradition, which has an extensive history in American literary scholarship, emphasises a Romantic and Puritan sensibility, continuing into Emersonian Transcendentalism, in which Nature is both divine and palpable, revealing in the landscape, seasons and elements signs of Godly intent. He finds traces of this 'authentic past' in some of Mamet's writings, which, however, 'stop short of providing a redemptive future' because Mamet is too much of a postmodernist to accept uncritically a view of Nature as benevolent teacher.[10] For example, while it is a cliché that Mamet is unusual for an American dramatist in setting the action not in the home but in the workplace, Roudané further observes that the urban spaces (in *Glengarry*, for example) are not downtown but in desolate suburbs, heightening the sense of a decentred alienation quite at odds with the American tradition of Nature. This contributes to a particular kind of realism that deconstructs itself by insistently bringing to mind a 'negative space', 'a figurative, imaginative world that's only hinted at' in ways that 'contribute to a nonrealistic atmosphere *and* call attention to the playwright's quarrel with American culture' (Roudané's emphasis).[11] This is one of the reasons why the 'detectable optimism' of *Writing in Restaurants*, his first collection of essays, is largely absent from the plays.[12]

What connects these multiple personae is, perhaps, a stance towards the dominant culture that appears both typical and oppositional at the same time. Michael L. Quinn places Mamet within a long tradition of American liberal dissenters who position themselves as outsiders, rejecting contemporary 'American culture in the name of American values'. Mamet rejects the bourgeoisie, 'banal social realists and the formalist avant-garde',[13] against whom he constructs himself as an individual, partly by writing about his experiences in a way that suggests he has come from an earlier time than he really has, an effect which is particularly noticeable in his writings about Chicago. From this vantage point he projects an ideal if masculine community, of truth, friendship and uncomplicated social interaction, rather like those proposed by Jefferson or Jean-Jacques Rousseau (1712–78). This America can never exist, however, so in accepting its absence the author creates an impression of realism. Quinn gives a short analysis of selected plays to show how recurring scenes – the business scam, the character who has dropped out or is in hiding, the reluctance to commit to love, the exposure of an illusion – dramatise this dynamic, setting up an ideal before exposing the lie beneath. In other words, these are speech-act plays: they do not represent situations (as a realist playwright would) but constitute them, and in the process they 'dramatize the moments in peoples' lives when their performances seem to come undone'. Like Elizabeth Klaver in her analysis of *House of Games* (see Chapter 9 of this Guide), Quinn argues that a properly deconstructive analysis would show that this apparently definitive unravelling is in fact just another stage in an infinite regression, yet in appearing to be true it appeals to a contemporary American culture which 'values such creative rejections'; this could change, and, therefore, Mamet's present popularity could decline.[14]

Indeed, within a few years of Quinn's essay of 1996 Mamet did become temporarily less fashionable, although not for this reason. Much of his work between *The Winslow Boy* and *The Unit* is marked not only by a kind of modernist difficulty in which the text's coherence, such as it is, is generated by an authorial consciousness that may pay little heed to the conventions of realism or the partialities of the audience, but also by the postmodern awareness that one always speaks from a particular position. There can be few who would now maintain, as did Marc Silverstein and others in the wake of *Oleanna*, that Mamet masks a particular political ideology as common American culture; it is all too clear that in works such as *The Wicked Son* he is uncompromisingly dedicated to a world-view that in certain ways is quite deliberately exclusive. Yet he is always both a moving and a multiple target; in the same year as *The Wicked Son* was published, *The Unit* exposed him to arguably his largest ever mainstream audience and achieved widespread critical acclaim, and before making it he committed himself to living and working long-term in Hollywood, a town he had previously characterised as 'a sink-hole of depraved venality'.[15]

Still more recently, as this book was going to press, Mamet published an article in the *Village Voice* on 11 March 2008 describing how his thinking changed as he was working on his latest play, *November*, which stages a political debate between a free-market, conservative President of the United States, and his leftish, female speechwriter. In Mamet's terms, the play is 'a disputation between reason and faith, or perhaps between the conservative (or tragic) view and the liberal (or perfectionist) view'.[16] The writer himself, who 'took the liberal view for many decades', has now changed his mind. He no longer accepts an ideology that takes a sufficiently idealistic view of human nature as constantly to be disappointed and angry about the ills of the country. Instead, the vicious self-interest displayed by his characters more accurately represents his view of people in general, who nevertheless are 'reasonably trying to maximize their comfort by getting along with each other'. Governments and Presidents of whatever complexion are corrupt, but also largely unnecessary, doing more harm than good by intervention, although the executive is held in check by the separation of powers enshrined in the Constitution. Consequently Mamet takes a much more benign view than previously of America itself, including its military and even its corporations.

Much of this is unsurprising. A positive perception of the military is apparent in *The Unit*, and Mamet's view of government, and indeed of authority in general, has been consistent through his career. In the *Village Voice* he compares government to a theatre director who damages the production by his very presence, since it induces the cast to act politically and appeal to authority rather than work through the problems of the play for themselves. The distinction appears to be less between liberalism and conservatism than between a libertarian sensibility and the managerial class that has consistently been an object of scorn, notably in *Glengarry Glen Ross*. What is new is the largely uncritical embrace of free-market economics. Again, some such position has been discernible for some time, and Johan Callens's analysis of *American Buffalo* in terms of the economic philosophy of Adam Smith seems more clear-sighted than ever. Yet something has changed when the author of *The Water Engine* is disinclined to take a critical view of corporate America, and cites approvingly the work of Milton Friedman (1912–2006) and even Paul Johnson (born 1928).

Who'd be a Mamet critic?

Notes

INTRODUCTION

1. C. Gerald Fraser, 'Mamet's Plays Shed Masculinity Myth', *New York Times* (5 July 1976), sec. 1, p. 7; Ross Wetzsteon, 'David Mamet: Remember That Name', *Village Voice* (5 July 1976), pp. 101–3.
2. John Ditsky, '"He Lets You See the Thought There": the Theatre of David Mamet', *Kansas Quarterly* 12.4 (1980), p. 26.
3. Richard Eder, 'David Mamet's New Realism', *New York Times*, magazine section (12 March 1978), p. 42.
4. Christopher C. Hudgins, 'Comedy and Humor in the Plays of David Mamet', in Leslie Kane, *David Mamet: A Casebook* (New York: Garland, 1992), p. 192.
5. Elaine Showalter, 'Acts of Violence: David Mamet and the Language of Men', *Times Literary Supplement* (6 November 1992), p. 17.
6. Hudgins (1992), p. 197.
7. David Mamet, *American Buffalo* (London: Methuen, 1984), p. 52.

CHAPTER ONE: EARLY PLAYS: *LAKEBOAT* (1970), *THE DUCK VARIATIONS* (1972), *SEXUAL PERVERSITY IN CHICAGO* (1974)

1. For a more detailed account of textual changes see Johan Callens, 'The 1970s', in Christopher Bigsby (ed.), *The Cambridge Companion to David Mamet* (Cambridge: Cambridge University Press, 2004), p. 42.
2. Carla J. McDonough, *Staging Masculinity: Male Identity in Contemporary American Drama* (Jefferson, NC: McFarland, 1997), pp. 80–5.
3. C. W. E. Bigsby, *David Mamet* (London: Methuen, 1985), p. 23.
4. Dennis Carroll, *David Mamet* (Basingstoke: Macmillan, 1987), pp. 83–90.
5. Michael Hinden, '"Intimate Voices": *Lakeboat* and Mamet's Quest for Community', in Leslie Kane (ed.), *David Mamet: A Casebook* (New York: Garland, 1992), p. 38.
6. David Mamet, *Lakeboat* (New York: Grove Press, 1981), p. 59.
7. Guido Almansi, 'David Mamet, a Virtuoso of Invective', in Marc Chénetier (ed.), *European Views of Contemporary American Literature* (Carbondale: Southern Illinois University Press, 1986), p. 194.
8. Jeanne-Andrée Nelson, '*Speed-the-Plow* or Seed the Plot? Mamet and the Female Reader', *Essays in Theatre* 10.1 (1991), pp. 71–82. Susan Harris Smith quotes the same line to support her general argument that the plays of Mamet, Sam Shepard and David Rabe are misogynistic, in 'En-Gendering Violence: Twisting "Privates" in the Public Eye', in Matthew C. Roudané (ed.), *Public Issue, Private Tensions: Contemporary American Drama* (New York: AMS, 1993), p. 123.
9. Steven Price, 'Disguise in Love: Gender and Desire in *House of Games* and *Speed-the-Plow*', in Christopher C. Hudgins and Leslie Kane (eds), *Gender and Genre: Essays on David Mamet* (New York: Palgrave, 2001), p. 41. See also Janet V. Haedicke, 'Plowing the Buffalo, Fucking the Fruits: (M)others in *American Buffalo* and *Speed-the-Plow*', in Hudgins and Kane, p. 27.
10. Almansi (1986), p. 199.
11. Almansi (1986), p. 193.

12. Henry I. Schvey, 'The Plays of David Mamet: Games of Manipulation and Power', *New Theatre Quarterly* 14.3 (1988), p. 78.

13. In Ross Wetzsteon, 'David Mamet: Remember That Name', *Village Voice* (5 July 1976), p. 101.

14. Robert Storey, 'The Making of David Mamet', *The Hollins Critic* 14.4 (1979), pp. 3–4.

15. Bigsby (1985), p. 28.

16. Carroll (1987), p. 76.

17. William Herman, *Understanding Contemporary American Drama* (Columbia: South Carolina University Press, 1987), p. 139.

18. Philip C. Kolin, 'David Mamet's *Duck Variations* as a Parody of a Socratic Dialogue', *American Drama* 9.1 (1999), pp. 21–32.

19. Pascale Hubert-Liebler, 'Dominance and Anguish: the Teacher–Student Relationship in the Plays of David Mamet', *Modern Drama* 31 (1988), p. 559.

20. Deborah R. Geis, *Postmodern Theatric(k)s: Monologue in Contemporary American Drama* (Ann Arbor: University of Michigan Press, 1993), p. 93.

21. David Skeele, 'The Devil and David Mamet: *Sexual Perversity in Chicago* as Homiletic Tragedy', *Modern Drama* 36 (1993), p. 514.

22. Skeele (1993), p. 514.

23. Douglas Bruster, 'David Mamet and Ben Jonson: City Comedy Past and Present', *Modern Drama* 33 (1990), p. 336.

24. Bruster (1990), p. 333.

25. Bruster (1990), p. 335.

26. Geis (1993), p. 96.

27. Bruster (1990), p. 341.

28. Bruster (1990), p. 342.

29. David Savran, 'New Realism: Mamet, Mann and Nelson', in Bruce King (ed.), *Contemporary American Theatre* (Basingstoke: Macmillan, 1991), pp. 64–5.

30. Bigsby (1985), p. 49.

31. Savran (1991), p. 69.

32. Carroll (1987), pp. 51–9.

33. Geis (1993), p. 95.

34. Savran (1991), p. 72.

35. Varun Begley, 'On Adaptation: David Mamet and Hollywood', *Essays in Theatre* 16.2 (1998), pp. 167–8.

36. Bruce Barton, *Imagination in Transition: Mamet's Move to Film* (Brussels: Peter Lang, 2005), p. 37.

37. Storey (1979), p. 4.

38. Barton (2005), p. 52–4.

CHAPTER TWO: *AMERICAN BUFFALO* (1975)

1. Andrew Harris, *Broadway Theatre* (London: Routledge, 1994), p. 98.

2. Harris (1994), pp. 105–6.

3. Jack V. Barbera, 'Ethical Perversity in Chicago: Some Observations on David Mamet's *American Buffalo*', *Modern Drama* 24 (1981), p. 275.

4. Barbera (1981), pp. 271–2.

5. Barbera (1981), p. 274.

6. June Schlueter and Elizabeth Forsyth, 'America as Junkshop: the Business Ethic in David Mamet's *American Buffalo*', *Modern Drama* 26 (1983), pp. 492–500.

7. C. W. E. Bigsby, *David Mamet* (London: Methuen, 1985), p. 72.

8. Bigsby (1985), p. 74.

9. Bigsby (1985), p. 77.

10.   Thomas L. King, 'Talk and Dramatic Action in *American Buffalo*', *Modern Drama* 34.4 (1991), p. 545.

11.   Johan Callens, 'Mr. Smith Goes to Chicago: Playing out Mamet's Critique of Capitalism in *American Buffalo*', *European Journal of American Culture* 19.1 (1999), p. 19.

12.   Callens (1999), p. 21.

13.   Callens (1999), p. 24.

14.   Callens (1999), p. 26.

15.   Callens (1999), p. 28.

16.   William Little, 'Taking It Back: Crises of Currency in David Mamet's *American Buffalo*', *Mosaic* 37.3 (2004), p. 140.

17.   Little (2004), pp. 152–3.

18.   Jon Dietrick, ' "Real Classical Money": Naturalism and Mamet's *American Buffalo*', *Twentieth Century Literature* 52.3 (2006), p. 343–4.

19.   David Radavich, 'Man among Men: David Mamet's Social Order', *American Drama* 1.1 (1991), p. 51.

20.   Carla J. McDonough, *Staging Masculinity: Male Identity in Contemporary American Drama* (Jefferson, NC: McFarland, 1997), p. 91.

21.   Hersh Zeifman, 'Phallus in Wonderland: Machismo and Business in David Mamet's *American Buffalo* and *Glengarry Glen Ross*', in Leslie Kane (ed.), *David Mamet: A Casebook* (New York: Garland, 1992), p. 129.

22.   Robert Vorlicky, *Act Like a Man: Challenging Masculinities in American Drama* (Ann Arbor: University of Michigan Press, 1995), p. 214.

23.   Vorlicky (1995), p. 226.

24.   Jeanette R. Malkin, *Verbal Violence in Contemporary Drama* (Cambridge: Cambridge University Press, 1992), pp. 145–7.

25.   Christopher C. Hudgins, 'Comedy and Humor in the Plays of David Mamet', in Leslie Kane, *David Mamet: A Casebook* (New York: Garland, 1992), p. 202.

26.   Stanton B. Garner, Jr., *Bodied Spaces: Phenomenology and Performance in Contemporary Drama* (Ithaca: Cornell University Press, 1994), p. 129.

27.   Deborah R. Geis, *Postmodern Theatric(k)s: Monologue in Contemporary American Drama* (Ann Arbor: University of Michigan Press, 1993), p. 101.

28.   Bruce Barton, *Imagination in Transition: Mamet's Move to Film* (Brussels: Peter Lang, 2005), p. 63.

29.   Barton (2005), p. 60.

30.   Toby Silverman Zinman, 'Jewish Aporia: the Rhythm of Talking in Mamet', *Theatre Journal* 44 (1992), p. 213.

31.   Leslie Kane, *Weasels and Wisemen: Ethics and Ethnicity in the Work of David Mamet* (New York: St Martin's, 1999), p. 52.

32.   Alain Piette, 'The Flexing of Muscles and Tongues: Thug Rituals and Rhetoric in David Mamet's *American Buffalo*', in Marc Maufort and Franca Bellarsi (eds), *Crucible of Cultures: Anglophone Drama at the Dawn of a New Millennium* (Brussels: Peter Lang, 2002), pp. 91–100.

CHAPTER THREE: *A LIFE IN THE THEATRE* (1977), *THE WATER ENGINE* (1977), *MR. HAPPINESS* (1977)

1.   Anne Dean, *David Mamet: Language as Dramatic Action* (Rutherford, NJ: Fairleigh Dickinson University Press, 1990), p. 126.

2.   William Herman, *Understanding Contemporary American Drama* (Columbia: South Carolina University Press, 1987), p. 149.

3.   Dennis Carroll, *David Mamet* (Basingstoke: Macmillan, 1987), p. 83.

4.   Deborah R. Geis, *Postmodern Theatric(k)s: Monologue in Contemporary American Drama* (Ann Arbor: University of Michigan Press, 1993), p. 95.

5.   Geis (1993), p. 93.

6.   Pascale Hubert-Liebler, 'Dominance and Anguish: the Teacher–Student Relationship in the Plays of David Mamet', *Modern Drama* 31 (1988), p. 558.

7.   Hubert-Liebler (1988), p. 565.

8.   Mel Gussow, 'Real Estate World a Model for Mamet', *New York Times* (28 March 1984), p. C19.

9.   For further discussion of Mamet's theories of acting, see Bella Merlin, 'Mamet's Heresy and Common Sense: What's True and False in "True and False"', *New Theatre Quarterly* 16 (2000), pp. 249–54; Don Wilmeth, 'Mamet and the Actor', in Christopher Bigsby (ed.), *The Cambridge Companion to David Mamet* (Cambridge: Cambridge University Press, 2004), pp. 138–53; Yannis Tzioumakis, 'The Poetics of Performance in the Cinema of David Mamet: Against Embellishment', *Journal of the Midwest Modern Language Association* 39.1 (2006), pp. 88–99.

10.   Jerry Dickey, 'Mamet's Actors: *A Life in the Theater* and Other Writings on the Art of Acting', in Barbara Ozieblo and María Dolores Narbona-Carrión (eds), *Codifying the National Self: Spectators, Actors and the American Dramatic Text* (Brussels, Belgium: Peter Lang, 2006), p. 262.

11.   Carroll (1987), pp. 135–6.

12.   C. W. E. Bigsby, *David Mamet* (London: Methuen, 1985), pp. 88–9.

13.   Geis (1993), p. 63.

14.   Bigsby (1985), p. 91.

15.   Steven Price, 'AT & T: Anxiety, Telecommunications and the Theatre of David Mamet', *Cycnos* 12.1 (1995), p. 66; see also Steven Price, ' "Accursed Progenitor": Samuel Beckett, David Mamet, and the Problem of Influence', in Marius Buning and Lois Oppenheim (eds), *Beckett in the 1990s* (Amsterdam: Rodopi, 1993), pp. 77–85.

16.   Johan Callens, 'Remediation in David Mamet's *The Water Engine*', *American Drama* 14.2 (2005), p. 40.

17.   Callens (2005), p. 46.

18.   Callens (2005), p. 47.

19.   Callens (2005), p. 53.

20.   Steven H. Gale, 'David Mamet: the Plays, 1972–1980,' in Hedwig Bock and Albert Wertheim (eds), *Essays on Contemporary American Drama* (Munich: Max Hueber Verlag, 1981), p. 215.

21.   C. W. E. Bigsby, 'David Mamet', in *A Critical Introduction to Twentieth-Century American Drama*, vol. 3: *Beyond Broadway* (Cambridge: Cambridge University Press, 1985), p. 278.

22.   John Ditsky, ' "He Lets You See the Thought There": The Theatre of David Mamet', *Kansas Quarterly* 12.4 (1980), p. 31.

CHAPTER FOUR: OTHER 1970s PLAYS: *THE WOODS* (1977), *REUNION* (1976), *DARK PONY* (1977), CHILDREN'S PLAYS, *SQUIRRELS* (1974), *MARRANOS* (1975), *LONE CANOE* (1979)

1.   John Russell Taylor, 'The Woods, the West, and Icarus's Mother: Myth in the Contemporary American Theatre', *Connotations* 5.2–3 (1995–96), pp. 339–54.

2.   Dennis Carroll, *David Mamet* (Basingstoke: Macmillan, 1987), pp. 52–3.

3.   Deborah R. Geis, 'David Mamet and the Metadramatic Tradition: Seeing "the Trick from the Back" ', in Leslie Kane, *David Mamet: A Casebook* (New York: Garland, 1992), p. 59.

4.   C. W. E. Bigsby, *David Mamet* (London: Methuen, 1985), p. 58.

5.   Bigsby (1985), p. 59.

6.   Bigsby (1985), p. 39.

7.   Bruce Barton, *Imagination in Transition: Mamet's Move to Film* (Brussels: Peter Lang, 2005), p. 100.

8.   Thomas P. Adler, 'Mamet's *Three Children's Plays*: Where the Wilder Things Are', in Christopher C. Hudgins and Leslie Kane (eds), *Gender and Genre: Essays on David Mamet* (New York: Palgrave, 2001), pp. 15–26.

9.   Carroll (1987), p. 77.

10.   Toby Silverman Zinman, 'Jewish Aporia: the Rhythm of Talking in Mamet', *Theatre Journal* 44 (1992), pp. 207–8.

11.   Leslie Kane, *Weasels and Wisemen: Ethics and Ethnicity in the Work of David Mamet* (New York: St Martin's, 1999), pp. 11–23. An earlier version was published as ' "In blood, in blood thou shalt remember": David Mamet's *Marranos*', *Yearbook of English Studies* 24 (1994), pp. 157–71.

12.   Carroll (1987), p. 106.

CHAPTER FIVE: THE SCREENPLAYS, 1981–9: *THE POSTMAN ALWAYS RINGS TWICE* (1981), *THE VERDICT* (1982), *THE UNTOUCHABLES* (1987), *WE'RE NO ANGELS* (1989)

1.   Gay Brewer, *David Mamet and Film: Illusion/Disillusion in a Wounded Land* (Jefferson, NC: McFarland, 1993), pp. 95–6, 99.

2.   Bruce Barton, *Imagination in Transition: Mamet's Move to Film* (Brussels: Peter Lang, 2005), pp. 137–8.

3.   Dan Yakir, 'The Postman's Words', *Film Comment* (March/April 1981), pp. 21–4.

4.   In John Duka, 'Hollywood's Long-Running Romance with James M. Cain', *New York Times* (5 April 1981), sec. 2, p. 15.

5.   William Goldman, *Adventures in the Screen Trade: A Personal View of Hollywood and Screenwriting* [1983] (London: Futura, 1985), pp. 63–7; Sidney Lumet, *Making Movies* (New York: Alfred A. Knopf, 1995), p. 39. For Mamet's similar but condensed account of events, see Leslie Kane (ed.), *David Mamet in Conversation* (Ann Arbor: University of Michigan Press, 2001), p. 194.

6.   Dennis Carroll, *David Mamet* (Basingstoke: Macmillan, 1987), p. 91.

7.   Joseph Campbell, *The Hero with a Thousand Faces* (Princeton: Princeton University Press, 1949), p. 30.

8.   Additional examples that refer to *The Verdict* include Michael Hauge, *Writing Screenplays that Sell* (London: Elm Tree, 1989), pp. 99, 103; Robert McKee, *Story: Substance, Structure, Style, and the Principles of Screenwriting* (London: Methuen, 1997), p. 104.

9.   Thomas Pope, *Good Scripts, Bad Scripts: Learning the Craft of Screenwriting through 25 of the Best and Worst Films in History* (New York: Three Rivers Press, 1998), p. 135.

10.   Pope (1998), pp. 137–8.

11.   Paul Lucey, *Story Sense: Writing Story and Script for Feature Films and Television* (New York: McGraw-Hill, 1996), p. xv.

12.   Lucey (1996), pp. 130, 127.

13.   Art Linson, *A Pound of Flesh: Perilous Tales of How to Produce Movies in Hollywood* (London: André Deutsch, 1994), p. 67.

14.   Linson (1994), p. 69.

15.   Gaylord Brewer, '*Hoffa* and *The Untouchables*: Mamet's Brutal Orders of Authority', *Literature/Film Quarterly* 28:1 (2000), pp. 31–2.

16.   Dennis Carroll, 'The Recent Mamet Films: "Business" versus Communion', in Leslie Kane (ed.), *David Mamet: A Casebook* (New York: Garland, 1992), p. 180.

17.   Brewer (1993), p. 126.

18.   Brewer (2000), p. 28.

19.   Brewer (1993), p. 129.

CHAPTER SIX: *EDMOND* (1982)

1.   Henry I. Schvey, 'The Plays of David Mamet: Games of Manipulation and Power', *New Theatre Quarterly* 14.3 (1988), p. 84.

2.   David Savran, 'New Realism: Mamet, Mann and Nelson', in Bruce King (ed.), *Contemporary American Theatre* (Basingstoke: Macmillan, 1991), p. 76.

3. Alain Piette, 'In the Loneliness of Cities: The Hopperian Accents of David Mamet's *Edmond*', *Studies in the Humanities* 24.1–2 (1997), pp. 43–51.

4. Gay Brewer, *David Mamet and Film: Illusion/Disillusion in a Wounded Land* (Jefferson, NC: McFarland, 1993), p. 95.

5. Johan Callens, review of *Edmond* (Théâtre Varia, Brussels, 16 January 1995), *Journal of Dramatic Theory and Criticism* 11.1 (1996), pp. 127–31.

6. Savran (1991), pp. 75–7.

7. Piette (1997), pp. 44–6.

8. C. W. E. Bigsby, *David Mamet* (London: Methuen, 1985), p. 108.

9. Robert Combs, 'Slaughtering Lambs: The Moral Universe of David Mamet and Wallace Shawn', *Journal of American Drama and Theatre* 13:1 (2001), pp. 73–81.

10. Daniel Dervin, '*Edmond*: Is There Such a Thing as a Sick Play?', *Psychoanalytic Review* 73.1 (1986), pp. 111–19.

11. Alisa Solomon, 'Weeping for Racists, Rapists, and Nazis', *Performing Arts Journal* 7.1 (1983), pp. 81–3.

12. Savran (1991), p. 75.

13. Jon Tuttle, ' "Be What You Are": Identity and Morality in *Edmond* and *Glengarry Glen Ross*', in Leslie Kane (ed.), *David Mamet's 'Glengarry Glen Ross': Text and Performance* (New York: Garland, 1996), p. 160.

14. Dennis Carroll, *David Mamet* (Basingstoke: Macmillan, 1987), p. 98.

15. Carroll (1987), pp. 103–4.

16. Bigsby (1985), p. 107.

17. Savran (1991), p. 76.

18. Dervin (1986), p. 119.

19. Bigsby (1985), p. 102.

20. Bigsby (1985), p. 108.

21. Bigsby (1985), p. 101.

22. Richard Brucher, 'Prophecy and Parody in *Edmond*', in Christopher C. Hudgins and Leslie Kane (eds), *Gender and Genre: Essays on David Mamet* (New York: Palgrave, 2001), p. 64.

23. Brucher (2001), p. 67.

24. Carla J. McDonough, *Staging Masculinity: Male Identity in Contemporary American Drama* (Jefferson, NC: McFarland, 1997), p. 80.

25. Piette (1997), p. 48.

26. McDonough (1997), p. 79.

27. Bruce Barton, *Imagination in Transition: Mamet's Move to Film* (Brussels: Peter Lang, 2005), p. 80.

28. Barton (2005), p. 92.

CHAPTER SEVEN: *GLENGARRY GLEN ROSS* (1983)

1. C. W. E. Bigsby, *David Mamet* (London: Methuen, 1985), pp. 111–26.

2. Matthew C. Roudané, 'Public Issues, Private Tensions: David Mamet's *Glengarry Glen Ross*', *South Carolina Review* 19.1 (1986), p. 39.

3. Matthew C. Roudané, 'Mamet's Mimetics', in Leslie Kane (ed.), *David Mamet: A Casebook* (New York: Garland, 1992), pp. 3–32.

4. Richard Brucher, 'Pernicious Nostalgia in *Glengarry Glen Ross*', in Leslie Kane (ed.), *David Mamet's* Glengarry Glen Ross: *Text and Performance* (New York: Garland, 1996), p. 212.

5. David Kennedy Sauer, 'The Marxist Child's Play of Mamet's Tough Guys and Churchill's *Top Girls*', in Kane (1996), p. 137.

6. Steven Price, 'Negative Creation: the Detective Story in *Glengarry Glen Ross*', in Kane (1996), p. 8.

7. Elizabeth Klaver, 'David Mamet, Jean Baudrillard and the Performance of America', in Kane (1996), p. 177.

8. Klaver (1996), p. 180.

9. Linda Dorff, 'Things (Ex)change: the Value of Money in David Mamet's *Glengarry Glen Ross*', in Kane (1996), p. 198.

10. Dorff (1996), p. 203.

11. Dorff (1996), p. 205.

12. David Sauer and Janice A. Sauer, 'Misreading Mamet: Scholarship and Reviews', in Christopher Bigsby (ed.), *The Cambridge Companion to David Mamet* (Cambridge: Cambridge University Press, 2004), p. 230.

13. Hersh Zeifman, 'Phallus in Wonderland: Machismo and Business in David Mamet's *American Buffalo* and *Glengarry Glen Ross*', in Kane (1992), p. 124.

14. Jason Berger and Cornelius B. Pratt, 'Teaching Business-Communication Ethics with Controversial Films', *Journal of Business Ethics* 17.16 (1998), p. 1821.

15. Eugene Garaventa, 'Drama: a Tool for Teaching Business Ethics', *Business Ethics Quarterly* 8.3 (1998), pp. 535–45.

16. Tony J. Stafford, 'Visions of a Promised Land: David Mamet's *Glengarry Glen Ross*', in Kane (1996), pp. 191–2.

17. Leslie Kane, *Weasels and Wisemen: Ethics and Ethnicity in the Work of David Mamet* (New York: St Martin's, 1999), pp. 57–102.

18. Deborah R. Geis, ' "You're Exploiting My Space": Ethnicity, Spectatorship, and the (Post)Colonial Condition in Mukherjee's "A Wife's Story" and Mamet's *Glengarry Glen Ross*', in Kane (1996), p. 127.

19. Zeifman (1992), p. 132.

20. Carla J. McDonough, *Staging Masculinity: Male Identity in Contemporary American Drama* (Jefferson, NC: McFarland, 1997), p. 98.

21. Robert Vorlicky, *Act Like a Man: Challenging Masculinities in American Drama* (Ann Arbor: University of Michigan Press, 1995), p. 82.

22. Vorlicky (1995), p. 85.

23. Vorlicky (1995), p. 93.

24. Jeanne-Andrée Nelson, 'So Close to Closure: the Selling of Desire in *Glengarry Glen Ross*', *Essays in Theatre* 14.2 (1996), p. 113.

25. Nelson (1996), p. 110.

26. Jeanette R. Malkin, *Verbal Violence in Contemporary Drama* (Cambridge: Cambridge University Press, 1992), pp. 159–60.

27. David Worster, 'How to Do Things with Salesmen: David Mamet's Speech–Act Play', *Modern Drama* 37 (1994), pp. 375–90.

28. Barry Goldensohn, 'David Mamet and Poetic Language in Drama', *Agni* 49 (1999), pp. 139–49.

29. Jonathan S. Cullick, ' "Always Be Closing": Competition and the Discourse of Closure in David Mamet's *Glengarry Glen Ross*', *Journal of Dramatic Theory and Criticism* 8.2 (1994), pp. 23–36.

30. Philip C. Kolin, 'Mitch and Murray in David Mamet's *Glengarry Glen Ross*', *Notes on Contemporary Literature* 18.2 (1998), p. 3.

31. Karen Blansfield, 'Women on the Verge, Unite!', in Christopher C. Hudgins and Leslie Kane (eds), *Gender and Genre: Essays on David Mamet* (New York: Palgrave, 2001), pp. 125–42.

32. Dorothy H. Jacobs, 'Levene's Daughter: Positioning of the Female in *Glengarry Glen Ross*', in Kane (1996), p. 115.

33. Robert I. Lublin, 'Differing Dramatic Dynamics in the Stage and Screen Versions of *Glengarry Glen Ross*', *American Drama* 10.1 (2001), p. 46.

34. Christopher C. Hudgins, ' "By Indirections Find Directions Out": Uninflected Cuts, Narrative Structure, and Thematic Statement in the Film Version of *Glengarry Glen Ross*', in Kane (1996), p. 31.

35. Hudgins (1996), p. 41.

CHAPTER EIGHT: *PRAIRIE DU CHIEN* (1978), THE SHAWL (1985)

1. Dennis Carroll, *David Mamet* (Basingstoke: Macmillan, 1987), p. 128.
2. Deborah R. Geis, *Postmodern Theatric(k)s: Monologue in Contemporary American Drama* (Ann Arbor: University of Michigan Press, 1993), p. 109.
3. Ilkka Joki, *Mamet, Bakhtin, and the Dramatic: The Demotic as a Variable of Addressivity* (Åbo, Finland: Åbo Akademi University Press, 1993), pp. 132–5.
4. Philip C. Kolin, 'Revealing Illusions in David Mamet's *The Shawl*', *Notes on Contemporary Literature* 16 (March 1986), pp. 9–10.
5. Henry I. Schvey, 'The Plays of David Mamet: Games of Manipulation and Power', *New Theatre Quarterly* 14.3 (1988), p. 78.
6. Carroll (1987), pp. 113–14.
7. C. W. E. Bigsby, *Modern American Drama, 1945–1990* (Cambridge: Cambridge University Press, 1992), p. 203.
8. Carroll (1987), p. 115.
9. Geis (1993), p. 111.
10. Geis (1993), p. 90.
11. Geis (1993), p. 65.
12. Bruce Barton, *Imagination in Transition: Mamet's Move to Film* (Brussels: Peter Lang, 2005), p. 115.
13. Barton (2005), p. 119.

CHAPTER NINE: *HOUSE OF GAMES* (1987)

1. William F. Van Wert, 'Psychoanalysis and Con Games: *House of Games*', *Film Quarterly* 43:4 (1990), p. 8.
2. Van Wert (1990), p. 2.
3. Richard Combs, 'Framing Mamet', *Sight and Sound* 1:7 (1991), p. 17.
4. Van Wert (1990), p. 10.
5. 'Controversy and Correspondence', *Film Quarterly* 44.3 (1991), pp. 61–3.
6. Ann C. Hall, 'Playing to Win: Sexual Politics in David Mamet's *House of Games* and *Speed-the-Plow*', in Leslie Kane (ed.), *David Mamet: A Casebook* (York: Garland, 1992), p. 139.
7. Hall (1992), p. 144.
8. Hall (1992), pp. 148–9.
9. Diane M. Borden, 'Man without a Gun: Mamet, Masculinity, and Mystification', in Christopher C. Hudgins and Leslie Kane (eds), *Gender and Genre: Essays on David Mamet* (New York: Palgrave, 2001), p. 236.
10. Borden (2001), p. 251.
11. Bruce Barton, *Imagination in Transition: Mamet's Move to Film* (Brussels: Peter Lang, 2005), p. 144.
12. Barton (2005), pp. 153–4.
13. Barton (2005), p. 150.
14. Barton (2005), pp. 172–3.
15. Barton (2005), p. 144.
16. Laura Kipnis, 'One Born Every Minute', *Jump Cut* 36 (1991), p. 26.
17. Kipnis (1991), p. 29.
18. Marina deBellagente LaPalma, 'Driving Doctor Ford', *Literature/Film Quarterly* 24 (1996), p. 58.
19. Kipnis (1991), p. 27.
20. Kipnis (1991), p. 31.
21. LaPalma (1996), pp. 59, 62.
22. Kipnis (1991), p. 27.
23. LaPalma (1996), pp. 60–2.

24. Kipnis (1991), p. 25.

25. LaPalma (1996), p. 60.

26. LaPalma (1996), p. 58.

27. Kipnis (1991), p. 31.

28. Michael L. Quinn, 'Anti-Theatricality and American Ideology: Mamet's Performative Realism', in William W. Demastes (ed.), *Realism and the American Dramatic Tradition* (Tuscaloosa: University of Alabama Press, 1996), p. 243.

29. Elizabeth Klaver, 'David Mamet's *House of Games* and the Allegory of Performance', in Leslie Kane (ed.), *The Art of Crime: The Plays and Films of David Mamet and Harold Pinter* (New York: Routledge, 2004), p. 186.

30. Steven Price, 'Disguise in Love: Gender and Desire in *House of Games* and *Speed-the-Plow*', in Hudgins and Kane (2001), pp. 41–59.

31. Roger Ebert, 'House of Games', *Chicago Sun-Times*, 31 October 1999.

CHAPTER TEN: *SPEED-THE-PLOW* (1988)

1. Tony J. Stafford, '*Speed-the-Plow* and *Speed the Plough*: the Work of the Earth', *Modern Drama* 36 (1993), pp. 38–9.

2. Leslie Kane, *Weasels and Wisemen: Ethics and Ethnicity in the Work of David Mamet* (New York: St Martin's, 1999), p. 130.

3. Kane (1999), p. 119.

4. Kane (1999), p. 139.

5. Ruby Cohn, 'How Are Things Made Round?', in Leslie Kane (ed.), *David Mamet: A Casebook* (New York: Garland, 1992), p. 119.

6. Cohn (1992), p. 112.

7. In Ross Wetzsteon, 'David Mamet: Remember That Name', *Village Voice* (5 July 1976), pp. 101–3.

8. Cohn (1992), pp. 110–11.

9. Cohn (1992), pp. 116–17.

10. Toby Silverman Zinman, 'Jewish Aporia: the Rhythm of Talking in Mamet', *Theatre Journal* 44 (1992), pp. 207–15.

11. Christopher C. Hudgins, 'Comedy and Humor in the Plays of David Mamet', in Kane (1992), pp. 224–5.

12. David Radavich, 'Man among Men: David Mamet's Homosocial Order', *American Drama* 1.1 (1991), pp. 56–7.

13. Quoted in Carla J. McDonough, *Staging Masculinity: Male Identity in Contemporary American Drama* (Jefferson, NC: McFarland, 1997), p. 94.

14. Marcia Blumberg, 'Staging Hollywood, Selling Out', in Kimball King (ed.), *Hollywood on Stage: Playwrights Evaluate the Culture Industry* (New York: Garland, 1997), p. 73.

15. Blumberg (1997), p. 74.

16. Katherine H. Burkman, 'The Myth of Narcissus: Shepard's *True West* and Mamet's *Speed-the-Plow*', in King (1997), p. 117.

17. Burkman (1997), p. 120.

18. Jeanne-Andrée Nelson, '*Speed-the-Plow* or Seed the Plot? Mamet and the Female Reader', *Essays in Theatre* 10.1 (1991), p. 74.

19. David Mamet, 'The Bridge', *Granta* 16 (1985), pp. 167–73.

20. Janet V. Haedicke, 'Plowing the Buffalo, Fucking the Fruits: (M)others in *American Buffalo* and *Speed-the-Plow*', in Christopher C. Hudgins and Leslie Kane (eds), *Gender and Genre: Essays on David Mamet* (New York: Palgrave, 2001), pp. 27–8.

21. Haedicke (2001), pp. 34–6.

22. Ann C. Hall, 'Playing to Win: Sexual Politics in David Mamet's *House of Games* and *Speed-the-Plow*', in Kane (1992), p. 139.

23. Steven Price, 'Disguise in Love: Gender and Desire in *House of Games* and *Speed-the-Plow*', in Hudgins and Kane (2001), pp. 41–59.

24. Hall (1992), p. 157.

25. Nelson (1991), pp. 80, 77.

CHAPTER ELEVEN: *THINGS CHANGE* (1988)

1. In Minty Cinch, 'Mamet Plots His Revenge', *Observer*, magazine section (22 January 1989), p. 49.

2. Dennis Carroll, 'The Recent Mamet Films: "Business" versus Communion', in Leslie Kane (ed.), *David Mamet: A Casebook* (New York: Garland, 1992), p. 184.

3. Linda Dorff, 'Things (Ex)change: The Value of Money in David Mamet's *Glengarry Glen Ross*', in Leslie Kane (ed.), *David Mamet's* Glengarry Glen Ross: *Text and Performance* (New York: Garland, 1996), p. 197.

4. Gay Brewer, *David Mamet and Film: Illusion/Disillusion in a Wounded Land* (Jefferson, NC: McFarland, 1993), p. 75.

5. Brewer (1993), p. 89.

6. Brewer (1993), p. 76.

7. Philip French, 'David Mamet and Film', in Christopher Bigsby (ed.), *The Cambridge Companion to David Mamet* (Cambridge: Cambridge University Press, 2004), p. 186.

8. Brewer (1993), p. 65.

9. Leslie Kane, *Weasels and Wisemen: Ethics and Ethnicity in the Work of David Mamet* (New York: St Martin's, 1999), p. 266.

10. Kane (1999), p. 268.

11. Kane (1999), p. 264.

12. Brewer (1993), p. 67.

13. Bruce Barton, *Imagination in Transition: Mamet's Move to Film* (Brussels: Peter Lang, 2005), p. 177.

14. Barton (2005), p. 18.

15. Jonathan Rosenbaum, 'Mamet & Hitchcock: the Men Who Knew Too Much', *Scenario* 4.1 (1999), p. 153.

CHAPTER TWELVE: THE 'BOBBY GOULD' PLAYS (c.1989)

1. Toby Silverman Zinman, 'So dis is Hollywood: Mamet in Hell', in Kimball King (ed.), *Hollywood on Stage: Playwrights Evaluate the Culture Industry* (New York: Garland, 1997), pp. 103–5.

2. Zinman (1997), p. 111.

3. Leslie Kane, *Weasels and Wisemen: Ethics and Ethnicity in the Work of David Mamet* (New York: St Martin's, 1999), pp. 227–59, esp. 227.

4. Jeanne-Andrée Nelson, 'A Machine out of Order: Indifferentiation in David Mamet's *The Disappearance of the Jews*', *Journal of American Studies* 25 (1991), p. 467.

5. Toby Silverman Zinman, 'Jewish Aporia: the Rhythm of Talking in Mamet', *Theatre Journal* 44 (1992), p. 212.

6. C. W. E. Bigsby, *David Mamet* (London: Methuen, 1985), p. 41.

7. Kane (1999), p. 232.

8. Kane (1999), p. 235.

9. Kane (1999), p. 237.

10. Zinman (1992), p. 209.

11. Zinman (1992), p. 213.

12. Kane (1999), p. 255.

13. Deborah R. Geis, *Postmodern Theatric(k)s: Monologue in Contemporary American Drama* (Ann Arbor: University of Michigan Press, 1993), p. 115.

14. David Skeele, 'The Devil and David Mamet: *Sexual Perversity in Chicago* as Homiletic Tragedy', *Modern Drama* 36 (1993), pp. 512–18.

15. Kane (1999), p. 229.

16. Leslie Kane, ' "It's the way that you are with your children": The Matriarchal Figure in Mamet's Late Work', in Christopher C. Hudgins and Leslie Kane (eds), *Gender and Genre: Essays on David Mamet* (New York: Palgrave, 2001), p. 160.

17. Kane (1999), pp. 253–4.

18. Howard Pearce, 'David Mamet's *Old Neighborhood*: Journey and Geography', *American Drama* 14.1 (2005), p. 54.

19. Pearce (2005), p. 58; Zinman (1997), p. 108.

CHAPTER THIRTEEN: *HOMICIDE* (1991)

1. Rogers and Cowan International, press information on David Mamet's *Homicide*, 11 October 1991.

2. John Lahr, 'Fortress Mamet', *New Yorker* (17 November 1997), pp. 70–82.

3. J. Hoberman, 'Rootless', *Village Voice* (15 October 1991), p. 61. A slightly different version of the same piece appeared as 'Identity Parade', *Sight and Sound* 1.7 (1991), pp. 14–16.

4. Philip Hanson, 'Against Tribalism: the Perils of Ethnic Identity in Mamet's *Homicide*', *CLIO* 31.3 (2002), pp. 257–8.

5. Alain Piette, 'Canon with a Vengeance? The (Re)-Affirmation of David Mamet's Ethnicity', in Christophe den Tandt (ed.), *Reading without Maps? Cultural Landmarks in a Post-Canonical Age* (Brussels: Peter Lang, 2005), p. 198.

6. Warren Rosenberg, *Legacy of Rage: Jewish Masculinity, Violence, and Culture* (Amherst: University of Massachusetts Press, 2001), p. 209; quoted in Piette (2005), p. 199.

7. Piette (2005), p. 200.

8. Toby Silverman Zinman, 'Jewish Aporia: the Rhythm of Talking in Mamet', *Theatre Journal* 44 (1992), p. 212.

9. Joel Streicker, 'How at Home? American Jewish (Male) Identities in Mamet's *Homicide*', *Shofar* 12.3 (1994), pp. 46–7.

10. Ranen Omer, 'The Metaphysics of Lost Jewish Identity in Mamet's *Homicide*', *Yiddish/Modern Jewish Studies* 11.3–4 (1999), p. 43.

11. Streicker (1994), p. 65.

12. Omer (1999), p. 42.

13. Hanson (2002), p. 265.

14. Adam Zachary Newton, *Facing Black and Jew: Literature as Public Space in Twentieth-Century America* (Cambridge: Cambridge University Press, 1999), p. 150.

15. Hanson (2002), p. 263.

16. Hanson (2002), p. 269.

17. Hanson (2002), p. 275.

18. Leslie Kane, *Weasels and Wisemen: Ethics and Ethnicity in the Work of David Mamet* (New York: St Martin's, 1999), p. 287.

19. Richard Combs, 'Framing Mamet', *Sight and Sound* 1:7 (1991), p. 17.

20. Alain Piette, 'Canon with a Vengeance? The (Re)-Affirmation of David Mamet's Ethnicity', in Christophe den Tandt (ed.), *Reading without Maps? Cultural Landmarks in a Post-Canonical Age* (Brussels: Peter Lang, 2005), p. 196.

21. Omer (1999), p. 49.

22. William Van Wert, 'Conspiracy Theory in Mamet', *Western Humanities Review* 49:2 (1995), pp. 140–1.

23. Van Wert (1995), p. 137.

24. Newton (1999), p. 144.
25. Newton (1999), p. 148.
26. Newton (1999), p. 150.
27. Zinman (1992), p. 210.
28. Omer (1999), pp. 46–9.
29. Kane (1999), p. 284.
30. Kane (1999), p. 294.
31. Laurence Roth, *Inspecting Jews: American Jewish Detective Stories* (New Brunswick, NJ: Rutgers University Press, 2004), pp. 193–4.
32. Roth (2004), p. 196.
33. Bruce Barton, *Imagination in Transition: Mamet's Move to Film* (Brussels: Peter Lang, 2005), p. 180.
34. Barton (2005), pp. 190–1.
35. Piette (2005), p. 194.

CHAPTER FOURTEEN: *OLEANNA* (1992)

1. Richard Badenhausen, 'The Modern Academy Raging in the Dark: Misreading Mamet's Political Incorrectness in *Oleanna*', *College Literature* 25.3 (1998), p. 11.
2. Carla J. McDonough, *Staging Masculinity: Male Identity in Contemporary American Drama* (Jefferson, NC: McFarland, 1997), p. 95.
3. Badenhausen (1998), p. 3.
4. Katherine H. Burkman, 'Misogyny and Misanthropy: Anita Hill and David Mamet', in Ann C. Hall (ed.), *Delights, Desires, and Dilemmas: Essays on Women and the Media* (Westport, CT: Praeger, 1998), pp. 117, 120.
5. Harry J. Elam, Jr, ' "Only in America": Contemporary American Theater and the Power of Performance', in Marc Maufort and Jean-Pierre van Noppen (eds), *Voices of Power: Co-operation and Conflict in English Language and Literatures* (Liège: English Department, University of Liège, 1997), p. 161.
6. Sandra Tomc, 'David Mamet's *Oleanna* and the Way of All Flesh', *Essays in Theatre* 15.2 (1997), p. 173.
7. Tomc (1997), pp. 166–7.
8. Tomc (1997), pp. 171–3.
9. Thomas E. Porter, 'Postmodernism and Violence in Mamet's *Oleanna*', *Modern Drama* 43 (2000), pp. 13–31.
10. David Sauer, '*Oleanna* and *The Children's Hour*: Misreading Sexuality on the Post/Modern Realistic Stage', *Modern Drama* 43 (2000), p. 436.
11. Sauer (2000), p. 429.
12. Thomas H. Goggans, 'Laying Blame: Gender and Subtext in David Mamet's *Oleanna*', *Modern Drama* 40 (1997), p. 436.
13. Goggans (1997), pp. 438–9.
14. Leslie Kane, *Weasels and Wisemen: Ethics and Ethnicity in the Work of David Mamet* (New York: St Martin's, 1999), p. 142.
15. Kane (1999), p. 172.
16. Kane (1999), p. 145.
17. Kane (1999), p. 147.
18. Roger Bechtel, 'PC Power Play: Language and Representation in David Mamet's *Oleanna*', *Theatre Studies* 41 (1996), p. 47. Similar arguments are advanced in Alain Piette, 'The Devil's Advocate: David Mamet's *Oleanna* and Political Correctness', in Marc Maufort (ed.), *Staging Difference: Cultural Pluralism in American Theatre and Drama* (New York: Peter Lang, 1995), pp. 173–87.
19. Burkman (1998), p. 118.
20. Porter (2000), p. 14.

21. Marc Silverstein, ' "We're Just Human": *Oleanna* and Cultural Crisis', *South Atlantic Review* 60.2 (1995), p. 115.

22. Silverstein (1995), p. 118.

23. Stanton B. Garner, Jr, 'Framing the Classroom: Pedagogy, Power, *Oleanna*', *Theatre Topics* 10.1 (2000), pp. 39–52; Richard C. Raymond, 'Rhetoricizing English Studies: Students' Ways of Reading *Oleanna*', *Pedagogy* 3.1 (2003), pp. 53–71.

24. David Mamet, *Oleanna* (London: Methuen, 1993), p. 80.

25. Ira Nadel, 'The Playwright as Director: Pinter's *Oleanna*', *The Pinter Review: Collected Essays 2001 and 2002* (Tampa, FL: University of Tampa Press, 2002), pp. 121–8.

26. Burkman (1998), pp. 113, 119.

27. Burkman (1998), pp. 114–15.

28. Burkman (1998), pp. 120, 114.

29. Katherine H. Burkman, 'The Web of Misogyny in Mamet's and Pinter's Betrayal Games', in Katherine H. Burkman and Judith Roof (eds), *Staging the Rage: The Web of Misogyny in Modern Drama* (Cranbury: Fairleigh Dickinson University Press, 1998), p. 35.

30. McDonough (1997), p. 96.

31. McDonough (1997), p. 98.

32. Kellie Bean, 'A Few Good Men: Collusion and Violence in *Oleanna*', in Christopher C. Hudgins and Leslie Kane (eds), *Gender and Genre: Essays on David Mamet* (New York: Palgrave, 2001), p. 109.

33. Bean (2001), p. 115.

34. Bean (2001), p. 122.

35. Bean (2001), p. 123.

36. Elaine Showalter, 'Acts of Violence: David Mamet and the Language of Men', *Times Literary Supplement* (6 November 1992), p. 17.

37. Robert Skloot, '*Oleanna*, or the Play of Pedagogy', in Hudgins and Kane (2001), pp. 95–109.

38. Badenhausen (1998), p. 14.

39. Verna Foster, 'Sex, Power, and Pedagogy in Mamet's *Oleanna* and Ionesco's *The Lesson*', *American Drama* 5.1 (1995), pp. 41–2.

40. Badenhausen (1998), p. 7.

41. Michael Mangan, ' "Appalling Teachers": Masculine Authority in the Classroom in *Educating Rita* and *Oleanna*', in Daniel Meyer-Dinkgräfe (ed.), *The Professions in Contemporary Drama* (Bristol: Intellect 2003), pp. 19–36.

42. Badenhausen (1998), p. 10.

43. Jean Jacques Weber, 'Three Models of Power in David Mamet's *Oleanna*', in Jonathan Culpepper, Mick Short and Peter Verdonk (eds), *Exploring the Language of Drama: From Text to Context* (London: Routledge, 1998), pp. 112–27.

44. Steven Ryan, '*Oleanna*: David Mamet's Power Play', *Modern Drama* 39.3 (1996), pp. 392–403.

45. Foster (1995), p. 43.

46. Craig Stewart Walker, 'Three Tutorial Plays: *The Lesson*, *The Prince of Naples*, and *Oleanna*', *Modern Drama* 40 (1997), pp. 158–9.

47. Christine MacLeod, 'The Politics of Gender, Language and Hierarchy in David Mamet's *Oleanna*', *Journal of American Studies* 29.2 (1995), p. 204.

48. MacLeod (1995), p. 202.

49. MacLeod (1995), pp. 210–11.

50. MacLeod (1995), p. 206.

51. MacLeod (1995), p. 213.

52. Kenneth Womack, *Postwar Academic Fiction* (Basingstoke: Palgrave, 2002), pp. 107–8.

53. David Mamet, *Oleanna*, with commentary and notes by Daniel Rosenthal (London: Methuen, 2004).

CHAPTER FIFTEEN: *THE CRYPTOGRAM* (1994)

1. Leslie Kane, '"It's the way that you are with your children": the Matriarchal Figure in Mamet's Late Work', in Christopher C. Hudgins and Leslie Kane (eds), *Gender and Genre: Essays on David Mamet* (New York: Palgrave, 2001), pp. 148–9.

2. Kane (2001), p. 145.

3. Leslie Kane, *Weasels and Wisemen: Ethics and Ethnicity in the Work of David Mamet* (New York: St Martin's, 1999), p. 190.

4. Kane (1999), p. 199.

5. Kane (1999), p. 195.

6. Kane (1999), p. 224.

7. Kane (2001), p. 157.

8. Martin Schaub, 'Magic Meanings in Mamet's Cryptogram', *Modern Drama* 42 (1999), p. 328.

9. Schaub (1999), pp. 331–4.

10. Janet V. Haedicke, 'Decoding Cipher Space: David Mamet's *The Cryptogram* and America's Dramatic Legacy', *American Drama* 9.1 (1999), p. 2.

11. Haedicke (1999), p. 9.

12. Haedicke (1999), p. 16.

13. Howard Pearce, '"Loving Wrong" in the Worlds of Harold Pinter's *Moonlight* and David Mamet's *Cryptogram*', *Journal of Dramatic Theory and Criticism* 15.1 (2000), p. 74.

14. Thomas P. Adler, 'More Uses of the Knife as Signifier in *The Cryptogram, The Old Religion,* and *The Edge*', in Leslie Kane (ed.), *The Art of Crime: The Plays and Films of David Mamet and Harold Pinter* (New York: Routledge, 2004), pp. 189–202.

15. Linda Dorff, 'Reinscribing the "Fairy": The Knife and the Mystification of Male Mythology in *The Cryptogram*', in Hudgins and Kane (2001), p. 177.

16. C. Gerald Fraser, 'Mamet's Plays Shed Masculinity Myth', *New York Times* (5 July 1976), sec. 1, p. 7.

17. Dorff (2001), pp. 176–9.

18. Dorff (2001), p. 188.

CHAPTER SIXTEEN: *THE SPANISH PRISONER* (1997), *THE EDGE* (1997),
WAG THE DOG (1997)

1. Jonathan Rosenbaum, 'Mamet & Hitchcock: the Men Who Knew Too Much', *Scenario* 4.1 (1999), p. 179.

2. Mike Digou, 'Hitchcock's MacGuffin in the Works of David Mamet', *Literature/Film Quarterly* 31.4 (2003), pp. 270–5.

3. Leslie Kane, 'Suckered Again: The Perfect Patsy and *The Spanish Prisoner*', in Leslie Kane (ed.), *The Art of Crime: The Plays and Films of David Mamet and Harold Pinter* (New York: Routledge, 2004), p. 219.

4. Jeffrey O. McIntire-Strasburg, 'Performing Pedagogy: Teaching and Confidence Games in David Mamet's *House of Games* and *The Spanish Prisoner*', *Journal of the Midwest Modern Language Association* 38.1 (2005), pp. 31–7.

5. Miriam Hardin, 'Lessons from the Lesson: Four Post-Ionescan Education Plays', *CEA Magazine* 12 (1999), pp. 30–46; Robert Skloot, '*Oleanna*, or the Play of Pedagogy', in Christopher C. Hudgins and Leslie Kane (eds), *Gender and Genre: Essays on David Mamet* (New York: Palgrave, 2001), pp. 95–109.

6. Todd F. Davis and Kenneth Womack, 'David Mamet's Altered Ethics: Finding Forgiveness, or Something Like It, in *House of Games, The Spanish Prisoner,* and *State and Main*', in Anna Fahraeus and AnnKatrin Jonsson (eds), *Textual Ethos Studies or Locating Ethics* (New York: Rodopi, 2005), pp. 283–4.

7. Davis and Womack (2005), pp. 292–3.

8. Davis and Womack (2005), p. 287.

9. Davis and Womack (2005), p. 288.

10. Temenuga Trifonova, 'Time and Point of View in Contemporary Cinema', *Cineaction* 58 (2003), p. 22.

11. Trifonova (2003), p. 13.

12. Claire Magaha, 'A Theater of the Self: Mamet's *The Edge* as a *Figura* of Otherness', in Kane (2004), pp. 203–5.

13. Leslie Kane, *Weasels and Wisemen: Ethics and Ethnicity in the Work of David Mamet* (New York: St Martin's, 1999), p. 296.

14. Kane (1999), p. 306.

15. Thomas P. Adler, 'More Uses of the Knife as Signifier in *The Cryptogram, The Old Religion*, and *The Edge*', in Kane (2004), p. 200.

16. Adler (2004), p. 201.

17. Kane (1999), p. 305.

18. Magaha (2004), p. 216.

19. Art Linson, *What Just Happened? Bitter Hollywood Tales from the Front Line* (London: Bloomsbury, 2002), p. 26.

20. Linson (2002), p. 32.

21. Michele Ronnick, 'David Mamet at Play: Paronomasia, the Berlin Soldier Conrad Schumann (1942–1998) and *Wag the Dog'*, *Germanic Notes and Reviews* 33.1 (2002), p. 28.

22. Tom Stempel, 'The Collaborative Dog: *Wag the Dog* (1997)', *Film and History* 35.1 (2005), pp. 60–4.

23. Mary Johnson, 'Deconstructing the Dog', *Creative Screenwriting* 5.3 (1998), pp. 20–3.

CHAPTER SEVENTEEN: *THE WINSLOW BOY* (1999) AND AFTER: *STATE AND MAIN* (2000), *HEIST* (2001), *SPARTAN* (2004), *BOSTON MARRIAGE* (1999)

1. Irene Morra, 'Performing the Edwardian Ideal: David Mamet and *The Winslow Boy'*, *Modern Drama* 48 (2005), p. 745.

2. Morra (2005), p. 753.

3. Ira Nadel, 'Lie Detectors: Pinter/Mamet and the Victorian Concept of Crime', in Leslie Kane (ed.), *The Art of Crime: The Plays and Films of David Mamet and Harold Pinter* (New York: Routledge, 2004), p. 132.

4. Nadel (2004), p. 131.

5. Yannis Tzioumakis, 'Marketing David Mamet: Institutionally Assigned Film Authorship in Contemporary American Cinema', *Velvet Light Trap* 57 (2006), p. 61.

6. Tzioumakis (2006), pp. 70–1.

7. Maurice Charney, 'Parody and Self-Parody in David Mamet', *Connotations* 13.1–2 (2003), p. 82.

8. Morra (2005), p. 748.

9. Morra (2005), p. 748.

10. Charney (2003), p. 84.

11. Janet V. Haedicke, 'David Mamet: an American on the American Stage', in David Krasner (ed.), *A Companion to Twentieth-Century American Drama* (Oxford: Blackwell, 2005), p. 420.

12. Christopher Bigsby, 'David Mamet's Fiction', in Christopher Bigsby (ed.), *The Cambridge Companion to David Mamet* (Cambridge: Cambridge University Press, 2004), p. 217.

13. Charney (2003), p. 87.

CONCLUSION

1. Ilkka Joki, *Mamet, Bakhtin, and the Dramatic: The Demotic as a Variable of Addressivity* (Åbo, Finland: Åbo Akademi University Press, 1993), p. 3.

2. Thomas P. Adler, 'More Uses of the Knife as Signifier in *The Cryptogram, The Old Religion*, and *The Edge*', in Leslie Kane (ed.), *The Art of Crime: The Plays and Films of David Mamet and Harold Pinter* (New York: Routledge, 2004), p. 190.

3. Ilkka Joki, 'Mamet's Novelistic Voice', in Christopher C. Hudgins and Leslie Kane (eds), *Gender and Genre: Essays on David Mamet* (New York: Palgrave, 2001), pp. 191–208.

4. Joki (1993), pp. 140–53.

5. Steven Ryan, 'David Mamet's *A Wasted Weekend*', *American Drama* 10.1 (2001), pp. 56–65.

6. Franz Wieselhuber, 'Mamet and Television', in Christiane Schlote and Peter Zenzinger (eds), *New Beginnings in Twentieth-Century Theatre and Drama* (Trier: Wissenschaftlicher, 2003), p. 463.

7. Warren Rosenberg, *Legacy of Rage: Jewish Masculinity, Violence, and Culture* (Amherst: University of Massachusetts Press, 2001), p. 233.

8. Donald Weber, 'David Mamet's Jewish Turn', *Chronicle of Higher Education*, 3 November 2006.

9. Rosenberg (2001), p. 246.

10. Matthew C. Roudané, 'Mamet's Mimetics', in Leslie Kane (ed.), *David Mamet: A Casebook* (New York: Garland, 1992), p. 25.

11. Roudané (1992), p. 23.

12. Roudané (1992), p. 27.

13. Michael L. Quinn, 'Anti-Theatricality and American Ideology: Mamet's Performative Realism', in William W. Demastes (ed.), *Realism and the American Dramatic Tradition* (Tuscaloosa: University of Alabama Press, 1996), pp. 236–8.

14. Quinn (1996), p. 252.

15. David Mamet, *A Whore's Profession: Notes and Essays* (London: Faber, 1994), p. 164.

16. David Mamet, 'Why I Am No Longer a "Brian-Dead Liberal"', *Village Voice* 11 March 2008.

Select Bibliography

An exhaustive bibliography of Mamet's works is beyond the scope of this Guide. Here I have included only published material (several screenplays and stage plays remain unpublished), and omitted some minor published plays and short stories not referred to elsewhere in this study. The book-length collections of Mamet's essays are quite comprehensive, but Leslie Kane's *David Mamet in Conversation* necessarily contains only a representative selection of the most important interviews. The section on criticism below is restricted to material considered in this guide. For further reading in all areas save film, see Sauer and Sauer (2003); the bibliography in Kane's *Weasels and Wisemen* (1999) is also exceptionally thorough.

WORKS BY DAVID MAMET

Plays
Editions cited are for first UK publication except when the first US edition is significantly earlier.

Sexual Perversity in Chicago and *The Duck Variations* (New York: Samuel French, 1977).
American Buffalo (New York: Grove, 1977).
A Life in the Theatre (New York: Grove, 1977).
The Revenge of the Space Pandas; or, Binky Rudich and the Two-Speed Clock (Chicago: Dramatic Publishing Company, 1978).
The Water Engine: An American Fable, and *Mr. Happiness* (New York: Grove, 1978).
The Woods (New York: Grove, 1979).
Reunion and *Dark Pony* (New York: Grove, 1979).
Lakeboat (New York: Grove, 1981).
The Poet and the Rent (New York: Samuel French, 1981).
Prairie du Chien, in *Short Plays and Monologues* (New York: Dramatists Play Service, 1981), pp. 21–38.
Squirrels (New York: Samuel French, 1982).
Edmond (New York: Grove, 1983).
The Frog Prince (New York: Samuel French, 1983).
Glengarry Glen Ross (London: Methuen, 1984).
The Shawl (New York: Samuel French, 1985).
Three Jewish Plays [*The Disappearance of the Jews*, *Goldberg Street* and *The Luftmensch*] (New York: Samuel French, 1987).
Speed-the-Plow (London: Methuen, 1988).
Bobby Gould in Hell, in *Oh, Hell!: Two One-Act Plays* (New York: Samuel French, 1991).
Oleanna (London: Methuen, 1993).
The Cryptogram (London: Methuen, 1995).
The Old Neighborhood (London: Methuen, 1998).
Boston Marriage (London: Methuen, 2001).
Faustus (New York: Vintage, 2004).
Romance (London: Methuen, 2005).
The Voysey Inheritance (New York: Vintage, 2005).

Many of Mamet's plays have been reissued in the UK by Methuen in four collections:

Plays: 1 (1994) [*The Duck Variations, Sexual Perversity in Chicago, Squirrels, American Buffalo, The Water Engine, Mr. Happiness*]
Plays: 2 (1996) [*Reunion, Dark Pony, A Life in the Theatre, The Woods, Lakeboat, Edmond*]
Plays: 3 (1996) [*Glengarry Glen Ross, Prairie du Chien, The Shawl, Speed-the-Plow*]
Plays: 4 (2002) [*Oleanna, The Cryptogram, The Old Neighborhood*]

Screenplays and teleplays
House of Games (London: Methuen, 1987).
Things Change (New York: Grove, 1988).
Five Television Plays (New York: Grove, 1990).
Homicide (New York: Grove, 1992).
The Spanish Prisoner and *The Winslow Boy* (London: Faber, 1999).

Films directed by David Mamet
House of Games (1987).
Things Change (1988).
Homicide (1991).
Oleanna (1994).
The Spanish Prisoner (1997).
The Winslow Boy (1999).
State and Main (2000).
Heist (2001).
Spartan (2004).
Redbelt (2008).

For television, Mamet has also directed a version of Samuel Beckett's short play *Catastrophe* (1999), and episodes of the television series *The Shield* (2004) and *The Unit* (2006–present).

Fiction
'The Bridge', *Granta* 16 (1985), pp. 167–73.
The Village (London: Faber, 1994).
The Old Religion (London: Faber, 1997).
Wilson: A Consideration of the Sources (London: Faber, 2000).

Non-fiction
Writing in Restaurants (New York: Viking Penguin, 1986).
Some Freaks (London: Faber, 1989).
The Cabin: Reminiscence and Diversions (New York: Turtle Bay, 1992).
On Directing Film (London: Faber, 1992).
A Whore's Profession: Notes and Essays (London: Faber, 1994). [Collects *Writing in Restaurants, Some Freaks, The Cabin* and *On Directing Film*]
Make-Believe Town: Essays and Reminiscences (London: Faber, 1996).
True and False: Heresy and Common Sense for the Actor (London: Faber, 1998).
Three Uses of the Knife: On the Nature and Purpose of Drama (New York: Columbia University Press, 1998).
Jafsie and John Henry: Essays on Hollywood, Bad Boys and Six Hours of Perfect Poker (London: Faber, 2000).

The Wicked Son: Anti-Semitism, Self-Hatred, and the Jews (New York: Schocken, 2006).
Bambi vs. Godzilla: On the Nature, Purpose, and Practice of the Movie Business (New York: Scribner, 2007).

Interviews
Kane, Leslie, *David Mamet in Conversation* (Ann Arbor: University of Michigan Press, 2001).

CRITICISM: BOOKS DEVOTED TO DAVID MAMET

Barton, Bruce, *Imagination in Transition: Mamet's Move to Film* (Brussels: Peter Lang, 2005).

Bigsby, C[hristopher]. W. E., *David Mamet* (London: Methuen, 1985).

Bigsby, Christopher (ed.), *The Cambridge Companion to David Mamet* (Cambridge: Cambridge University Press, 2004).

Brewer, Gay[lord], *David Mamet and Film: Illusion/Disillusion in a Wounded Land* (Jefferson, NC: McFarland, 1993).

Carroll, Dennis, *David Mamet* (Basingstoke: Macmillan, 1987).

Dean, Anne, *David Mamet: Language as Dramatic Action* (Rutherford, NJ: Fairleigh Dickinson University Press, 1990).

Hudgins, Christopher C., and Leslie Kane (eds), *Gender and Genre: Essays on David Mamet* (New York: Palgrave, 2001).

Joki, Ilkka, *Mamet, Bakhtin, and the Dramatic: The Demotic as a Variable of Addressivity* (Åbo, Finland: Åbo Akademi University Press, 1993).

Kane, Leslie (ed.), *David Mamet: A Casebook* (New York: Garland, 1992).

Kane, Leslie (ed.), *David Mamet's* Glengarry Glen Ross*: Text and Performance* (New York: Garland, 1996).

Kane, Leslie, *Weasels and Wisemen: Ethics and Ethnicity in the Work of David Mamet* (New York: St Martin's, 1999).

Kane, Leslie (ed.), *The Art of Crime: The Plays and Films of David Mamet and Harold Pinter* (New York: Routledge, 2004).

Sauer, David Kennedy, and Janice A. Sauer, *David Mamet: A Research and Production Sourcebook* (Westport, CT: Praeger, 2003).

CRITICISM: ESSAYS AND BOOK CHAPTERS ON DAVID MAMET
General

Adler, Thomas P., 'More Uses of the Knife as Signifier in *The Cryptogram, The Old Religion,* and *The Edge*', in Leslie Kane (ed.), *The Art of Crime: The Plays and Films of David Mamet and Harold Pinter* (New York: Routledge, 2004), pp. 189–202.

Almansi, Guido, 'David Mamet, a Virtuoso of Invective', in Marc Chénetier (ed.), *European Views of Contemporary American Literature* (Carbondale: Southern Illinois University Press, 1986), pp. 191–207.

Bigsby, C[hristopher]. W. E., *A Critical Introduction to Twentieth-Century American Drama*, vol. 3: *Beyond Broadway* (Cambridge: Cambridge University Press, 1985), pp. 251–90.

Bigsby, C[hristopher]. W. E., *Modern American Drama, 1945–1990* (Cambridge: Cambridge University Press, 1992), pp. 195–229.

Bigsby, C[hristopher]. W. E., 'David Mamet's Fiction', in Bigsby (2004), pp. 194–219.

Blansfield, Karen, 'Women on the Verge, Unite!', in Hudgins and Kane (2001), pp. 125–42.

Borden, Diane M., 'Man without a Gun: Mamet, Masculinity, and Mystification', in Hudgins and Kane (2001), pp. 235–54.

Brewer, Gaylord, '*Hoffa* and *The Untouchables*: Mamet's Brutal Orders of Authority', *Literature/Film Quarterly* 28.1 (2000), pp. 28–33.

Burkman, Katherine H., 'The Web of Misogyny in Mamet's and Pinter's Betrayal Games', in Katherine H. Burkman and Judith Roof (eds), *Staging the Rage: The Web of Misogyny in Modern Drama* (Cranbury, NJ: Fairleigh Dickinson University Press, 1998), pp. 27–37.

Carroll, Dennis, 'The Recent Mamet Films: "Business" versus Communion', in Kane (1992), pp. 175–89.

Cohn, Ruby, 'How Are Things Made Round?', in Kane (1992), pp. 109–21.

Davis, Todd F., and Kenneth Womack, 'David Mamet's Altered Ethics: Finding Forgiveness, or Something Like It, in *House of Games*, *The Spanish Prisoner*, and *State and Main*', in Anna Fahraeus and AnnKatrin Jonsson (eds), *Textual Ethos Studies or Locating Ethics* (New York: Rodopi, 2005), pp. 281–95.

Ditsky, John, ' "He Lets You See the Thought There": the Theatre of David Mamet', *Kansas Quarterly* 12.4 (1980), pp. 25–34.

Eder, Richard, 'David Mamet's New Realism', *New York Times* (12 March 1978), magazine section, pp. 40–7.

French, Philip, 'David Mamet and Film', in Bigsby (2004), pp. 171–93.

Gale, Steven H., 'David Mamet: The Plays, 1972–1980', in Hedwig Bock and Albert Wertheim (eds), *Essays on Contemporary American Drama* (Munich: Max Hueber Verlag, 1981), pp. 207–23.

Garner, Stanton B., Jr, *Bodied Spaces: Phenomenology and Performance in Contemporary Drama* (Ithaca, NY: Cornell University Press, 1994), pp. 128–30.

Geis, Deborah R., 'David Mamet and the Metadramatic Tradition': Seeing "the Trick from the Back" ', in Kane (1992), pp. 49–68.

Geis, Deborah R., *Postmodern Theatric(k)s: Monologue in Contemporary American Drama* (Ann Arbor: University of Michigan Press, 1993), pp. 89–115.

Goldensohn, Barry, 'David Mamet and Poetic Language in Drama', *Agni* 49 (1999), pp. 139–49.

Haedicke, Janet V., 'Plowing the Buffalo, Fucking the Fruits: (M)others in *American Buffalo* and *Speed-the-Plow*', in Hudgins and Kane (2001), pp. 27–40.

Haedicke, Janet V., 'David Mamet: an American on the American Stage', in David Krasner (ed.), *A Companion to Twentieth-Century American Drama* (Oxford: Blackwell, 2005), pp. 406–22.

Hall, Ann C., 'Playing to Win: Sexual Politics in David Mamet's *House of Games* and *Speed-the-Plow*', in Kane (1992), pp. 137–60.

Herman, William, 'Theatrical Diversity from Chicago: David Mamet', in *Understanding Contemporary American Drama* (Columbia: South Carolina University Press, 1987), pp. 125–60.

Hubert-Liebler, Pascale, 'Dominance and Anguish: the Teacher–Student Relationship in the Plays of David Mamet', *Modern Drama* 31 (1988), pp. 557–70.

Hudgins, Christopher C., 'Comedy and Humor in the Plays of David Mamet', in Kane (1992), pp. 191–228.

Kane, Leslie, "'It's the way that you are with your children": the Matriarchal Figure in Mamet's Late Work', in Hudgins and Kane (2001), pp. 143–73.

King, Kimball (ed.), *Hollywood on Stage: Playwrights Evaluate the Culture Industry* (New York: Garland, 1997).

Lahr, John, 'Fortress Mamet', *New Yorker* (17 November 1997), pp. 70–82.

McDonough, Carla J., *Staging Masculinity: Male Identity in Contemporary American Drama* (Jefferson, NC: McFarland, 1997), pp. 71–101.

McIntire-Strasburg, Jeffrey O., 'Performing Pedagogy: Teaching and Confidence Games in David Mamet's *House of Games* and *The Spanish Prisoner*', *Journal of the Midwest Modern Language Association* 38.1 (2005), pp. 31–7.

Malkin, Jeanette R., *Verbal Violence in Contemporary Drama* (Cambridge: Cambridge University Press, 1992), pp. 145–62.

Piette, Alain, 'Canon with a Vengeance? The (Re)-Affirmation of David Mamet's Ethnicity', in Christophe den Tandt (ed.), *Reading without Maps? Cultural Landmarks in a Post-Canonical Age* (Brussels: Peter Lang, 2005), pp. 193–201.

Price, Steven, 'A. T. & T.: Anxiety, Telecommunications and the Theatre of David Mamet', *Cycnos* 12.1 (1995), pp. 59–67.

Price, Steven, 'Disguise in Love: Gender and Desire in *House of Games* and *Speed-the-Plow*', in Hudgins and Kane (2001), pp. 41–59.

Quinn, Michael L., 'Anti-Theatricality and American Ideology: Mamet's Performative Realism', in William W. Demastes (ed.), *Realism and the American Dramatic Tradition* (Tuscaloosa: University of Alabama Press, 1996), pp. 235–54.

Radavich, David, 'Man among Men: David Mamet's Social Order', *American Drama* 1.1 (1991), pp. 46–60.

Rosenbaum, Jonathan, 'Mamet & Hitchcock: the Men Who Knew Too Much', *Scenario* 4.1 (1999), pp. 152–3, 179–80.

Rosenberg, Warren, *Legacy of Rage: Jewish Masculinity, Violence, and Culture* (Amherst: University of Massachusetts Press, 2001), pp. 233–46.

Roudané, Matthew C., 'Mamet's Mimetics', in Kane (1992), pp. 3–32.

Sauer, David Kennedy, and Janice A. Sauer, 'Misreading Mamet: Scholarship and Reviews', in Bigsby (2004), pp. 220–42.

Savran, David, 'New Realism: Mamet, Mann and Nelson', in Bruce King (ed.), *Contemporary American Theatre* (Basingstoke: Macmillan, 1991), pp. 63–79.

Schvey, Henry I., 'The Plays of David Mamet: Games of Manipulation and Power', *New Theatre Quarterly* 14.3 (1988), pp. 77–89.

Storey, Robert, 'The Making of David Mamet', *The Hollins Critic* 14.4 (1979), pp. 1–11.

Tuttle, Jon, ' "Be What You Are": Identity and Morality in *Edmond* and *Glengarry Glen Ross*', in Kane (1996), pp. 157–69.

Tzioumakis, Yannis, 'Marketing David Mamet: Institutionally Assigned Film Authorship in Contemporary American Cinema', *Velvet Light Trap* 57 (2006), pp. 60–75.

Vorlicky, Robert, *Act Like a Man: Challenging Masculinities in American Drama* (Ann Arbor: University of Michigan Press, 1995), pp. 25–56, 213–29.

Weber, Donald, 'David Mamet's Jewish Turn', *Chronicle of Higher Education* (3 November 2006).

Wetzsteon, Ross, 'David Mamet: Remember That Name', *Village Voice* (5 July 1976), pp. 101–3.

Zeifman, Hersh, 'Phallus in Wonderland: Machismo and Business in David Mamet's *American Buffalo* and *Glengarry Glen Ross*', in Kane (1992), pp. 123–35.

Zinman, Toby Silverman, 'Jewish Aporia: The Rhythm of Talking in Mamet', *Theatre Journal* 44 (1992), pp. 207–15.

Zinman, Toby Silverman, 'So dis is Hollywood: Mamet in Hell', in King (1997), pp. 101–12.

Individual works

The section divisions below correspond to the chapters of this Guide.

CHAPTER 1: *LAKEBOAT, THE DUCK VARIATIONS, SEXUAL PERVERSITY IN CHICAGO*

Begley, Varun, 'On Adaptation: David Mamet and Hollywood', *Essays in Theatre* 16.2 (1998), pp. 165–76.

Bruster, Douglas, 'David Mamet and Ben Jonson: City Comedy Past and Present', *Modern Drama* 33 (1990), pp. 333–46.

Hinden, Michael, ' "Intimate Voices": *Lakeboat* and Mamet's Quest for Community', in Kane (1992), pp. 33–48.

Kolin, Philip C., 'David Mamet's *Duck Variations* as a Parody of a Socratic Dialogue', *American Drama* 9.1 (1999), pp. 21–32.

Skeele, David, 'The Devil and David Mamet: *Sexual Perversity in Chicago* as Homiletic Tragedy', *Modern Drama* 36 (1993), pp. 512–18.

CHAPTER 2: *AMERICAN BUFFALO*

Barbera, Jack V., 'Ethical Perversity in Chicago: Some Observations on David Mamet's *American Buffalo*', *Modern Drama* 24 (1981), pp. 270–5.

Callens, Johan, 'Mr. Smith Goes to Chicago: Playing out Mamet's Critique of Capitalism in *American Buffalo*', *European Journal of American Culture* 19.1 (1999), pp. 17–29.

Dietrick, Jon, ' "Real Classical Money": Naturalism and Mamet's *American Buffalo*', *Twentieth Century Literature* 52.3 (2006), pp. 330–46.

Harris, Andrew, *Broadway Theatre* (London: Routledge, 1994), pp. 97–111.

King, Thomas L., 'Talk and Dramatic Action in *American Buffalo*', *Modern Drama* 34.4 (1991), pp. 538–48.

Little, William, 'Taking It Back: Crises of Currency in David Mamet's *American Buffalo*', *Mosaic* 37.3 (2004), pp. 139–55.

Piette, Alain, 'The Flexing of Muscles and Tongues: Thug Rituals and Rhetoric in David Mamet's *American Buffalo*', in Marc Maufort and Franca Bellarsi (eds), *Crucible of Cultures: Anglophone Drama at the Dawn of a New Millennium* (Brussels: Peter Lang, 2002), pp. 91–100.

Schlueter, June, and Elizabeth Forsyth, 'America as Junkshop: The Business Ethic in David Mamet's *American Buffalo*', *Modern Drama* 26 (1983), pp. 492–500.

CHAPTER 3: *A LIFE IN THE THEATRE, THE WATER ENGINE*

Callens, Johan, 'Remediation in David Mamet's *The Water Engine*', *American Drama* 14.2 (2005), pp. 39–55.

Dickey, Jerry, 'Mamet's Actors: *A Life in the Theater* and Other Writings on the Art of Acting', in Barbara Ozieblo and María Dolores Narbona-Carrión (eds), *Codifying the National Self: Spectators, Actors and the American Dramatic Text* (Brussels: Peter Lang, 2006), pp. 251–64.

CHAPTER 4: OTHER 1970s PLAYS

Adler, Thomas P., 'Mamet's *Three Children's Plays*: Where the Wilder Things Are', in Hudgins and Kane (2001), pp. 15–26.

Taylor, John Russell, 'The Woods, the West, and Icarus's Mother: Myth in the Contemporary American Theatre', *Connotations* 5.2–3 (1995–6), pp. 339–54.

CHAPTER 5: THE SCREENPLAYS, 1981–9

Chase, Chris, 'At the Movies', *New York Times* (20 March 1981), p. C6. [*The Postman Always Rings Twice*]

Duka, John, 'Hollywood's Long-Running Romance with James M. Cain', *New York Times* (5 April 1981), sec. 2, p. 15. [*The Postman Always Rings Twice*]

Goldman, William, *Adventures in the Screen Trade: A Personal View of Hollywood and Screenwriting* [1983] (London: Futura, 1985), pp. 62–7. [*The Verdict*]

Linson, Art, *A Pound of Flesh: Perilous Tales of How to Produce Movies in Hollywood* (London: André Deutsch, 1994), pp. 65–75. [*The Untouchables*]

Lucey, Paul, *Story Sense: Writing Story and Script for Feature Films and Television* (New York: McGraw-Hill, 1996), pp. 109–37. [*The Verdict*]

Lumet, Sidney, *Making Movies* (New York: Knopf, 1995), pp. 39–40. [*The Verdict*]

Pope, Thomas, *Good Scripts, Bad Scripts: Learning the Craft of Screenwriting through 25 of the Best and Worst Films in History* (New York: Three Rivers Press, 1998), pp. 133–9. [*The Verdict*]

Yakir, Dan, 'The Postman's Words', *Film Comment* (March/April 1981), pp. 21–4. [*The Postman Always Rings Twice*]

CHAPTER 6: *EDMOND*

Brucher, Richard, 'Prophecy and Parody in *Edmond*', in Hudgins and Kane (2001), pp. 61–75.

Callens, Johan, Review of *Edmond*, Théâtre Varia, Brussels, 16 January 1995, *Journal of Dramatic Theory and Criticism* 11.1 (1996), pp. 127–31.

Combs, Robert, 'Slaughtering Lambs: the Moral Universe of David Mamet and Wallace Shawn', *Journal of American Drama and Theatre* 13.1 (2001), pp. 73–81.

Dervin, Daniel, '*Edmond*: is There Such a Thing as a Sick Play?', *Psychoanalytic Review* 73.1 (1986), pp. 111–19.

Piette, Alain, 'In the Loneliness of Cities: the Hopperian Accents of David Mamet's *Edmond*', *Studies in the Humanities* 24.1–2 (1997), pp. 43–51.

Solomon, Alisa, 'Weeping for Racists, Rapists, and Nazis', *Performing Arts Journal* 7.1 (1983), pp. 78–83.

CHAPTER 7: *GLENGARRY GLEN ROSS*

Berger, Jason, and Cornelius B. Pratt, 'Teaching Business-Communication Ethics with Controversial Films', *Journal of Business Ethics* 17.16 (1998), pp. 1817–23.

Brucher, Richard, 'Pernicious Nostalgia in *Glengarry Glen Ross*', in Kane (1996), pp. 211–25.

Cullick, Jonathan S., ' "Always Be Closing": Competition and the Discourse of Closure in David Mamet's *Glengarry Glen Ross*', *Journal of Dramatic Theory and Criticism* 8.2 (1994), pp. 23–36.

Dorff, Linda, 'Things (Ex)change: The Value of Money in David Mamet's *Glengarry Glen Ross*', in Kane (1996), pp. 195–209.

Garaventa, Eugene, 'Drama: a Tool for Teaching Business Ethics', *Business Ethics Quarterly* 8.3 (1998), pp. 535–45.

Geis, Deborah R., ' "You're Exploiting My Space": Ethnicity, Spectatorship, and the (Post)Colonial Condition in Mukherjee's "A Wife's Story" and Mamet's *Glengarry Glen Ross*', in Kane (1996), pp. 123–30.

Gussow, Mel, 'Real Estate World a Model for Mamet', *New York Times* (28 March 1984), p. C19.

Hudgins, Christopher C., ' "By Indirections Find Directions Out": Uninflected Cuts, Narrative Structure, and Thematic Statement in the Film Version of *Glengarry Glen Ross*', in Kane (1996), pp. 19–45.

Jacobs, Dorothy H., 'Levene's Daughter: Positioning of the Female in *Glengarry Glen Ross*', in Kane (1996), pp. 107–22.

Kolin, Philip C., 'Mitch and Murray in David Mamet's *Glengarry Glen Ross*', *Notes on Contemporary Literature* 18.2 (1998), pp. 3–5.

Lublin, Robert I., 'Differing Dramatic Dynamics in the Stage and Screen Versions of *Glengarry Glen Ross*', *American Drama* 10.1 (2001), pp. 38–55.

Nelson, Jeanne-Andrée, 'So Close to Closure: the Selling of Desire in *Glengarry Glen Ross*', *Essays in Theatre* 14.2 (1996), pp. 107–16.

Price, Steven, 'Negative Creation: the Detective Story in *Glengarry Glen Ross*', in Kane (1996), pp. 3–17.

Roudané, Matthew C., 'Public Issues, Private Tensions: David Mamet's *Glengarry Glen Ross*', *South Carolina Review* 19.1 (1986), pp. 35–47.

Sauer, David Kennedy, 'The Marxist Child's Play of Mamet's Tough Guys and Churchill's *Top Girls'*, in Kane (1996), pp. 131–55.

Stafford, Tony J., 'Visions of a Promised Land: David Mamet's *Glengarry Glen Ross'*, in Kane (1996), pp. 185–94.

Worster, David, 'How to Do Things with Salesmen: David Mamet's Speech-Act Play', *Modern Drama* 37 (1994), pp. 375–90.

CHAPTER 8: *THE SHAWL*

Kolin, Philip C., 'Revealing Illusions in David Mamet's *The Shawl'*, *Notes on Contemporary Literature* 16.2 (1986), pp. 9–10.

CHAPTER 9: *HOUSE OF GAMES*

Ebert, Roger, 'House of Games', *Chicago Sun-Times* (31 October 1999).

Kipnis, Laura, 'One Born Every Minute', *Jump Cut* 36 (1991), pp. 25–31.

Klaver, Elizabeth, 'David Mamet's *House of Games* and the Allegory of Performance', in Kane (2004), pp. 175–88.

LaPalma, Marina deBellagente, 'Driving Doctor Ford', *Literature/Film Quarterly* 24 (1996), pp. 57–62.

Van Wert, William F., 'Psychoanalysis and Con Games: *House of Games'*, *Film Quarterly* 43.4 (1990), pp. 2–10.

CHAPTER 10: *SPEED-THE-PLOW*

Blumberg, Marcia, 'Staging Hollywood, Selling Out', in King (1997), pp. 71–82.

Burkman, Katherine H., 'The Myth of Narcissus: Shepard's *True West* and Mamet's *Speed-the-Plow'*, in King (1997), pp. 113–23.

Nelson, Jeanne-Andrée, '*Speed-the-Plow* or Seed the Plot?: Mamet and the Female Reader', *Essays in Theatre* 10.1 (1991), pp. 71–82.

Stafford, Tony J., '*Speed-the-Plow* and *Speed the Plough*: the Work of the Earth', *Modern Drama* 36 (1993), pp. 38–47.

CHAPTER 11: *THINGS CHANGE*

Cinch, Minty, 'Mamet Plots His Revenge', *Observer* (22 January 1989), magazine section, p. 49.

CHAPTER 12: THE 'BOBBY GOULD' PLAYS

Nelson, Jeanne-Andrée, 'A Machine out of Order: Indifferentiation in David Mamet's *The Disappearance of the Jews'*, *Journal of American Studies* 25 (1991), pp. 461–7.

Pearce, Howard, 'David Mamet's *Old Neighborhood*: Journey and Geography', *American Drama* 14.1 (2005), pp. 46–62.

CHAPTER 13: *HOMICIDE*

Combs, Richard, 'Framing Mamet', *Sight and Sound* 1.7 (1991), p. 17.

Hanson, Philip, 'Against Tribalism: the Perils of Ethnic Identity in Mamet's *Homicide'*, *CLIO* 31.3 (2002), pp. 257–77.

Hoberman, J., 'Rootless', *Village Voice* (15 October 1991), p. 61.

Newton, Adam Zachary, *Facing Black and Jew: Literature as Public Space in Twentieth-Century America* (Cambridge: Cambridge University Press, 1999), pp. 142–51.

Omer, Ranen, 'The Metaphysics of Lost Jewish Identity in Mamet's *Homicide'*, *Yiddish/Modern Jewish Studies* 11.3–4 (1999), pp. 37–50.

Roth, Laurence, *Inspecting Jews: American Jewish Detective Stories* (New Brunswick, NJ: Rutgers University Press, 2004), pp. 173–98.

Streicker, Joel, 'How at Home? American Jewish (Male) Identities in Mamet's *Homicide*', *Shofar* 12.3 (1994), pp. 46–65.

Van Wert, William F., 'Conspiracy Theory in Mamet', *Western Humanities Review* 49.2 (1995), pp. 133–42.

CHAPTER 14: *OLEANNA*

Badenhausen, Richard, 'The Modern Academy Raging in the Dark: Misreading Mamet's Political Incorrectness in *Oleanna*', *College Literature* 25.3 (1998), pp. 1–19.

Bean, Kellie, 'A Few Good Men: Collusion and Violence in *Oleanna*', in Hudgins and Kane (2001), pp. 109–23.

Bechtel, Roger, 'P.C. Power Play: Language and Representation in David Mamet's *Oleanna*', *Theatre Studies* 41 (1996), pp. 29–48.

Burkman, Katherine H., 'Misogyny and Misanthropy: Anita Hill and David Mamet', in Ann C. Hall (ed.), *Delights, Desires, and Dilemmas: Essays on Women and the Media* (Westport, CT: Praeger, 1998), pp. 111–22.

Elam, Harry J., Jr, ' "Only in America": Contemporary American Theater and the Power of Performance', in Marc Maufort and Jean-Pierre van Noppen (eds), *Voices of Power: Co-operation and Conflict in English Language and Literatures* (Liège: English Department, University of Liège, 1997), pp. 151–63.

Foster, Verna, 'Sex, Power, and Pedagogy in Mamet's *Oleanna* and Ionesco's *The Lesson*', *American Drama* 5.1 (1995), pp. 36–50.

Garner, Stanton B., Jr, 'Framing the Classroom: Pedagogy, Power, *Oleanna*', *Theatre Topics* 10.1 (2000), pp. 39–52.

Goggans, Thomas H., 'Laying Blame: Gender and Subtext in David Mamet's *Oleanna*', *Modern Drama* 40 (1997), pp. 433–41.

MacLeod, Christine, 'The Politics of Gender, Language and Hierarchy in David Mamet's *Oleanna*', *Journal of American Studies* 29.2 (1995), pp. 199–213.

Mangan, Michael, ' "Appalling Teachers": Masculine Authority in the Classroom in *Educating Rita* and *Oleanna*', in Daniel Meyer-Dinkgräfe (ed.), *The Professions in Contemporary Drama* (Bristol: Intellect, 2003), pp. 19–36.

Nadel, Ira, 'The Playwright as Director: Pinter's *Oleanna*', *The Pinter Review: Collected Essays 2001 and 2002* (Tampa, FL: University of Tampa Press, 2002), pp. 121–8.

Porter, Thomas E., 'Postmodernism and Violence in Mamet's *Oleanna*', *Modern Drama* 43 (2000), pp. 13–31.

Raymond, Richard C., 'Rhetoricizing English Studies: Students' Ways of Reading *Oleanna*', *Pedagogy* 3.1 (2003), pp. 53–71.

Ryan, Steven, '*Oleanna*: David Mamet's Power Play', *Modern Drama* 39.3 (1996), pp. 392–403.

Sauer, David Kennedy, '*Oleanna* and *The Children's Hour*: Misreading Sexuality on the Post/Modern Realistic Stage', *Modern Drama* 43 (2000), pp. 421–41.

Showalter, Elaine, 'Acts of Violence: David Mamet and the Language of Men', *Times Literary Supplement* (6 November 1992), pp. 16–17.

Silverstein, Marc, ' "We're Just Human": *Oleanna* and Cultural Crisis', *South Atlantic Review* 60.2 (1995), pp. 103–20.

Tomc, Sandra, 'David Mamet's *Oleanna* and the Way of All Flesh', *Essays in Theatre* 15.2 (1997), pp. 163–75.

Walker, Craig Stewart, 'Three Tutorial Plays: *The Lesson*, *The Prince of Naples*, and *Oleanna*', *Modern Drama* 40 (1997), pp. 149–62.

Weber, Jean Jacques, 'Three Models of Power in David Mamet's *Oleanna*', in Jonathan Culpepper, Mick Short and Peter Verdonk (eds), *Exploring the Language of Drama: From Text to Context* (London: Routledge, 1998), pp. 112–27.

Womack, Kenneth, *Postwar Academic Fiction* (Basingstoke: Palgrave, 2002), pp. 101–8.

CHAPTER 15: *THE CRYPTOGRAM*

Dorff, Linda, 'Reinscribing the "Fairy": the Knife and the Mystification of Male Mythology in *The Cryptogram*', in Hudgins and Kane (2001), pp. 175–90.

Haedicke, Janet V., 'Decoding Cipher Space: David Mamet's *The Cryptogram* and America's Dramatic Legacy', *American Drama* 9.1 (1999), pp. 1–20.

Pearce, Howard, ' "Loving Wrong" in the Worlds of Harold Pinter's *Moonlight* and David Mamet's *Cryptogram*', *Journal of Dramatic Theory and Criticism* 15.1 (2000), pp. 61–79.

Schaub, Martin, 'Magic Meanings in Mamet's *Cryptogram*', *Modern Drama* 42 (1999), pp. 326–37.

CHAPTER 16: *THE SPANISH PRISONER, THE EDGE, WAG THE DOG*

Kane, Leslie, 'Suckered Again: The Perfect Patsy and *The Spanish Prisoner*', in Kane (2004), pp. 217–31.

Johnson, Mary, 'Deconstructing the Dog', *Creative Screenwriting* 5.3 (1998), pp. 20–23.

Linson, Art, *What Just Happened? Bitter Hollywood Tales from the Front Line* (London: Bloomsbury, 2002), pp. 25–33. [*The Edge*]

Magaha, Claire, 'A Theater of the Self: Mamet's *The Edge* as a *Figura* of Otherness', in Kane (2004), pp. 203–16.

Ronnick, Michele, 'David Mamet at Play: Paronomasia, the Berlin Soldier Conrad Schumann (1942–1998) and *Wag the Dog*', *Germanic Notes and Reviews* 33.1 (2002), pp. 26–8.

Stempel, Tom, 'The Collaborative Dog: *Wag the Dog* (1997)', *Film and History* 35.1 (2005), pp. 60–4.

Trifonova, Temenuga, 'Time and Point of View in Contemporary Cinema', *Cineaction* 58 (2003), pp. 11–31. [*The Spanish Prisoner*]

CHAPTER 17: *THE WINSLOW BOY, BOSTON MARRIAGE*

Charney, Maurice, 'Parody and Self-Parody in David Mamet', *Connotations* 13.1–2 (2003), pp. 77–88. [*Boston Marriage*]

Morra, Irene, 'Performing the Edwardian Ideal: David Mamet and *The Winslow Boy*', *Modern Drama* 48 (2005), pp. 744–57.

Nadel, Ira, 'Lie Detectors: Pinter/Mamet and the Victorian Concept of Crime', in Kane (2004), pp. 119–36. [*The Winslow Boy*]

CONCLUSION: NOVELS AND TELEPLAYS

Bigsby, Christopher, 'David Mamet's Fiction', in Bigsby (2004), pp. 194–291.

Joki, Ilkka, 'Mamet's Novelistic Voice', in Hudgins and Kane (2001), pp. 191–208.

Ryan, Steven, 'David Mamet's *A Wasted Weekend*', *American Drama* 10.1 (2001), pp. 56–65.

Wieselhuber, Franz, 'Mamet and Television', in Christiane Schlote and Peter Zenzinger (eds), *New Beginnings in Twentieth-Century Theatre and Drama* (Trier: Wissenschaftlicher, 2003), pp. 451–64.

Index